SPAIN IN THE WEST
IX

From New Spain by Sea
to the
Californias
1519 - 1668

by
MAURICE G. HOLMES, PH.D.
Brigadier General, USMC (Retired)

The Arthur H. Clark Company
Glendale, California
1963

TO
ALICE S. HOLMES

Contents

Illustrations

Acknowledgments

I wish to express profound gratitude to all who have assisted me in producing this work. My particular thanks go to those whose names are given below in the sequence of their contributions.

Dr. Donald C. Cutter, History Department, University of Southern California, was the first who encouraged me to work toward the PH.D. degree in history and demonstrated the practicability of a plan thereto. He also encouraged me to go to Spain for research and fifteen months' investigations there are reflected in my dissertation which is embodied by this work.

Major General William A. Worton, USMC, Retired, presented me most favorably to the Del Amo Foundation toward a grant in aid for this research. His efforts in my behalf induced the support of Mr. Eugenio Cabrero, secretary of that organization, who assisted me consistently thereafter.

Dr. Joaquín de Entrambasaguas y Peña, *Catedrático* of the University of Madrid, oriented me toward the principal research facilities in Spain. He procured admission for me to the Museo Naval and the Biblioteca de Palacio in that city under the most favorable working conditions.

Rear Admiral Julio F. Guillén y Tato, Spanish Navy, Director of the Museo Naval, and his staff, gave me unstinted support in every respect. They were especially helpful in guiding me through the wealth of research material in that unique depository.

The Marqués de Villa Alcázar, one of the Board of Directors of the Del Amo Foundation, gave me every encouragement in my work. He was instrumental in amplifying the Foundation's grant to afford an extension of my research period.

Dr. José de la Peña, Director of the Archivo General de Indias, Sevilla, afforded me every courtesy during my research there. He also went outside his archives in order to place me in contact with contemporary authors in kindred fields.

Dr. Donald W. Rowland of the History Department, University of Southern California, guided me invaluably in revising the first drafts of the successive chapters of my work. Such continuity as this effort reveals is due largely to his touches.

Mr. Frank G. Forward, then President of the Union Title Insurance Company, San Diego, used his plant's facilities in preparing illustration copy for this work. He was the first to indicate to me the existence of the 1859 chart of San Diego Bay.

Mr. Richard F. Pourade, Editor Emeritus of the *San Diego Union,* was most helpful with suggestions as to changes in title and chapter headings. He also revised the introduction and the conclusion in my work.

San Diego.   MAURICE G. HOLMES

Introduction

The discoveries of Christopher Columbus from 1492 to 1502 opened a century of exploration that sent many Spanish expeditions along the coasts of the peninsula of Baja California, in Mexico, and of California itself. The vast treasure captured by Hernán Cortés in his conquest of Mexico helped the great conquistador in building, equipping and manning ships for further explorations by sea. He hoped that these would sail from Mexico's Pacific Coast to other lands as fantastically rich as those he had reached by sailing from Cuba, and not much farther away. His sea captains never found any such realms of ready-to-hand wealth; outside of Mexico and Peru, there weren't any.

While the general course of these Spanish explorations, and of others by sea along the coasts of the two Californias during the sixteenth and seventeenth centuries, have been known for many years, a wealth of new material has turned up on the character, motivation and rivalry of such leaders as Hernán Cortés, Pedro de Alvarado, Juan Rodríguez Cabrillo, and the first viceroy of Mexico, Antonio de Mendoza. New light has come on the strange flotilla of non-Spanish vessels sighted off the Mexican coast in 1573, and on the attempt to found a settlement in Lower California and which illustrated why such ventures invariably failed.

Nearly all of these explorers were in some way connected with the establishment of Spain's hegemony over the West Indies, and, in certain cases, they were involved in the conquest of Perú. For example, Hernán Cortés; his impetuous lieutenant, the red-haired Pedro de Alvarado whom the Aztecs named *Tonatiuh,* meaning "Sun"; and Juan Rodríguez Cabrillo, the discoverer of Alta California's coast, all were related to some degree to the Spanish overthrow of the Inca Empire. But it all began on the island which the Spanish knew as Hispaniola, and which now forms the Republic of Haiti and the Dominican Republic. In 1493, Diego Velásquez went with Columbus to Hispaniola where he became most active in subduing rebellious natives on that island. In 1504, Hernán Cortés arrived there and got his baptism in fire. Pedro de Alvarado and his four doughty brothers arrived in 1510.

Diego Columbus, Christopher's son and heir, was governor of Hispaniola when Pedro de Alvarado arrived. It has been related that he twitted young Pedro – he was only nineteen – because he was wearing inside out a doublet upon which the insignia of Knight Commander of the Order of Santiago had left traces. Santiago was one of Spain's four preeminent military orders, and an uncle of Pedro's, a knight commander in it, had given the doublet charitably to the needy nephew. Pedro got poetic justice about eighteen years later, however; he was invested with that same insignia by the Emperor, Charles I of Spain and Charles V of Austria.

In Hispaniola, all these men won or were just beginning to win their spurs. By 1511, Diego Velázquez had so distinguished himself in action against the aborigines there that Diego Columbus sent him in command of an expedition to conquer Cuba and to assume its governorship. He took Cortés and the Alvarado brothers with him and many more whose names acquired international renown in the years to come. By 1514, all who remained alive from that expedition had become veterans as also many others who pushed into Cuba after its conquest began.

Bernal Díaz del Castillo [1] was among the latter; he has stated that he had been one of one hundred and ten soldiers who went to Cuba from Tierra Firme, now Panamá, in 1514. They had sailed to the isthmus from Spain under the newly-appointed governor, Pedro Arias de Avila, commonly called Pedrarias, who was to succeed Vasco Núñez de Balboa who had gone there in 1510. When they reached Nombre de Dios, a settlement which was probably near Porto Bello, Panamá, they learned that Pedrarias' predecessor, the discoverer of the Pacific Ocean, had conquered the country already to such an extent that their numbers were neither neces-

---

[1] Bernal Díaz del Castillo, *Historia verdadera de la conquista de la Nueva España* (Madrid, 1928), vol. I, pp. 6-61. All the following, including Cortés' selection to command the third Cuba-Mexico expedition, is based thereon. It will be designated *Historia verdadera* hereinafter.

Extremely widespread use of this work has given it a ranking among the most highly prized sources of information concerning the conquest of Mexico. In pp. xv-xvii of the prologue to Bernal Díaz del Castillo, *Verdadera y notable relación del descubrimiento y conquista de la Nueva España y Guatemala* in *Biblioteca "Goathemala" de la Sociedad de Geografía e Historia* (Guatemala City, 1933-1934), vols. x and xi, Eduardo Mayora stated that the *Historia verdadera* was first published in 1632 under the direction of P. Fray Alonso Remón from the manuscript finished in 1568. According to Mayora, Friar Remón found the manuscript in possession of Lorenzo Ramírez de Prado, a member of the Council of the Indies, and that Remón adulterated the text in order to exalt his religious order, the Mercedarians. Mayora said that one of Díaz' descendents, Francisco Antonio de Fuentes y Guzmán, compared Remón's edition with the original, finding suppressions here and additions there. Others, including Genaro García, have found the same things also. Mayora granted that Díaz' heirs may have stricken out, but Remón undoubtedly made the additions. The writer has not been able to find any difference between the *Veradera y notable relación* and the *Historia verdadera*.

sary nor desirable. So, Pedrarias very graciously gave them permission to move to Cuba.

Again they arrived too late for the main events. When they had cooled their heels about three years in the greatest island of the Antilles, Díaz and his companions and some other late arrivals became impatient for action, gain, and glory. Accordingly, they concerted a scheme for discovery and conquest under Francisco Hernández de Córdoba into which Governor Velázquez entered with aid and blessing.

In February 1517, they put to sea in three ships; twenty-one days later, they sighted Cape Cotoche in Yucatán, Mexico. From the outset, hostilities ensued between them and the natives and waxed warmer to such a degree that, wherever they went, they could scarcely remain ashore long enough to fill up their water casks. By the time they got back on board at Champotón, Campeche, they had been used so badly that they decided to go back to Cuba. In order to gain the wind more advantageously, they headed for the Gulf coast of Florida where the chief pilot, Antón de Alaminos, said he had been in 1513 with Juan Ponce de León, governor of Puerto Rico, who discovered Florida and so named it because it was Easter at the time.

Córdoba's expedition brought back to Cuba some gold dust and accounts of stone and mortar houses – *casas de cal y canto*. These animated Velázquez anew and in April 1518, he sent out four ships under a kinsman, Juan de Grijalva, since Córdoba had died shortly after his return to Cuba of wounds the Mexicans had inflicted upon him. Three of these ships were commanded respectively by Alonso Dávila, Francisco de Montejo, and Pedro de Alvarado, names to be perpetuated in the history of Mexico and Central America.

Grijalva's expedition made its first landfall at Cozumel Island, just off the northeast coast of the Yucatán Peninsula, whence he sailed along Córdoba's course of the year before. Upon arriving at Champotón, history repeated itself, for the Indians met them at the beach in great force with vim and vigor. The Spaniards this time, however, were better prepared; they had boat guns, falconets, to cover the landing and a heavy proportion of crossbows and arquebuses. According to Díaz there were so many little locusts flying around the battlefield that with Indian arrows coming in swarms also, they often mistook one for the other, raising their shields to ward off locusts and leaving the shields low when arrows were flying at them. The Spaniards won this fight, nevertheless, driving the Indians pell-mell into nearby swamps for refuge.

As they fared along coastwise, Pedro de Alvarado gave the first demonstration of the lack of discipline or impetuosity which twice was to cost him his commanding officer's displeasure, once a terrible sentence by the *Audiencia* [2] of Mexico, and, finally, his life. Without asking Grijalva's permission, he went ahead of the flotilla and started up a river which the natives called Papaloaba and the Spaniards named Río de Alvarado as it is yet designated. As this escapade angered Grijalva greatly, he consequently reprimanded Alvarado very severely.

It probably led in turn also to Alvarado's detachment from the force, for Grijalva wanted to establish a settlement in Mexico and didn't care to have Alvarado "in his hair." As the expedition, originally small at best,

---

[2] The *Audiencia* was a body with legislative, judicial, and executive or administrative powers, responsible directly to the Spanish crown, which has no counterpart in English. It will be designated Audiencia hereinafter.

had been reduced by battle casualties and sickness, Grijalva decided to ask Velázquez for reinforcements in men and materials and chose Alvarado for that mission. He transferred all the sick and wounded to Alvarado's ship, the "San Sebastián," and put aboard her as well a large portion of the treasure they had acquired. The ships' captains wrote their respective reports of the expedition up to that point and gave these to Alvarado for delivery to Velázquez.

After Alvarado's departure, however, Grijalva changed his decision to establish a settlement because he deemed his means too scanty. Velázquez became more determined than ever to do so for the sight of gold worth about twenty thousand pesos, the total for which the expedition accounted, whetted his appetite for more and the accounts of stone and mortar cities and a great Aztec empire convinced him that great realms lay just beyond the western horizon. As the imagination of all Cuba caught fire, the job got too big for Grijalva and called for Hernán Cortés, who had become one of the most influential men in Cuba.

While the course of events in that island was leading toward epochal deeds, so also it was in Spain. In 1517, a Portuguese seafarer, Fernão Magalhães, or Ferdinand Magellan, transferred his allegiance from Portugal to Spain because he felt that his services in the East Indies and in Morocco had not been rewarded properly. He convinced the emperor that the Moluccas or Spice Islands of the East Indies lay outside the hemisphere which had been assigned to Portugal by the Treaty of Tordesillas in 1494, and that he could find a westward passage to those islands. It might seem a far-fetched idea that this development could affect Cortés in any way in consideration of the great divergence between the courses he and Magellan were to steer and the thousands of miles of Pacific Ocean which lay between their destinations. As will be seen later, however, it was to affect Cortés very definitely by diverting his ships from the purposes for which he had built them. The result of this diversion was, consequently, to delay the projection of nautical exploration toward the coasts of the two Californias. Cortés and Magellan sailed westward the same year; the former from Cuba on February 18, the latter from Spain on September 20, 1519.

Until 1540, the great conquistador was to send many sails into the Gulf of California and the Pacific Ocean, and some believe that one of his ships, the "Trinidad," under Francisco de Ulloa, may have sighted the Alta California coast near San Diego. By the end of 1539, however, a great competitor, Antonio de Mendoza, the first viceroy of Mexico, had checkmated Cortés in the land he had conquered. Mendoza and Pedro de Alvarado joined forces and Alvarado's shift from allegiance to his former commanding officer took Juan Rodríguez Cabrillo into Mendoza's service and, in 1542, he became the first European to make port in Alta California. In that same year, a part of the Mendoza-Alvarado fleet was dispatched to the Philippines under Ruy López de Villalobos.

From this time onward, numerous expeditions and some attempts to found settlements in Baja California were projected into the Gulf of California; the most important of these will be mentioned in the course of this study. One of them, led in 1668 by Francisco de Lucenilla, will be treated in detail because it shows the reasons why so many of them were failures.

The next occasion when Alta California's coast is known to have been sighted, however, came in 1565

when Friar Andrés de Urdaneta ran along a goodly
portion of it while returning to Mexico from the
Philippines where he had gone for the express purpose
of establishing the most feasible sailing directions for
the Manila Galleon. In 1573, a report of eight sails
sighted off the coast of Jalisco or Tepic prompted the
King of Spain to order the Audiencia of Nueva Galicia [3] to make a formal inquiry into the matter. It was
proved that five ships of high freeboard, *alto bordo,*
and three lesser craft which resembled Galician caravels had been sighted; yet, their nationality, their
mission, and their destination were never established.
In 1579, Sir Francis Drake sailed into the Pacific via
the Strait of Magellan, and cruised about seven degrees
in latitude along the Alta California coast which then
included Oregon from possibly forty-five degrees north
down to Drake's Bay. With his galleon, the "Golden
Hind," carrying Spanish gold and silver as ballast, he
fared westward to England and thus circumnavigated
the world. There was no question this time as to nationality, mission, and destination although the Spaniards
did fear that Drake might have found the mythical
Strait of Anián; returned through it into the Atlantic;
and, that England and Spain's other enemies might
thenceforth place her Pacific possessions in greater
jeopardy than ever.

In 1584, Francisco de Gali, sailing from the Philippines, sighted the Alta California coast much as Urdaneta had done nineteen years earlier. Pedro de Unamuno, sailing likewise, explored some of that coast in

---

3 This was a territorial subdivision which embraced an area approximately
equivalent to the current Mexican states of Jalisco, Aguascalientes, Zacatecas,
Sinaloa, Durango, and a part of San Luis Potosí. Tepic was then part of
Jalisco. The area was partially conquered in 1530 by one of Cortés' inveterate
enemies, Nuño de Guzmán, of whom more will be said later.

1587, and Sebastián Rodríguez Cermeño, leading survivors from the wreck of the "San Agustín," made a partial survey of it in 1595. In 1602-1603, Juan Sebastián Vizcaíno's expedition went up as far as Cape Mendocino, largely retracing Cabrillo's 1542-1543 courses.

Despite the fact that English and Dutch freebooters became very active off the South Sea coasts of Mexico, Central and South America during the early years of the seventeenth century,[4] Spain did not develop any operating or supporting bases on the Pacific seaboard north of Cape San Lucas. In fact, from 1603 to 1769, Spain abandoned Alta California to the Indians.

These piratical incursions into the Pacific in general and Spain's other international relations have borne so little influence upon her early projections toward Alta California that they can hardly be considered germane to the framework of this paper. No trespassing occurred on her Pacific littoral comparable to the foreign incursions into what is now the United States and Canada which began shortly before the defeat of the Invincible Armada in 1588 and ensued very rapidly thereafter as Spain lost control of the sea. Between 1588 and 1801, there were no non-Spanish settlements on the Pacific coast of North America to be countered as the English and Huguenot settlements on the Atlantic side had been attacked.

Perhaps it is well to say that the original motivation toward Alta California was the lure of possibly another kingdom comparable to the Aztec and the Inca realms. Next, the need for a base to support the Manila Galleon on her return voyage, her *tornaviaje,* was argued. Per-

[4] Peter Gerhard, *Pirates on the West Coast of New Spain, 1575-1742.* (Glendale, Calif., 1960), pp. 57-132.

meating both of these motivations and concomitant with them, was the ever-present urge to evangelize the natives; in fact, no early Spanish nautical exploration was attempted which did not go hand in glove with this objective. All these elements will become evident in the course of this work, which begins with the movement toward California initiated by Hernán Cortés.

Except where specified otherwise, all biographical data in this paper will have been taken from current editions of *The Century Dictionary and Cyclopedia* and *The Encyclopaedia Britannica.*

From New Spain by Sea to the Californias

I

To California with Cortes

Many characters comprised the casts which were staged into nautical expeditions to the Californias' coasts. Of these casts, the first impresario was the great conquistador, Hernán Cortés, whose career, as partially outlined in the introduction to this book, included his selection to lead the third expedition which Diego Velázquez, governor of Cuba, was to send from that island to Mexico in 1519. This expedition was the most ambitious of all because Velázquez intended to occupy Mexico and thus extend vastly the scope of his domain.[1] Cortés had two adherents, Andrés del Duero, secretary, and Amador de Lares, paymaster, on Velázquez' staff who spared no pains extolling Cortés' merits to their chief; yet, there were others, particularly the governor's relatives, who were equally sedulous trying to discredit the leader he had chosen. They even employed a sort of court jester to tell Velázquez that Cortés would bilk him of any gains there might be from their enterprise.

Cortés, although not born into wealth, was nevertheless a nobleman. He was so established by the four sides of descent on account of the standing as *hidalgos* enjoyed by the families Cortés, Pizarro, Monroy, and Altamirano. And, as adherents flocked to his banner and

---

[1] Díaz del Castillo, *Historia verdadera,* vol. I, pp. 58 *et seq.* Except where specified otherwise, this account will be based upon these pages.

more ships were acquired, Cortés began to act, dress, and live in the grand manner.

In all the preparation and organization of this expedition, Cortés demonstrated commendable energy and skill together with keen appreciation of seafaring matters. His zeal led him to extend his credit to the fullest extent, borrowing 4,000 pesos in gold, more than $20,000, and as many more in merchandise, in order to equip and supply the ships properly. Throughout the course of these activities, he preserved the appearance of excellent relations with Governor Velázquez although, indeed, he was warned constantly by Andrés del Duero that Velázquez was undergoing a change of heart toward his captain because of constant importunings by the Velázquez clan.

Acting upon Duero's recommendation, Cortés left the capital, Santiago de Cuba, and sailed northwesterly to Trinidad, about three hundred miles away, where he soon had eleven ships assembled. There, also, he enrolled the brothers Alvarado, Velázquez de León, Cristóbal de Olid, and Hernández de Puertocarrero.[2] In the meantime, Velázquez finally yielded to accusations against the leader of his expedition. One of these, constantly repeated, was that Cortés would rise against the governor in revenge for the affront he had suffered some years previously when Velázquez cast him into prison.

At any rate, Velázquez revoked Cortés' commission; ordered all the ships embargoed; and, directed that Cortés be returned to Santiago under arrest. The effect of this was indeed according to what Velázquez had been warned; Cortés rebelled, creating a breach be-

---

[2] Jean Descola, translated from French by Malcolm Barnes, *The Conquistadors* (New York, 1957), pp. 138-139.

tween himself and his former chief which was never closed, an act which was to plague them both the rest of their lives. As Velázquez' officials in Trinidad did not dispose of force sufficient to cope with Cortés' contingent, the Governor's orders were futile. Cortés dispatched two ships to the north coast of Cuba to take aboard additional supplies and personnel and ordered a rendezvous for all eleven of his vessels in the vicinity of Cape San Antonio at the west end of the island. They were to proceed thence in company to Cozumel Island, off Yucatán where, as noted above, Grijalva made his landfall in 1518, the previous year.

Pedro de Alvarado was in command for the second time of the "San Sebastián," one of the two ships which had been sent to the north coast. For the second time also, he advanced without authority and again he brought down wrath upon his head.

Despite Cortés' orders, Alvarado did not wait at Cape San Antonio; he sailed right on to Cozumel Island. Here, he arrived two days ahead of Cortés who, coming up, found Alvarado just returning to the anchorage with all his landing force. Alvarado had disembarked upon anchoring at Cozumel; looted foodstuffs and trinkets ashore; and, had scattered all the Indians into the bush except two men and a woman whom he captured.

When Cortés grasped the situation, he ordered one Camacho, Alvarado's pilot, clapped into irons for failure to make the rendezvous, and reprimanded Alvarado very severely for the same offense and also for his incursion into Cozumel Island, telling him among other things, that robbing the natives was no way to pacify a country. As if this weren't enough, Cortés required him to return everything he had looted. In the case of about forty hens which couldn't be returned because the Spaniards had eaten them, Alvarado had to pay their former owners with beads and jingle bells. He was required also to release the three prisoners whom Cortés sent into the woods to call the caciques and their followers into conference. Returning the loot was indeed punishment for Alvarado and his followers because, under the prevailing system, that was the only compensation they received for their services.

From Cozumel Island, Cortés retraced the tracks of Córdoba and Grijalva as far as they had gone, then proceeded to present day Vera Cruz. In all his relations with the natives, in hostilities as well as conferences, he was infinitely more successful than his predecessors had been. All the steps in his progress to Mexico City are not germane to the purview of this paper; yet, the picture of Cortés as a seafaring impresario would be incomplete unless instances of his appreciation of matters nautical were not cited in the meantime.

Shortly after his ships had come to anchor at Vera Cruz, Cortés decided to march on the Aztec capital. In accordance with this decision, he resolved first to beach all the ships which had borne his expedition; to beach, not scuttle, if one may believe Bernal Díaz, and his contentions seem most reasonable. Cortés, indeed, showed every desire to salvage from these vessels everything worth using later, such as all forms of hardware, rigging, cordage, canvas, spars, sound timbers, and equipment, particularly aids to navigation. Scuttling would certainly have been at cross purposes with such desires.

However, no great strain on the imagination is necessary to fancy Cortés beaching his ships just in order to prevent their total loss by sinking; especially so is such understandable on the part of anyone who has witnessed the swift ravages of the *broma* or marine borer, *teredo navalis*. All those hulls, at and below the water line, very probably presented the appearance of honeycombs instead of matched planking.

At any rate, Cortés did salvage material which was to stand him in good stead later and, besides this, he added about one hundred sailing masters, pilots, artificers, and seamen to what remained of the five hundred and eight soldiers who were mustered at Cozumel Island. And Bernal Díaz declared that nearly all of these mariners proved later to be valiant and staunch fighting men as the Spaniards, by dint of greater military skill, superior defensive armor, steel, gunpowder, and horses, went on to conquer tribes tributary to the Aztec monarch and to win vast numbers of these as their allies against the central authority.

As the Spaniards moved into Mexico City, Cortés developed a splendid appreciation of the military situation which that lacustrine city presented. Its lake and causeway features, the only communications with the mainland, prompted him to build four *bergantines*[3] in 1519, shortly after he had imprisoned the Aztec emperor, Montezuma. He had foreseen the possibility of withdrawal under attack; even a disaster as the *Noche Triste* or Sad Night was designated later; so, he prepared for a relatively safe withdrawal by water.

One should note at this point that some disagreement

[3] The apparent English equivalent, brigantine or brig, does not seem to portray this type of craft adequately. Bergantine will be used in reference to this vessel hereinafter.

prevails with respect to this, Cortés' first essay in bergantín construction. Pedro Mártir said that Cortés

> constructed in the salt lagoon four little two-oared craft, called
> bergantines, in order that, if any necessity whatever supervened,
> he could withdraw to the mainland at one time twenty comrades
> with their horses.[4]

According to Bernal Díaz, two were built, and these
were constructed under the directions of "our master
shipbuilders, named Martín López and one Andrés
Núñez," and that "Martín López was a very outstanding Master." He related, too, that they were manned
by experienced seamen from their force and proved to
be very swift sailers and very steady craft. When Cortés
took the great Montezuma for an outing in one of them,
they quickly outdistanced all of the Mexican canoes; it
did not matter how large the canoes were nor how many
paddles were used, all were left far behind.[5]

In the writer's opinion, Cortés himself provided the
best evidence that four of these vessels were built, albeit

---

[4] Pedro Mártir de Anglería, *Décadas del Nuevo Mundo,* translated from
Latin to Spanish by Joaquín Torres Asensio (Buenos Aires, 1944), p. 395.
This author, called also Pietro Martyr d'Anghiera, an Italian by birth, lived
1455-1526, held several offices in Spain becoming a member of the Council
of the Indies in 1524. His principal historical works cover the first thirty
years of Spanish intervention in Mexico.

[5] Díaz del Castillo, *Historia verdadera,* vol. I, pp. 358-361. In addition to
information given previously regarding this author, it may be noted that he
was among the most widely experienced conquistadores of Mexico as he participated in the three successive expeditions from Cuba to that country;
fought through its conquest; took part in Cortés' lengthy campaign into Central America; and, went thereafter into Pedro de Alvarado's service in
Guatemala where he was resident the rest of his life. After the appearance
of Francisco López de Gómara, *Historia general de las Indias* (Zaragoza,
1552-1553), he began his *True History* in order to correct what he deemed
inaccuracies in Gómara's work and to render credit to personnel subordinate
to Cortés whom he said Gómara ignored in order to signalize the leader's
deeds. If there is any weakness in this work, such must be chargeable to the
fact that he wrote from memory so many years after the events he related.

he indicated capabilities for them far in excess of Mártir's statement. Cortés said:

> Perceiving that, if the inhabitants wanted to practise any treachery against us, they had plenty of opportunity because the said city being built as I have described, they might, by raising the bridges at the exits and entrances, starve us without our being able to reach land, as soon as I entered the city, I made great haste to build four brigantines, which I had completed in a short time, capable whenever we might wish, of taking three hundred men and the horses to land.[6]

In view of Cortés' saying that three hundred men and the horses could be moved by four bergantines, the writer is inclined to favor the larger dimensions of these craft; this question will be discussed shortly. In this respect, Gardiner has uncovered rather specific evidence in Ms, Patronato 57, no. 1, ramo 1, fols. 3 and 17r., Archivo General de Indias, Sevilla.[7] As recorded in this document, the builder, Martín López, testified that each bergantine was between twenty-five and twenty-six cubits in length and his testimony was corroborated by workman Gómez de Herrera. Gardiner, giving the cubit eighteen inches, found that each of these vessels was between thirty-seven and one-half and thirty-nine feet long. It is regrettable that he did not give the source of his eighteen-inch cubit; apparently, he used English measure for, as far as the writer is aware, no Spanish cubit measures eighteen inches. The writer is inclined to believe that Martín López used a

---

[6] Francis Augustus MacNutt, translator and editor, *Letters of Cortés: The Five Letters of Relation from Fernando Cortés to the Emperor Charles V* (New York, 1908), vol. I, p. 257.

[7] C. Harvey Gardiner, *Naval Power in the Conquest of Mexico* (Austin, 1956), p. 62. The Archivo General de Indias, Sevilla, will be designated hereinafter AGI.

cubit measuring slightly more than 22.11 [8] inches and, as a consequence, the bergantines were between 46.6 and 47.9 feet long.

In the construction of the bergantines, Cortés' foresight in salvaging materials from the ships he beached at Vera Cruz returned very fine dividends. Using the *tameme,* the Aztec term for human pack animals, he brought to Mexico City practically all he needed for building them except the timber which was available in the capital's environs. Montezuma assisted him by providing workmen to bring in the lumber and carpenters to work it into shape under the directions of Martín López and his assistants.

It isn't to be wondered that outings in the bergantines should have been offered the Aztec ruler in the light of his cooperation with the Spaniards. As a matter of fact, Cortés and several of his officers enjoyed the monarch's company anyway. Bernal Díaz said that Cortés and Montezuma used to play a game the Mexicans called *totoloque,* described as something resembling quoits. Alvarado kept score for Cortés while one of Montezuma's nephews scored for him. The Aztec remarked laughingly one day that he didn't like to have Tonatiuh score for Cortés because he did so always with much *yxoxol,* meaning that he cheated. As a matter of fact,

---

[8] Successive royal decrees in the sixteenth century tended more to standardize prevailing practices than to introduce innovations. Measurements of vessels had been fixed sometime prior to 1587 in *codos* [cubits], each *codo* equal to two feet or two thirds of a *vara.* See Gervasio de Artiñano y de Galdácano, *La Arquitectura Naval Española (en madera): Bosquejo de sus condiciones y rasgos de su evolución* (Barcelona, 1920), p. 306. Extracts from Diego de Palacio, *Instrucción Náutica* (No place: no publisher, 1587). While the *vara* varied even from one province to another in Spain and likewise in the New World, the writer thinks that a fair mean has been struck in assigning it 835.9 millimeters or a trifle more than 33.17 inches, two-thirds of which give the *codo* slightly more than 22.11 inches. See Real Academia Española, *Diccionario manual e ilustrado de la lengua española* (Madrid, 1950).

according to Díaz, Alvarado always made one more mark for Cortés than he had actually earned. All burst out laughing uproariously at Alvarado's expense.[9]

Montezuma's cooperation with the Spaniards in bergantín construction was merely in keeping with many other favors he showed them for he had housed them handsomely; fed them from the fat of the land; provided them Aztec maidens for service and companionship; and, besides a vast number of lesser presents, he had given them a tremendous treasure in gold which Cortés had persuaded him to collect from the caciques as tribute to their overlord in common, the Emperor of Spain.[10] This idyllic situation which Montezuma had provided for the Spaniards was rapidly drawing to an end, however, and Cortés was soon to feel the first blight which the plague ensuing from his definance of Diego Velázquez was to bring upon him.

As Velázquez became aware of the immensity of Cortés' gains in Mexico, he seethed with urges to avenge his former captain's insubordination. Although the Cuban governor had grown obese and heavy, this did not deter his travelling from town to town over Cuba, even to Guaniguanico, more than seventy leagues from Havana, in order to recruit a force sufficiently ample to deal with Cortés. He assembled nineteen ships in order to carry fourteen hundred soldiers whose striking power included twenty pieces of artillery, ninety crossbowmen, seventy arquebusmen, and eighty cavalry with their mounts.

When news of Velázquez' preparations reached the Audiencia of Santo Domingo, that body forbade his

[9] Díaz del Castillo, *Historia verdadera*, vol. I, pp. 353-354.
[10] *Ibid.*, pp. 302-332, 380-384.

proceeding farther against Cortés. So great, however, was Velázquez' support in Spain by Juan Rodríguez de Fonseca, Bishop of Burgos, Archbishop of Rosano, and President of the Council of the Indies, whose power was absolute while the emperor was in Flanders, that the governor of Cuba snapped his fingers at the Audiencia's orders and dispatched his expedition to Vera Cruz with the mission to seize Cortés and his followers or to destroy them.[11] Active as Velázquez had been while organizing his means of vengeance upon Cortés, however, he did not choose to lead that force in person; rather, he entrusted its command to one Pánfilo de Narváez who had gone to Cuba in 1511 and had become prominent in that island's conquest.

As soon as Cortés learned that Narváez had arrived at Vera Cruz and what the latter's intentions were, he left eighty of his followers under command of Pedro de Alvarado to garrison Mexico City and hurried with the remainder of his Spaniards, about two hundred sixty-six, to come to grips with his fellow countrymen who outnumbered his force about five to one. Most unfortunately for Cortés, however, while he was seizing the hapless Narváez and winning over most of that leader's followers, Pedro de Alvarado's rashness or impetuosity impelled him and his little garrison into a dire situation inside the Aztec capital. Alvarado provoked the Aztecs into open rebellion by leading the cold-blooded massacre of a large number of unarmed chieftains while they were dancing in celebration of the traditional festivity of Huitzilopochtli, a gathering for which Alvarado himself had given permission.

When Alvarado had reported the situation to his chief, Cortés asked him about the matter of having

---

[11] *Ibid.*, pp. 397-399.

given the Aztec leaders permission to hold their celebration. Alvarado answered yes, he had, then explained
that he had been informed by a native priest, two
leaders, and other Mexicans that the Indians had
formed a scheme to massacre all the Spaniards as soon
as they had propitiated their war god, Vichilobos,
(Bernal Díaz' spelling), by the dance; he had made a
purely preventive attack in order to thwart their plot.
When Cortés heard that explanation, he flew into a
rage and said that it was a very bad thing to do, an
immense blunder, and that there was little truth in the
situation Alvarado described.[12]

Thus, an otherwise triumphant return to the Aztec
capital for Cortés became through Alvarado's rashness
an entrance into a situation as grave as any the great
leader could have foreseen when he ordered Martín
López to build the four bergantines. And, as if nothing
were to be lacking in order to portray a completely
hopeless situation to Cortés, even the succor he had
intended the bergantines to provide him was lost because, as a prerequisite toward exterminating the
Spaniards, the Indians had burned these vessels. If
these bergantines had been available when the *Noche
Triste,* that sad night of withdrawal, inevitably ensued,
Cortés might have withdrawn with much less than
almost disastrous losses in personnel; certainly, he could
have evacuated much of the millions of dollars in
treasure he left in the city or lost under attack along
the causeway to the mainland.

In the interim between the *Noche Triste* and the
assault Cortés led against Mexico City, two important

---

[12] *Ibid.,* pp. 464-465. A footnote here reads: "Testado en el original: 'e poca
verdad.'" Luckily, the original manuscript has remained extant to show the
liberties taken with it when it was first edited for publication.

actors among the early stagings for California came upon the scene. One of these was a Juan Páez who, very probably, wrote the report of the first authenticated cruise to the coast of Alta California. The other was Juan Rodríguez Cabrillo who led that cruise and, like Magellan, died of combat injuries during the outbound voyage. The records indicate that Páez [13] and Cabrillo [14] went to Mexico in 1520 as followers of Pánfilo de Narváez; then entered the conquest under Cortés.

As for Juan Páez, he became the objective of Cortés' wrath shortly after the retreat from Mexico City, probably in late July 1520. The episode between him and Cortés has been related in part as follows:

> Now that Cortés had reposed and diverted himself somewhat, Joan Páez, his Captain, whom he had left in Tlaxcala when he passed on to Mexico to reinforce Pedro de Alvarado, came to see him . . . Cortés . . . had learned from some who had told him so, how Magiscacin, understanding that the Mexicans had rebelled, said to Joan Páez: "if you dare to go to your General's relief with those Spaniards you have, I will give you one hundred thousand warriors, and see here; I believe there will be need, because the Mexicans are infinite and highly treacherous and so hostile to Christians, that it would not matter at all to them if ten thousand of theirs should die in order to kill one Christian and little by little none of these be left." [15]

---

[13] Real Academia de la Historia, *Colección de documentos inéditos relativos al descubrimiento, conquista y organización de las antiguas posesiones españolas de América y Oceanía* (Madrid, 1870), Serie I, vol. 35, p. 130. Hereinafter, these publications will be designated *Documentos inéditos*.

[14] Ms, Justicia 286, fol. 18, AGI.

[15] Francisco Cervantes de Salazar, *Crónica de la Nueva España* (Madrid, 1914), p. 512. On p. v, prologue, M. Magallón indicated this author as the "Dean Cervantes" whom Herrera listed among writers of works on New Spain, and stated that Herrera consulted Cervantes' work while writing his *Décadas*. On p. xi, Magallón said: "Dr. Cervantes began to write his Crónica in 1560, the same year in which he had been appointed Chronicler of the imperial city of México. Cervantes was born about 1514."

Herrera told this story likewise in essentials but with some interesting details besides. He said that Cortés found Captain Juan Páez in "Tlascala" where he had left Páez with eighty Castilians, casualties of the forced march from Vera Cruz to Alvarado's relief. After they had exchanged greetings, Páez assured his chief that Maxiscatzin, Cacique of Tlaxcala, was his true friend, but that Xicotencatl the Lad, Maxiscatzin's heir-apparent, did not like Cortés. When Cortés learned from Páez that Maxiscatzin had offered a hundred thousand troops to go with Páez's eighty Castilians to support the Spaniards in Mexico City, he flew into a violent rage. Páez tried to justify his inaction, saying that he had merely obeyed orders, knowing, as he did, that Cortés was a very strict commander. Cortés, thereupon, insulted Páez, calling him a coward, unworthy of a captain's rank, and that he deserved to be hanged. Valiant captains, according to Cortés, never stuck to the letter of their orders in such perilous situations but came up where their need was greatest. If Páez should ever open his mouth again to Cortés on this subject, he would be executed.

Cortés' rage and despondency over the terrible disaster he had suffered during the Noche Triste, which might have been averted or, at least, mitigated if Páez and the Indian allies had supported him, so aggravated the effects of a serious head injury he had received while skirmishing between Otumba and Tlaxcala, that he became critically ill.[16] As his losses in withdrawing from Mexico City have been estimated as between one-third and a little more than two-thirds of his Spaniards,

---

[16] Antonio de Herrera, *Historia general de los hechos de los castellanos en las islas y tierra firme del mar océano* (Madrid: Nicolás Rodríguez Franco, 1730), Década II, 273, I, Chap. XIV.

and, as he lost forever the immense treasure he had been unable to carry off, his subsequent mental turmoil must seem only an entirely human reaction.

Madariaga has related the incident between "Captain Juan Páez or Pérez" substantially as Herrera did, and this is the sole variant in surname which the writer has yet encountered.[17]

Bancroft, referring to this passage between Cortés and Páez, said:

> . . . According to Herrera, Captain Juan Paez – Torquemada writes Perez – was one of the invalids at Tlascala and to him 100,000 warriors had been offered to go to the aid of his general; but he declined, on the ground that his strict orders were to remain with his 80 men at Tlascala. For this he was naturally upbraided by Cortés as a coward, fit for hanging. The story is not very probable, dec. ii. lib. x. cap. xiv.; *Torquemada,* i. 512.[18]

When Cortés recovered health and strength from the serious illness which his rage at Juan Páez had brought upon him, he began to plan the capture of the city from which he had been ejected so painfully. Although he had lost the services of his first bergantines and while he was foiled in his plan for a safe retreat thereby, the lessons they provided him, nevertheless, were to stand him in good stead thereafter. The speed and steadiness they had demonstrated indicated excellent combat qual-

---

[17] Salvador de Madariaga, *Hernán Cortés* (Buenos Aires, 1945), pp. 467-468, note 2; 704, 512. Several Spanish scholars have told the writer that they thought Peláez was probably the etymon of Páez. Madariaga noted that, while Bernal Díaz has not mentioned this episode, Cervantes de Salazar did, and so did Torquemada in his *Monarchía Indiana.* "It is almost certain," said Madariaga, "that it comes from Ojeda, eyewitness to the events."

[18] Hubert Howe Bancroft, *History of Mexico, 1516-1521,* (San Francisco, 1883), p. 507, note 52. With due respect for Bancroft, one notes, withal, that Francisco Cervantes de Salazar did not appear in that most formidable list, "Authorities Quoted in the History of Mexico," which occupies pp. xxi-cxii in the work just cited.

ities; they were proved prototypes for larger scale construction.

Displaying a high order of military ability in his estimate of the situation under the self-assigned mission to regain control of the Aztec Empire's seat of authority, Cortés decided that dominance of the water surrounding that lacustrine city was indispensable to its seizure. That he earned high standing among the progenitors of the modern amphibious assault appears incontrovertible in history's perspective. Then, putting his decision into execution, Cortés initiated construction of thirteen bergantines in order to destroy or neutralize the thousands of Mexican canoes which had been thorns in his flesh and to isolate the city from personnel and logistic support. That the Mexicans were thoroughly aware of the dire threat the bergantines posed is indicated by the fact that they tried three times to burn them while under construction.[19]

It was during the construction of the bergantines that Juan Rodríguez Cabrillo first identified himself with shipbuilding in the New World as far as any record now extant is concerned, as far as the writer has been able to discover. Bernal Díaz said that, as the Spaniards had no pitch for caulking the bergantines, and as the Indians couldn't make it, Cortés sent four seamen to some good pine groves near Guaxalcingo to do so. On the same page, a footnote begins with the all too familiar, *"Tachado en el original,"* or stricken out of the original. In the stricken text, Díaz said:

I remember that the man who had charge of and went as captain was one Juan Rodríguez Cabrillo, who was a good soldier in the Mexican campaign, who later was a resident of Guatimala, a very honorable person, and he was captain and admiral of thirteen ships in Pedro de Alvarado's behalf and he served His

[19] Díaz del Castillo, *Historia verdadera*, vol. II, pp. 5-6.

Majesty very well in everything which presented itself to him, and died in his royal service.[20]

As wooden ships in the early sixteenth century could not remain afloat without proper caulking, it is obvious that Cabrillo's production of pine tar was indispensable to the watertight integrity of Cortés' bergantines and, consequently, to the very life of these vessels.

It is extremely difficult to form a good picture of these bergantines. The illustration following this page is an artist's conception, indeed interesting, yet so inaccurate historically as to annul its representative value.[21] Some of the able writers, manifestly scholars, have attempted to convey ideas of their size with very uncertain results like the following:

> In order to be able to calculate the dimensions, I will say that all carried a small gun with its corresponding supply of powder and ball, six oars on either side, twelve arquebusiers, and the captain. As for how much support and benefit these embarkations provided during the ninety-three days the siege of Mexico lasted, that may be seen in the pertinent histories; I shall say in order to wind up this subject that the craft commanded by García Holguín, a native of Cáceres, captured Guatemozín and his wife when, fleeing from Mexico, they left the city at the point of surrender.[22]

---

[20] *Ibid.*, vol. I, pp. 536-537.

[21] It has been included in order to illustrate the variance between fancy and fact: the vessels were not carried overland; their separate timbers were. If they were to have been moved intact, however, an able engineer like Martín López would certainly have used skids and rollers, a practice possibly antedating the pyramids of Egypt. The bergantine sails were not lateen – they were square – they had no bowsprits.

[22] Ricardo Cappa, *Estudios críticos acerca de la dominación española en América* (Madrid, 1894) vol. XI, pp. 188-189. Speaking of this author, Clarence Henry Haring, *Trade and Navigation Between Spain and the Indies in the Time of the Hapsburgs* (Cambridge, Mass., 1918), p. xxi, said: "A Peruvian Jesuit, Ricardo Cappa, has written a series of studies on early Spanish American society . . . volumes vii to x of which treat of the beginnings of manufacturing industries in the colonies. They include many details which it is difficult or impossible to find elsewhere."

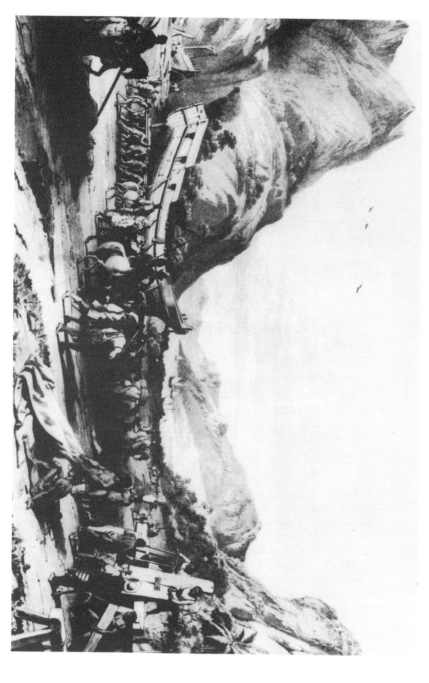

An Artist's Conception of the Launching of Cortés' Bergantines

Courtesy of the Museo Naval, Madrid.

It is keenly regretted that artists like those figuring in the codices might not have drawn their illustrations in proper proportion even if they had not developed perspective. Like standing a life-sized baby doll in a dishpan, they showed the head of a man, standing on forecastle or poop, almost level with the masthead. For instance, one drawing with hull, masts, spars, men, and gun in true size ratio would have been invaluable in comparison with the scant worth depicted by the twelve bergantines in the Codex Florentino.[23]

All seems to have been left to Gardiner to form the really splendid picture of these vessels. In his verbal reconstruction of the bergantín, he has performed a service of outstanding merit, a boon to students of the amphibious attack. And, in fairness to Aztec artists, one may assume that they were bent upon conveying information, not showing everything in true perspective. After all, it must be said that they did provide Gardiner with some specific details essential indeed to his able reconstruction, "conjectural" as he belittled it. It is not germane to the purpose of this work to quote verbatim the approximately three and a half pages he has devoted to the picture; yet, as some reference to Spanish ship proportions may appear from time to time in the course of this effort, it is deemed fitting now to indicate some salient bergantín characteristics.

---

[23] This is the title of the illustrations drawn by an Aztec artist for Bernadino de Sahagún, *Historia general de las cosas de Nueva España,* Carlos María de Bustamante, editor, (Mexico City, 1829-1830). The editor says Sahagún was one of the first missionaries to reach Mexico. He suggests that the work he edited was a reformation of the original which probably portrayed the outrages which the conquistadores inflicted upon the natives too vividly for Spanish taste. Prints of the Aztec pictures of the bergantines may be seen in Gardiner, *Naval Power in the Conquest of Mexico,* p. 118, and in George C. Vaillant, *Aztecs of Mexico: Origin, Rise, and Fall of the Aztec Nation* (Garden City, N.Y., 1953), pp. 257-258.

The over-all dimensions of the brigantines of the conquest can be approximated. The length is known, being about forty-two feet for each of twelve of the thirteen brigantines and forty-eight feet for the flagship. Our best index to the beam, beyond knowledge of the length, is the fact that the Texcoco canal through which they had to move to the lake proper had a width of twelve feet. Counterpoising that limiting factor, it must be remembered that a mast was mounted in the well, space was required for a double row of oarsmen – six on each side of the vessel – and minimum passageway had to be maintained for the free movement of gunners and bowmen about the ship. All such matters being taken into consideration, it is quite feasible to assume that the vessels had a beam of between eight and nine feet. Thus the brigantines, with the ratio of length to beam approximating five to one, might fall in the not uncommon class of five-beam vessels.[24]

---

[24] Gardiner, *op. cit.*, p. 130. With no desire whatever to detract anything from Gardiner's picture but, rather to enhance credit felt due Martín López, the writer feels it appropriate to show how length-beam ratio was usually fixed in those days. The prevailing rule in Spanish construction was *tres, dos y as* or "three, two, and one." To the writer, it seems simpler to express it "one, two, and three" and, in fact, the Spaniards so expressed it in illustrating their system of *arqueamiento* or gross tonnage measurement. At any rate, all measurements inboard, "one" referred to *puntal*, depth of hull at maximum beam; in decked vessels, depth was measured from the upper deck. "Two" referred to *manga* or maximum beam; "three' was *eslora*, length from stem to sternpost. Thus, if puntal were eight cubits, manga would be sixteen, and eslora forty-eight. See Cesáreo Fernández Duro. *A la mar madera: Libro quinto de las disquisiciones náuticas* (Madrid, 1880), pp. 11-12. Obviously, this called for a very tubby type craft.

To Martín López' credit, be it said, he was building finer lined vessels more than fifty years before anyone of real weight in Spanish naval construction had begun to advocate greater length ratio. In 1572, Cristóbal de Barros, Superintendent of Factories, Forests, and Plantations, began insisting upon increasing length in ratio to beam saying, "the warship must be just like the racehorse, long and big-backed." See *ibid.*, pp. 19-20.

While the writer would have expected a wider beam in Cortés' bergantines, say ten or, possibly, eleven feet, in order to give adequate space to the oarsmen, Gardiner believed that they more likely used paddles instead of oars. That, naturally, would economize space and allow the finer lines. The writer does wish, however, that Gardiner had conjectured the purpose of what, apparently, were portholes as shown in the *Codex Florentino*. Ten of the twelve bergantines portrayed show them, in varying numbers, relatively near the gunwales. Did they serve as oarlocks or loopholes?

However the bergantines may have been in size and type, withal, they accomplished their mission; possibly they went beyond Cortés' fondest hopes for them. They isolated Mexico City from powerful satellites on the mainland; by arquebus and crossbow fire, they reduced the speed of even the fastest enemy canoes; then, by gunfire and ramming, they destroyed thousands of those hostile hulls. In direct support of Spaniards and their allies advancing along the causeways, they breached barricades by gunfire and outflanked the defending Aztecs, rapidly thinning their ranks by enfilading fire with all their weapons. In short, they extracted the canoe thorns from their great captain's flesh.

About two months after the fall of Mexico City, Cortés began dispatching detachments of Spaniards with large contingents of Indian allies attached to subdue yet hostile tribes who had been tributary or satellite to the Aztecs.[25] Juan Rodríguez Cabrillo saw rather extensive service in these incursions, going with Francisco de Orozco to the conquest of Oaxaca. He went next under Pedro de Alvarado to subjugate Tututepeque, Chontales, and Mijes. When he returned to Mexico City, Cortés offered him employment there, but Cabrillo did not accept Cortés' bread because he wanted to fare into further conquests with Pedro de Alvarado.[26]

The record regarding Cabrillo's comrade, Juan Páez, is not as explicit regarding his services during this period as Cabrillo's record is. In the case of Páez, it is shown that he "had gone upon some incursions into the province of Mexico" and afterward came with Pedro de Alvarado to explore Guatemala and to "put it under-

[25] Díaz del Castillo, *Historia verdadera*, vol. II, p. 163.
[26] Ms, Justicia 290, fols. 43v.-44, AGI.

neath the royal crown of His Majesty." The names of
the officers under whom he served and the localities
where they went are not mentioned.[27]

In the meantime, Cortés had sent Juan Rodríguez de
Villafuerte to pacify and settle the Zacatula area, and
to establish a shipyard there. One may find in Cortés'
own words what motivated his action:

> As God, Our Lord, had well guided this business, and fulfilled
> my desire to serve Your Majesty on this South Sea, being as it
> is of such importance, I have provided with so much diligence
> that, in one of three places where I discovered the sea, two
> medium-sized caravels and two brigantines are being built: the
> caravels for the purpose of discovering, and the brigantines to
> follow the coast. For this purpose, I sent under a reliable person,
> forty Spaniards, amongst whom go ship-masters, ship-carpenters,
> wood-sawyers, blacksmiths, and seamen; and I have sent to the
> city [Mexico City] for nails, sails, and other things necessary
> for the said ships, and all possible haste will be used to finish and
> launch them. Your Majesty may believe that it will be a great
> thing to accomplish this, and the greatest service since the Indies
> have been discovered will be thus rendered to Your Majesty.[28]

When Cortés began building his caravels and bergantines,

> Most of the men who were responsible for his unusual nautical
> achievements were still at his disposal after 1521. When a
> former brigantine skipper, Juan Rodríguez de Villafuerte, served
> at the coastal settlement of Zacatula in the dual role of com-
> mandant of the Spanish garrison and director of the earliest of
> Cortés' shipbuilding programs on the Pacific, Cortés was clearly
> relating past experience to future program.[29]

Zacatula lies close to the mouth of the Río de las
Balsas near the northwest extremity of Guerrero province, about one hundred seventy miles up the coast from

27 Ms, Patronato 68, no. 2, ramo 3, fol. 11v., AGI.
28 MacNutt, Letters of Cortés, vol. II, p. 144, from Cuyoacan, May 15, 1522.
29 Gardiner, Naval Power in the Conquest of Mexico, p. 202.

Acapulco. Its location alone offers eloquent evidence of the difficulties facing Cortés who said that it was "two hundred leagues, and even more, from the ports on the North Sea where all material which arrives in this New Spain is delivered." He spoke also of very steep mountain passes and wide streams over which material had to be carried, and of the fact that everything ships comprised except wood had to be imported from Spain at that time.[30] Besides the length of transport and the harshness of the route, the means were painfully slow, a great handicap which the paucity of carriers posed. Despite their advances otherwise, the Aztecs had not developed the wheel beyond its use as a toy, an ornament, or a calendar, nor a beast of burden or traction. The *tamemes* were the only carriers.

As if such obstacles sufficient to daunt the most stouthearted weren't enough, Cortés' shipbuilding was set back by misfortune. As he related the situation,

> Another thing also happened, which was that when I had got together the sails, cordage, nails, anchors, tar, tallow, tow, bitumen, oil, and everything else required, and stored them in a house in that port, it took fire and everything was burned, except the anchors, which could not burn. I have now again begun, as a ship arrived from Castile, four months since, bringing me everything necessary for the ships; as, foreseeing the possibility of what had happened, I had already ordered material to be sent. . . I attach more importance to these ships than I can say, for I am positive that – God willing – I shall discover for Your Majesty more kingdoms and dominions than all those discovered up till now, and that, with His guidance, my projects may succeed according to my desires, and Your Highness will become the Sovereign of the world.[31]

---

[30] MacNutt, *op. cit.,* vol. II, p. 199.

[31] *Ibid.,* vol. II, p. 200. Cortés did not give the date when this fire occurred. It must have been sometime between the date on his third letter, May 15, 1522, and that on his fourth, from which the matter of the fire was quoted, and bears date October 15, 1524.

Cortés, withal, had been given a good antidote against depressive agents for,

In October 1522, fourteen months after the fall of Mexico, he received letters from Charles v recognizing his conquest, absolving him from blame for having thrown off Velázquez's authority, and appointing him Governor and Captain-General of New Spain. The Emperor, however, sent out four officials, a Treasurer, an Accountant, a Trade Agent and an Inspector, whose duty it was to report to him and to look after his interests. Cortés ceased to be an independent ruler and became an official governor within the Spanish administrative system.[32]

At any rate, Cortés renewed his efforts, as he told the emperor he would, and laid the keels of four more ships. Besides his desire to find more realms for his emperor, he was given a mission which really fired the imagination as His Majesty ordered him in 1523 to search for the mythical Northwest Passage or Strait of Anián along both coasts of North America.[33]

As referred to above in connection with Cabrillo and Páez, Cortés, in December 1523, sent Pedro de Alvarado to conquer and settle Guatemala. For this purpose, Alvarado was provided a force of four hundred twenty Spaniards and several thousand Indian allies. While this expedition was being organized and lesser detachments were kept active in pacifying areas within current Mexico, Cortés heard that, in Honduras and contiguous areas, there were rich lands and good mines. Also, some pilots, who had cruised along that coast, told him that they believed there was a strait in the region which linked the Gulf of Mexico with the Pacific Ocean. These reports decided Cortés to conquer and

---

[32] Maurice Collis, *Cortés and Montezuma* (New York, 1955), p. 239.

[33] Alvaro del Portillo y Diez de Sollano, *Descubrimientos y exploraciones en las costas de California* (Madrid, 1947), p. 142.

explore that land so, in January 1524, he dispatched
one of his erstwhile outstanding captains, Cristóbal de
Olid, in command of a maritime expedition sailing
from Vera Cruz to accomplish his purpose. Olid's force
comprised five ships and a bergantín, all very well
gunned, and three hundred seventy soldiers.

Cortés' defection from Diego Velázquez came home
then to plague him, for Olid succumbed to the tempta-
tion to emulate his chief and carve out an empire of his
own. He was encouraged thus to revolt by Velázquez
who was yet obsessed by burning desire to take vengeance upon Cortés, a second case after the Narváez
incident to be cited to Velázquez' discomfiture as a
gross disservice to his Majesty. The governor of Cuba
improved an opportunity to seduce Olid which had
been afforded when the flotilla touched at Cuban ports
to take aboard supplies which had been purchased by
Cortés' agents.

When news of Olid's treachery reached Cortés, he
quickly dispatched a strong expedition by sea, again
from Vera Cruz, under Francisco de las Casas to seize
his former captain. As months passed by without
Cortés' having learned that Casas had accomplished
the assassination of Olid, the governor, fearful of
further uprisings against his authority, decided to
march to Honduras in person to set his domain in order.
So, in October 1524, Cortés set out to execute a decision [34] which dealt his influence a blow from which it
could never recover.

During Cortés' prolonged absence – he did not return
to Mexico until April 1526 – his shipbuilding at Zacatula was entrusted to Juan Rodríguez de Villafuerte.

[34] Díaz del Castillo, *Historia verdadera,* vol. II, pp. 234-239; 305-306;
312-319.

He not only commanded the Spanish garrison that settled the town of Zacatula, but also had charge of the shipbuilding activity which was of prime importance in terms of the wider interests and plans of Hernando Cortés. In mid-1526 Rodríguez de Villafuerte met with other municipal procuradores [procurators] in Mexico City, the inference being that he was serving as a procurador for the town of Zacatula.[35]

Before Cortés had been gone a year, his enemies, led by the emperor's trade agent and his inspector, gained the upper hand in the government; circulated a report that Cortés had died; and, even went so far as to confiscate or embargo the great leader's property. In 1525, Pedro de Alvarado's brother, Jorge, and other Cortés partisans in Mexico wrote to Pedro urging him to return from Guatemala and assume the governorship.

The chance that the mantle of his great master might perhaps fall upon his own shoulders, made him anxious not to miss this opportunity, and he lost no time in beginning the journey. But it was already reported in Mexico that he would arrive there before long, and he had proceeded but a short distance when he received an intimation from the factor [trade agent] that he had better approach no further. If, however, he preferred to revisit the capital, Salazar informed him that he would gladly meet him on the way, and have the satisfaction of putting him to death.

Alvarado learned that the factor, Gonzalo de Salazar, had sent fifty horse and seventy foot troops against him. On account of a Cakchiquel Indian revolt at the time, Guatemala couldn't spare troops sufficient to cope with Salazar's force, so Alvarado retraced his steps. Near the end of 1525, Alvarado learned that Cortés was safe and marched to join him in Honduras. At Choluteca Malalaca (probably near Tegucigalpa) Luis Marín

---

[35] Gardiner, *Naval Power in the Conquest of Mexico*, p. 212.

met Alvarado and with their forces combined, they marched via Guatemala to Mexico where Cortés entertained them regally. Their great chief, sailing out of Honduras, had reached Mexico City long before they arrived.[36]

In the meantime, in 1525, the emperor issued a radical modification of his 1523 mission to Cortés, and in this change, Magellan's voyage weighed heavily although the great Portuguese navigator had been killed in the Philippine Islands in 1521. Cortés' new mission involved three tasks: (1) to find the "Trinidad"[37] of Magellan's flotilla, (2) to determine what had happened to García Jofre de Loaisa or Loaysa's expedition,[38] and (3) to get information regarding Sebastián Caboto or Cabot's voyage.[39] The first of these

[36] Hubert Howe Bancroft, *History of Central America*, vol. II (San Francisco, 1886), pp. 74 *et seq.*

[37] A short while before February 13, 1522, unanimous agreement in the "Victoria" and the "Trinidad," the survivors of five ships which began Magellan's cruise, decided that the "Victoria" under Juan Sebastián de Elcano would sail for Spain via the Cape of Good Hope and that the "Trinidad" under Gómez de Espinosa would sail eastward for Panamá. Both ships were then at Tidore Island in the Moluccas. The "Trinidad," unknown to the Spaniards, was seized by order of the King of Portugal. The "Victoria" arrived at Sanlúcar de Barrameda, Spain, September 6, 1522, carrying about twenty-six tons of spices whose sale not only paid all the costs of the expedition but also provided a surplus of about 500 gold ducats, approximately $2,000. Interest in the "Trinidad," possibly loaded with a like amount of spices, is readily understandable. *See* Stefan Zweig, *Magallanes: La Aventura más audaz de la Humanidad* (Buenos Aires, 1943), pp. 252-255, 261-265.

[38] Loaisa, commanding seven ships, sailed from Spain July 24, 1525 with orders to follow up Magellan's discoveries. Sailing via the Strait of Magellan into the Pacific, he died en route across that ocean and only one ship of his flotilla reached the Moluccas.

[39] He was born in England, 1474, son of Giovanni Caboto, an Italian navigator. In 1519, he entered Charles V's service and, in 1526, he sailed from Spain, commanding four ships, with orders to the Moluccas via the Strait of Magellan. He abandoned his mission, however, in favor of exploration in the Uruguay-Paraguay area in South America, and returned to Spain in 1530.

tasks was connected directly with Magellan's voyage; each of the others, in turn, was a follow-up of the voyage immediately preceding. In compliance with these orders, Cortés sent out three ships about the end of October 1527 under Alvaro de Saavedra. Only one reached the Moluccas; none returned.[40]

In the meantime, Pedro de Alvarado, who had met Cortés in Mexico City in 1526, sailed soon thereafter for Spain where he arrived early in 1527. Whatever his motivations toward this voyage might have been, his timing was excellent, for Gonzalo Mejía, colonial procurator, was preferring serious charges of embezzling the royal fifth of the gold he had extorted from the Indians and many other instances of malfeasance against him. His renown as a conquistador and his personal magnetism, however, developed powerful supporters at court, notably Francisco de los Cobos, the emperor's secretary, a portfolio equivalent in power to that of prime minister today.

Although Alvarado was betrothed to Cecilia Vázquez, Cortés' cousin, he paid suit, nevertheless, to Francisca de la Cueva, daughter of the Conde de Bedmar, and the ward of Cobos who gave her away at the wedding. She died en route to New Spain. Thus Alvarado indeed acquired a friend at court, and Cobos secured his acquittal from Mejía's charges, the return of fifteen thousand ducats Alvarado had posted as bond, and much additional favor from the emperor. He was made Knight Commander of Santiago as noted earlier; governor and captain-general of Guatemala; and, he was authorized to build ships on the south coast of Guatemala, and to explore the Spice Islands and to

---

[40] Alvaro del Portillo, *Descubrimientos y exploraciones en las costas de California*, pp. 142-143.

develop commerce on the Pacific.[41] His great leader in the conquest was no longer to have the monopoly over maritime enterprise in that part of the world; another impresario was to stage seafaring expeditions.

Cortés, however, was nothing if not persistent. Despite his severe setbacks, he put five more ships on the ways and, by 1528, these were well along toward completion. He found to his discomfiture, nevertheless, that he was to be restricted in authority within the very lands he had brought to the Spanish crown. The disorder which afflicted Mexico during his expedition to Honduras had led to supplanting the four representatives whom the emperor sent to the seat of government in 1522 by a much more powerful agency, a royal audiencia. This body opposed his launching any more expeditions so, in order to substantiate his rights, Cortés sailed to Spain.[42]

> Alvarado was now prepared to return to the western world, and on the 26th of May 1528, entered his appointments and despatches at the India House in Seville according to form. While he was there waiting to embark Cortés arrived at Palos. But the new adelantado [governor] was no longer so anxious to meet his former commander as he had been when he marched to his aid through the wilds of Honduras. He knew how deeply he had wounded his pride in the two most sensitive points, and he received with a feeling of relief the news that Cortés had gone direct to Madrid.[43]

In 1529, Cortés went back to Mexico, loaded with honors and vast New World riches; but nothing which cost the emperor any outlay. He had been created Marqués del Valle de Oaxaca; appointed captain-

---

[41] Hubert Howe Bancroft, *Central America,* vol. II, pp. 100-102.

[42] Charles E. Chapman, *A History of California* (New York, 1951), pp. 44, 48-49.

[43] Hubert Howe Bancroft, *Central America,* vol. II, pp. 102-103.

general of New Spain; endowed with *encomiendas* or vassalages of twenty-three thousand Indians; but, he was no longer and never again to be, governor of his conquest, an imperial act which indeed should rank among the most ironical in the history of monarchies. Besides these rewards – yet at no cost to the crown – he was armed with an imperial capitulation which authorized him, at his personal expense, risk, and responsibility, to search for and settle the islands of the South Sea, a lifetime governorship over them, and a twelfth of the land in what he might discover.[44] He forthwith repaired some of his ships; bought others; and, in 1532, dispatched two ships under Diego Hurtado de Mendoza from Acapulco to sail northward along the coast except when off Nueva Galicia, domain of Nuño de Guzmán, a bitter enemy. Hurtado was to stand well off that coast.

At this time a would-be nautical impresario entered the field, for Guzmán's hunger for riches, power, and fame had been whetted by his conquest of Nueva Galicia, and he yielded to the lure of shining cities just beyond the horizon. Was there an easier way to get ahead of Cortés than by hampering his operations or seizing his ships? So, when sea damage forced Hurtado into port in Guzmán's territory, Nuño would neither let Cortés' captain take supplies aboard nor remain long enough to overhaul his ships. While Hurtado was clawing off the coast, mutiny broke out. Some of the mutineers transferred to the other ship which then stood away to New Spain. She was stranded in Ban-

---

[44] Francisco López de Gómara, *Crónica general de las Indias: Historia de la Conquista de Méjico* (Madrid: Colección de Autores Españoles, 1852), vol. XXII, p. 426.

deras Bay, Tepic, where Guzmán seized her. Hurtado fared on his way, and disappeared.[45]

Antonio de Herrera appeared to believe that Hurtado was killed a few leagues upstream from the mouth of the Río Fuerte, Sinaloa. He said that a detachment of Nuño de Guzmán's men, exploring this river, encountered some Indians whose trinkets included items of Spanish origin; necklaces and bracelets made of studs from belts, some hiltless swords, knives, etc. They put many questions to an Indian woman in whose village they found a piece of a cape made of London cloth. She said it had belonged to some foreigners who were dead. Further inquiry among many Indians developed the story that Hurtado, greatly in need of supplies, had gone ashore with fifteen or twenty men and struck a trail which led to the villages. There, fatigue made them careless and, while sleeping, the Indians killed them. They killed also the men Hurtado had left on board the ship, but this account did not relate what happened to the vessel.[46] Perhaps Guzmán got her?

The main results of efforts thus far were gaining some knowledge of the Mexican shoreline up to Sonora and the discovery by Hurtado of the Tres Marías Islands, close beyond which was the beginning of the Californias. Cortés was not dismayed, however; he sent out two more ships in October 1533, the "Concepción" and the "San Lázaro." He gave command of these to a kinsman, Diego de Becerra, who sailed in the "Concepción," and placed Hernando de Grijalva in command of the "San Lázaro."

---

[45] Chapman, op. cit., pp. 49-50.

[46] Herrera, Historia general (Madrid, 1601), vol. III, Década v, Libro I, p. 19.

Upon sailing out of Tehuantepec where they were built,[47] these ships parted company and never rejoined. They had been ordered to search for Hurtado, then take to the high seas bound for discovery. Grijalva did discover an unpopulated island that he named Santo Tomé which was, perhaps, one of the Revillagigedo Islands, approximately two hundred nautical miles south of Cape San Lucas. His course had been widely divergent from the track Hurtado must have followed, and it is said that, after the two ships took departure from Tehuantepec, the weather soon became favorable for Grijalva's rejoining Becerra.

Diego de Becerra, however, has been portrayed as haughty, badly dispositioned, and hated by all hands; so, Grijalva, very likely, wanted no part at all in company with his chief. In this respect, it has been said that, shortly after they put to sea, Becerra had a falling out with his chief pilot, Fortún Jiménez.[48]

At any rate, Fortún Jiménez, his brother Pero, and several other Vizcayans, relatives and friends, decided to do something about "a certain gentleman from Estremadura who called himself Diego bezerra a man very trustworthy and expert in navigation." They "treacherously and traitorously in concert, serious, and with malice aforethought," set upon "the said Diego bezerra" who, at midnight, was sleeping soundly upon a chest. They cut and slashed him, wounding him in the head, the body, and the arms, and, as a result of this, he died, and they threw his body overboard.

---

47 While the writer has not seen any categorical statements as to why Cortés transferred his shipbuilding to Tehuantepec, one may presume he did so because the Isthmus of Tehuantepec afforded the shortest of all routes across Mexico. As far as Acapulco was concerned, Bancroft implied that Cortés abandoned it because "Acapulco was inaccessible to carts and pack animals." – Bancroft, *History of Mexico*, vol. II, p. 420.

48 Díaz del Castillo, *Historia verdadera*, vol. II, pp. 479-480.

In order, apparently, to do a thorough job, Fortún and his cohorts attacked other high officials on board, then marooned them and two Franciscan friars on a beach in Jalisco. Cortés petitioned the emperor to order every diligence to be employed toward arresting Fortún Jiménez and punishing him as his crime demanded.[49]

The emperor's minions, however, did not have a chance to do this even if the monarch had been disposed so to order, and the writer has not seen yet any evidence that he was. In short order, Fortún sailed across the Gulf of California into Santa Cruz Bay, now Bahía de la Paz, Lower California. Here, he went ashore with an escort, and promptly met death at the hands of Indians in that area. The survivors, the men left on board the "Concepción," sailed her to the "port of Jalisco" where they gave an account of these events, and reported that Santa Cruz Bay was "rich in pearls."[50]

Thus, as far as the writer has been able to discover in the records, Cortés' ship, the "Concepción," in 1533, carried the first Spaniards to reach one of the Californias. Insofar as nearly ten years' efforts to extend the conquest of Mexico City to like or greater realms were concerned, Cortés had realized only frustration. That, in reaching Lower California, he had encountered the vermiform appendix of a region greater in potential wealth than Mexico and Perú combined, was something he could not imagine. So, since Cortés did not have the consolation of knowing what the appendage hung from, one, even at this point, may begin to accept Bernal Díaz del Castillo's conclusion regarding the conqueror: ". . . and if we consider the matter care-

---

[49] Letter, Cortés to Charles V, no date, in MS, Patronato 180, ramo 52, AGI.
[50] Díaz del Castillo, *op. cit.*, vol. II, pp. 480-481.

fully, he wasn't fortunate in anything at all after we gained New Spain." [51]

Down the Pacific littoral, along the coast of Guatemala, formidable naval strength was being concentrated by means of constructing and commandeering ships. Another impresario in staging maritime expeditions had emerged, no longer to follow Cortés, but to emulate him by striking forth on his own account, for Pedro de Alvarado was going down in ships to the vast South Sea.

---

[51] *Ibid.,* p. 485.

II

Alvarado Emulates Cortes

In the preceding chapter, some account was given of Pedro de Alvarado's activities subsequent to the fall of Mexico City during the period, December 1523-May 1528. Cortés dispatched him upon the conquest of Guatemala in the former month; in the latter, he was waiting in Sevilla to embark for Mexico while Cortés was on his way from Palos to Madrid. While he was in Spain, Alvarado negotiated a contract with the emperor which authorized him to build ships in Guatemala and to explore and exploit certain areas in the Pacific.

In the interval between the foregoing dates, Alvarado had been penetrating much of Central America with great rapidity. He overran not only the territory which current Guatemala embraces, but also, most of present Honduras, all of El Salvador as constituted today, and, well into northwest Nicaragua.[1] While this campaign did not accomplish complete pacification of this region, Alvarado, nevertheless, set up a seat of its government at Santiago de Guatemala, near the Volcán de Agua, on July 25, 1524.

As noted also in the preceding chapter, Juan Rodríguez Cabrillo and Juan Páez were among the Spaniards whom Alvarado led into Guatemala and it has been recorded that both served him and His Majesty

---

[1] Bancroft, *Central America*, vol. II, map on p. 82, "Alvarado's March."

faithfully and well in that conquest where Cabrillo "was captain and chief of crossbowmen (fue capitan y cauo de ballesteros)."[2]

As far as the writer is aware, the specific military service Juan Páez performed in Guatemala has not been recorded. The extent of his participation is that "he served with his arms and horse (sirvio con sus armas e cauallo)."[3] At any rate it appears that he didn't do badly in Alvarado's estimation for the city council records of Santiago de Guatemala, under date of August 12, 1524, show that Juan Páez was received among the "vecinos de esta cibdad (residents of this city)." Juan Rodríguez Cabrillo, also, was so received the same date.[4]

Apparently, Juan Páez had expiated the lapse for which Cortés took him to task so severely in Tlaxcala shortly after the Noche Triste for, in 1525, "Letters of credence were given to Pedro de Alvarado . . . Juan Rodríguez de Villafuerte . . . Juan Páez . . . all qualified Persons, and principal Captains."[5] As recommendations for this recognition must

---

[2] Ms, Indiferente General 111, AGI.

[3] Ms, Patronato 68, no. 2, ramo 3, fol. 11v., AGI.

[4] Biblioteca "Goathemala" de la Sociedad de Geografía e Historia, *Libro viejo de la fundación de Guatemala y papeles relativos a D. Pedro de Alvarado* (Guatemala, 1934), vol. XII, p. 7. This work will be designated hereinafter, *Libro viejo*.

[5] Herrera, *Historia general* (Madrid, 1730), Déc. II, 273, I, cap. XIV. The writer has not established to his satisfaction the precise purpose of these *cartas de creencia*. That they constituted credentials cannot be doubted; yet, just how these could serve fighting men is not manifest. Possibly they were equivalent to regular commissions in the imperial army; perhaps they merely certified that the recipients were entitled to the rights and the immunities which were accorded hidalgos and, more still, hidalgos who were officers in His Majesty's armed forces. As for recognition just as an hidalgo, this meant much. For example, the City Council, Santiago de Guatemala, passed an act, dated June 20, 1529, which prescribed punishment for certain infractions of its ordinances: "And if a Spaniard should commit the said offense, he will

have required Cortés' approval, it seems obvious that he had forgiven Páez' failure to go to his support in Mexico City.

Juan Páez, the distinguished captain, had been serving his military chief, Pedro de Alvarado, since December 1524 in a civilian capacity for, at that time, he became the *escribano público* or notary public in the *cabildo* (city council) of Santiago de Guatemala.[6] While Cabrillo did not appear to have any official connection with the cabildo, his name appeared with Páez' in many instances where they attested the council's acts and proclamations. In late 1524 or in 1525, Cabrillo went to Spain where he married Beatriz Sánchez de Ortega, sister of one of his comrades among the conquistadores, Diego Sánchez de Ortega.[7]

As noted earlier, Pedro de Alvarado returned to Mexico from Spain in October 1528 as governor of Guatemala, but he was not to assume immediately the new functions which the emperor had granted him. The Audiencia of Mexico informed him that he was to face trial on thirty-four charges running from embezzling the royal fifth through cruelty and illegal warfare. He required so much time to extricate himself from the audiencia's clutches that he did not reach Santiago de Guatemala until April 11, 1530.[8]

In the meantime, Juan Rodríguez Cabrillo, manifestly, had gained a high level in Alvarado's esteem for, in 1529, Cabrillo was enjoying the tributes of Coban and, in company with his brother-in-law, was working

---

be fined a hundred pesos, applied in the manner aforesaid, if he is an hidalgo; and, if not, a hundred lashes . . ." See *Libro viejo*, p. 69. So, it paid to be an hidalgo!

[6] *Libro viejo*, p. 9.

[7] Ms, Justicia 286, fols. 17-17v., AGI.

[8] Bancroft, *Central America*, vol. II, pp. 103-104, 117.

mines along the Uzpantlan and Tequiçiztlan Rivers.[9]

When Pedro de Alvarado had resumed the governorship of Guatemala, he proceeded to build and acquire ships in order to comply with his contract with the crown. Instead of sending an expedition toward Especiería, however, he found a more attractive objective much closer at hand, for news had reached New Spain of the fabulous stores of gold which the brothers, Francisco and Gonzalo Pizarro, and their partner, Diego de Almagro, had encountered in their conquest of Perú. So, Alvarado, reasoning that Quito, now the capital of El Ecuador, lay outside the area which the emperor had proscribed in their contract,[10] prepared a formidable force to move upon that place.

News of Alvarado's plans and preparations, however, reached the Audiencia of Mexico and, in September 1532, that tribunal ordered him to cease fitting out twelve vessels of various types and tonnage which he was preparing for uninvited intervention in the former realm of the Inca. This order upset and angered Tonatiuh very much, and he appealed against it, complaining about Cortés who, he suspected, had intervened in the audiencia to prevent his making a cruise from which he expected great honor and much profit.[11]

---

[9] Ms, Justicia 290, folios unnumbered, AGI. This is from sworn testimony by Francisco de Castellanos, Treasurer of Guatemala, in the *probanza* of Juan Rodríguez Cabrillo in the suit between the Cabrillo heirs and Licentiate Gerónimo de Ulloa, State's Attorney. This is the Castellanos, "a man of spirit and ability," who redeemed the dire situation into which Guatemala had been plunged by the bullying and ineptitude of Francisco de Orduña, a judge appointed by the Audiencia of Mexico to take the *residencia,* or investigation, of Jorge de Alvarado, one of Pedro's brothers, who had been acting governor during Pedro's absence in Spain. Orduña suspended Jorge and assumed the governorship himself. See Bancroft, *Central America,* vol. II, pp. 105, 111-113.

[10] Ministerio de Fomento, *Cartas de Indias* (Madrid, 1877), pp. 708-709.

In 1534, in defiance of the Audiencia of Mexico, Alvarado proceeded with his expedition to Quito. After great exertions, much hardship, and many personnel and material casualties, he arrived at that place only to find himself checkmated by Marshal Diego de Almagro, who, at this juncture, could count upon complete support by the Pizarro forces. So, Alvarado had to compromise with his fellow-countrymen who, at that stage in their fortunes, considered his presence entirely gratuitous and superfluous.

In May 1535, Alvarado wrote the emperor a lengthy account of his trip to Quito with particular emphasis upon the hardships he had undergone, the tremendous expenses he had incurred, and the harsh treatment he had received from Almagro. The latter had inflicted almost irreparable injury upon him financially by practically forcing him to sell six splendid ships to the Almagro-Pizarro partners for a mere one hundred thousand *castellanos,* only about a third of their true value.[12]

---

[11] Antonio de Remesal, *Historia general de las Indias Occidentales y particular de la gobernación de Chiapa y Guatemala* (Guatemala, 1932. Reprinted from Madrid, 1619), vol. IV, p. 170.

[12] Ms, Audiencia de Guatemala 9, AGI. Under date October 12, 1534, however, Almagro had submitted an *interrogatorio* or deposition in which he attempted to prove that Alvarado had practically forced him to buy six ships, which he didn't need, for 100,000 castellanos whereas they couldn't have been worth more than 25,000 or 30,000. Perhaps, withal, the most serious stroke at Alvarado in this deposition was Item 19 which accused Alvarado's men of saying that their force was going on to Cuzco to take that place from Francisco Pizarro. See *Documentos inéditos,* Ser. I, vol. 10, pp. 152 *et seq.* Several Almagro witnesses confirmed this, thus establishing a rather strong case for their side because the 1532 capitulation between the crown and Alvarado provided that he could not occupy any places where governors had been established already. See *ibid.,* vol. 22, pp. 307 *et seq.* Alvarado's defense, relative to this charge, was that he had not intended to go farther than Quito which, he alleged, lay outside the Almagro-Pizarro territory. He lost.

What Alvarado's men said about their commander's intentions would hardly have surmounted the objection as "hearsay" before an English or an

The disposal of six of his ships in Perú, however, did not deter Alvarado in his determination to proceed as a maritime impresario. Upon his return to Guatemala from the Quito expedition, he set about reconstituting a potent flotilla. One of his first acts was to take a ship, the "San Antonio," from Juan Rodríguez Cabrillo at Acajutla, in or about September 1534. Cabrillo was rigging this ship in the river near Acajutla and, along the bank, he had supplies, cargo, horses, mares, and other items, to be sent to Perú in this vessel with Domingo del Castillo as master. Alvarado "took the said ship from me by force and against my will and sent her on discovery in the South Sea," thus preventing Cabrillo's accomplishing the voyage he had planned.[13] Cabrillo alleged further, that, at the time Alvarado seized his ship, she had cost him three thousand *castellanos de oro de minas*.[14]

Cabrillo claimed that failure to make the Perú voyage caused a loss to him of five thousand castillanos

---

American court, but Spanish records are alive with it. An eminent American jurist, Dr. Schoenrich, has made this comment upon Spanish practice: "Hearsay evidence was allowed, so that it was not uncommon for a witness to answer that some fact was 'public and notorious' or that 'he has heard it said that this was so,' but the witness was expected to explain whom he had heard make the statement. . ." *See* Otto Schoenrich, *The Legacy of Christopher Columbus* (Glendale, Calif., 1949), vol. I, p. 342.

The Audiencia of Mexico found against Alvarado, but the Emperor set aside the sentence to a 100,000 castellano fine among other penalties. It was "not for nothing" that, as noted earlier, Alvarado had a friend at court in Francisco de los Cobos, the Emperor's secretary. *See* Ministerio de Fomento, *Cartas de Indias*, pp. 709-710.

13 This charge was made by Cabrillo at a much later date, after Alvarado was dead.

14 Ms, Justicia 280, AGI. It is very difficult to say how much that sum would be worth in United States dollars now but, according to Haggard, it might be $15,384.40. He shows the gold castellano worth $5.1128 in 1500; $4.5574, as of December 13, 1612, both in U.S. currency of 1936. See J. Villasana Haggard, *Handbook for Translators of Spanish Historical Documents* (Oklahoma City, 1941), p. 99.

because, at that time, the "San Antonio" was to carry ten horses. These animals, he said, were worth then, in Perú, twelve hundred and thirteen hundred pesos apiece, and upward.[15] This seems reminiscent of the Klondike gold rush when, it has been said, hen eggs sold at a dollar apiece, or of the forty-niners' period when, in San Francisco, no one expected change for a quarter.

Cabrillo alleged also that after Alvarado went to Spain, leaving Licentiate Alonso Maldonado as governor of Guatemala, he requested justice; by this time, two years after the ship's seizure. Maldonado ordered the vessel returned to the plaintiff who found it so ruined, old, and broken, that it wasn't worth two hundred *pesos de oro*. And, just as it was when returned to him, he sold it later to Alvarado himself for one hundred fifty *pesos de oro de minas*. Thus, Cabrillo received 67,500 *maravedís*[16] or $675.00 for this ship.[17]

While Cabrillo's allegations with regard to the losses he sustained through Alvarado's seizure of his ship

[15] This is item 4, of Cabrillo's petition, *ad perpetuam rei memoriam*, or, for the perpetual remembrance of the thing, which Cabrillo submitted on September 1, 1541 to Luis de Castilla, Chief Justice and Inspector of New Spain, in Puerto de la Navidad, Colima. It forms part of MS, Justicia 280, folios unnumbered, AGI.

[16] Manuel Luengo Muñoz, "Regulación jurídica de la explotación y comercio de las perlas del Mar Caribe en el siglo XVI," (unpublished Doctor's dissertation, Universidad Central de España, Madrid, 1952), p. 137. Colonel Luengo (teniente coronel, Guardia Civil) said here that the *peso de oro de minas* was an imaginary unit which, after 1531, the Spaniards continued to consider as worth 450 maravedís. The writer suggests its analogy to the current British "guinea" worth twenty-one shillings, entirely imaginary, yet very real in usage.

[17] Villasana Haggard, *Handbook for Translators*, p. 97. Haggard showed here that the maravedí fluctuated from $0.1361, in 1324, to $0.0075, in 1454; and, that it rose to $0.0077, by 1550. If, for convenience only, it be considered as one cent in U.S. current money, the peso de oro de minas would be worth $4.50.

were substantiated by manifestly competent testimony, it appears that the governor was not entirely callous to his subjects' interests. In 1536, it was recorded that he gave Cabrillo in *encomienda*[18] the town of Teota é Cotela near Gracias a Dios together with everything thereunto appertaining.[19] While the writer has not seen any assessment levied upon this encomienda as approved by the cabildo of Santiago de Guatemala, its *tasación* in the terminology then used, the *tasaciónes* upon other encomiendas which Tonatiuh granted Cabrillo show that the governor was by no means niggardly toward those in his favor. For example, the *tasación* of Jicalapa at one time was two hundred fifty *xiquipiles* of cacao and other items besides to be delivered annually. The cacao alone from this single encomienda would have returned about twenty-two hundred dollars, current United States money, a year to its encomendero.[20]

18 Vassalage has been given earlier as the equivalent of encomienda. While this term is believed to be accurate literally, the Spaniards developed palliatives in order to harmonize somewhat the Indians' status with the fiction that they were subjects of the Emperor on the same footing as Spanish nationals. Solórzano deemed the terms encomienda and *encomendero* coined for the situation, tracing the practices they involved from Christopher Columbus' period in Santo Domingo. He said:

"As those who received allotments of Indians were charged with their instruction, and teaching in Religion, and good practices, commending to them their persons, and good treatment, these allotments began to be called Encomiendas, and those who thus received the Indians, *Encomenderos,* or *Comendatarios,* from the Latin word *Commendo,* which sometimes signifies receiving something in safekeeping and trust, at other times to receive it to shelter and protect, and as under their faith, and patronage, according to its rendering by many texts, and Authors who treat this subject." – Juan de Solórzano y Pereyra, *Política indiana* (Madrid, 1776), vol. I, pp. 225 *et seq.*

19 *Documentos inéditos,* Ser. I, vol. 15, p. 18.

20 Ms, Audiencia de Guatemala 128, fol. 100, AGI. The xiquipil or jiquipil, as it is written today, was an integer of 8,000. The Aztecs used cacao as money, 100 kernels being equivalent to a *real.* Even now, it is said, the Indians estimate the *libra,* a very close equivalent to the English pound in

While Pedro de Alvarado gave Cabrillo the encomienda of Teota é Cotela in 1536, it appears that he engaged the latter's services in ship construction prior to that date for, in his petition cited above, *ad perpetuam rei memoriam* of 1541, Item 6, Cabrillo asked,

> if they knew that it may be six years, more or less, when the aforesaid governor went to spain and at the time he was going he charged me with building an armada for him in the meantime and then I built it and served in making the said armada which is the one he brought to this port of la navidad and with my own means I built a ship named sant salvador which is anchored in this port and at my expense without the governor or his stewards' putting anything whatever into it say what they know about this.

This allegation was amply substantiated by several witnesses in the replies to this question.

As indicated above, Alvarado's expedition to Quito enmeshed him anew in the toils of the Audiencia of Mexico and, although extrication was a tedious and time-consuming struggle, it did not deter him from energetic measures in acquiring his new flotilla. By 1537, Francisco Marroquín, bishop of Guatemala, could inform the emperor, relative to Alvarado's ships,

---

weight, of cacao in a peso of eight *reales*. See Augusto Malaret, *Diccionario de americanismos* (San Juan, Puerto Rico, 1931).

The cacao of 1790 was given the equivalent in current United States money of $0.0011. The silver real of 1497 was $0.3546; the *real vellón,* an alloy of silver and copper, of 1609-1625, was $0.0212. *See* Villasana Haggard, *Handbook for Translators,* pp. 99, 107.

Thus, the variety of values for the real, and the *peseta* and the peso, in which it figured, is so great that an assignment of value to the cacao during the first half of the sixteenth century could never be completely accurate. Perhaps it may be just as well to assume that no important currency changes ensued in Guatemala between the early 1500's and 1790, thus enabling one to value a cacao kernel in 11/10,000ths of today's United States dollar. On this basis, a jiquipil of cacao represented to the Cabrillo encomienda, 8,000 x 11/10,000 (88,000/10,000) or $8.80. As Jicalapa was assessed in 250 jiquipiles, this encomienda would have provided an annual income of $2,200.00.

"that he has very good ones, the best constructed that sailed the sea." [21]

In order best to escape from the penalties the Audiencia of Mexico had imposed upon him – a hundred thousand castellano fine being the heaviest – Alvarado set out again for Spain in 1537. And again, the emperor's secretary, Francisco de los Cobos, was to come to Alvarado's rescue; through his recommendations, the monarch set aside the Audiencia of Mexico's sentence. Alvarado not only maintained his former tie with that powerful minister but also he strengthened it, for he again paid court to one of Cobos' nieces, his first wife's sister, Beatriz de la Cueva. Cobos approved Alvarado's suit and procured a Papal dispensation in order that he could marry her. [22]

After an examination of the record, one must say that Tonatiuh was thoroughgoing in his bid for influence at court. He had not only taken two nieces personally off Cobos' hands, but also he made provision for their brother, Francisco de la Cueva, Cobos' nephew, by engaging to take him to Guatemala to marry Alvarado's mestizo daughter, Leonor. [23] As if he wanted to ingratiate himself with more numerous, if not such powerful supporters in Spain, he arranged also to take twenty damsels of leading families to Guatemala in order to find husbands among the wealthy conquistadores in that province. [24] So, with these young ladies and an otherwise brilliant suite and many of the sinews of war and much equipment for ship construction and fitting-out, Alvarado sailed for his bailiwick in early 1539.

21 Letter, May 10, 1537, Bishop Marroquín to the Emperor, in Ministerio de Fomento, Cartas de Indias, pp. 421, 708-709.

22 Ministerio de Fomento, Cartas de Indias, pp. 709-710.

23 Díaz del Castillo Historia verdadera, vol. II, p. 500.

24 Bancroft, Central America, vol. II, p. 202.

It appeared that romance was to flower swiftly in the New World for Pedro the matchmaker for it even blossomed in Santo Domingo on the way to Guatemala. Alvarado stopped at that capital in order to enjoy the hospitality of the Columbus palace but more especially to visit family connections. Tonatiuh's wife, Doña Beatriz, was a niece by marriage of Juana Columbus Toledo, daughter of Christopher Columbus' son, Diego, by María de Toledo who, incidentally, was a niece of the Duke of Alba and a relative of the emperor. Juana Columbus Toledo had married Luis de la Cueva, and thus had become Doña Beatriz de la Cueva de Alvarado's aunt by marriage.

But, reverting to the romance, Don Luis Columbus, a youth about nineteen years old and heir apparent to the vast Columbus holdings in the New World, appeared to have a propensity toward marriage somewhat similar to that of certain wealthy American "playboys" of the current era. A young lady, María de Orozco, one of those in the Alvarado suite, caught Don Luis' fancy, and he soon managed by palace intrigue to get clandestine meetings with the object of his infatuation. At the second of these love feasts, they, "by words of the present" – *por palabras de presente* – celebrated a valid marriage, although the records do not show that it was consummated carnally; they mutually and reciprocally declared themselves husband and wife.[25]

Doña María de Toledo de Columbus was highly in-

---

[25] The steps of this romance and the family relationships are covered in Schoenrich, *Legacy of Christopher Columbus*, vol. I, pp. 253-262. The legality and validity of such marriages was based upon Part IV, Title I, Law V, of the Code of the *Siete Partidas* (Seven Parts), a code of laws prepared under the direction of King Alfonso X in the thirteenth century. See *ibid.*, pp. 46, 257. Its provisions were abrogated by the Council of Trent on November 11, 1563. *Ibid.*, p. 258.

censed and deeply distressed by her son's conduct; the Alvarado couple were profoundly mortified because a member of their suite had caused the hostess so much distress. The Alvarados quickly put a stop to further association between María de Orozco and Don Luis by incarcerating her and the maids privy to the intrigue in the palace chapel until they again embarked for Guatemala. The senior family parties agreed that it was more expedient to part the newlyweds definitively than to undergo the expense and great delay a Papal annulment of this impromptu marriage would require. The church frowned upon such unions anyway.

Don Luis tried to get in touch with María in Guatemala, but Alvarado frustrated all that young man's efforts. The governor then arranged a match between María and Francisco de Castellanos, treasurer of Guatemala, who has been introduced earlier in this book. It has been recorded that she bore him many children.

The other young ladies in the Alvarado suite were not as fortunate, apparently, as María de Orozco had been; they were sadly disillusioned by at least their first glimpse of prospective husbands.

> What! marry those old fellows? Let those wed them who choose; I will not; the devil take them! One would think by the way they are cut up that they just escaped from the infernal regions; for some are lame, some with but one hand, others without ears, others with only one eye, others with half their face gone, and the best of them with one or two cuts across the forehead.[26]

What a blow to anyone who had fancied the conquistadores as handsome young knights in shining armor!

---

[26] Bancroft, *Central America*, vol. II, p. 204.

Again in Guatemala, from April 4, 1539 onward, Alvarado transferred his ships' materials across that country to Acajutla on the Pacific Ocean, at a great sacrifice of *tamemes,* for many of the loads (such as guns and anchors) which they had to carry were enormous. With the delivery of ships' materials to Juan Rodríguez Cabrillo, construction and outfitting of the largest flotilla ever seen in the South Sea up to that time went on apace. As it will develop later, Alvarado was practically to bankrupt himself and his creditors in his self-assigned mission to emulate and supersede his former chieftain, Hernán Cortés, in bringing new and greater realms into His Majesty's domains. As for Cortés, who was left in Mexico in 1534 after his ships' first contact with Baja California, it is well now to return to the scene of his activities in nautical exploration.

III

Cortes and Mendoza as Rivals

Although the misfortunes which, in 1534, resulted in
the deaths of Becerra and Jiménez and left the "Concepción" in a missing status, Cortés, nevertheless, was
merely checked momentarily in his efforts toward nautical exploration. Grijalva returned to New Spain in
the "San Lázaro," and, shortly thereafter, Cortés got
word about what had happened to Becerra and to the
"Concepción" from two sailors, presumably Becerra's
men, who had arrived in a small craft sailing from
Jalisco. They reported that Nuño de Guzmán had
seized the "Concepción" and everything in her and that
he planned to send her to Santa Cruz Bay. Cortés complained to the audiencia, but got no satisfaction.[1]

Cortés decided to take matters into his own hands,
outfitting three ships for this purpose, and called for
volunteers to form a force which he would lead in person. So great yet was Cortés' prestige, that he was soon
swamped by volunteers. There is some disagreement,
however, on his procedure after he had assembled his
force and some colonists besides. Bernal Díaz said that,
"in order to avoid so much confusion by land, he
ordered that those who wished to embark in Tehuantepec should join the ships there while he would lead
the rest to the port from which the ships would finally
sail."[2]

---

[1] Herrera, *Historia general,* Déc. v, Lib. vi, p. 201.
[2] Díaz del Castillo, *Historia verdadera,* vol. ii, pp. 481-482.

On the other hand, Herrera said that Cortés sent off the three ships he had fitted out, the "San Lázaro," the "Santa Agueda," and the "Santo Tomás," while he, personally, marched on Nueva Galicia by land, leading a heavily armed force of horse and foot. Herrera said, moreover, that the scare which this movement threw into Nuño de Guzmán was, alone, ample compensation for Cortés' expense and trouble. When Cortés' column reached the "Concepción," however, they found her beached, broadside to, and looted; a loss estimated at more than twenty thousand ducats, a sum which today might approximate eighty thousand dollars. Guzmán had not lingered anywhere near Cortés' route of march for a reckoning.[3]

Bernal Díaz and Herrera agreed, however, on Cortés' subsequent movements. In 1535, he established a colony at La Paz Bay, then called Bahía de Santa Cruz. The barren nature of the land in that littoral and its consequent lack of produce made supply from the mainland imperative, and Cortés soon found himself and his ships wracked by the head winds from his sources of supply on the Mexican coast. When he did deliver supplies to his colony, he also found distressing deaths from dearth of victuals and disease.

While Cortés was engaged in these soul-trying efforts, the marchioness, his wife, fearing for his life, sent a ship under the command of Francisco de Ulloa to La Paz to deliver to him letters urging him to return to Mexico. Ulloa brought Cortés also the news that Don Antonio de Mendoza, the first viceroy of New Spain, had arrived to assume his office in that country.[4]

3 Herrera, *op. cit.,* vol. III, Déc. v, Lib. VIII, pp. 247-248.

4 Bancroft, *History of Mexico,* vol. II, p. 424. Díaz del Castillo, *op. cit.,* p. 483, said that Ulloa also brought Cortés letters to the same effect from Viceroy Mendoza.

In passing, it is interesting to note that Bernal Díaz, after dwelling upon the turns of bad luck which had been besetting Cortés, said: "And Cortés, in order not to see so much bad fortune confronting him, went to discover other lands, and they ran into California, which is a bay." [5] Díaz gave California a different meaning on the two pages following this quotation. After relating Cortés' return to Acapulco at the instances of his wife and Mendoza, Díaz said: "And besides this, all the soldiers and captains whom he had left in those islands, or bay, which they call California, came back next," a Cervantine touch, more than forty years before Don Quixote appeared.

As Ulloa brought the news that a viceroy had come to Mexico, Cortés was to learn that a rival, far more powerful than any other who had confronted him previously, had entered the scene in New Spain. Don Antonio de Mendoza, scion of a noble family enjoying great influence at court in Spain, came bountifully clothed with viceregal powers and provided by royal dispensation with ample means to maintain a state of princely dignity in office. The princely means, of course, were to be made available from the revenues which the emperor expected from Mexico. [6]

Although Cortés was the captain-general of New Spain, Mendoza, nevertheless, had been empowered to delegate at discretion the functions of that office to someone other than the Marqués del Valle. [7] Whether

---

[5] Díaz del Castillo, *loc. cit.*

[6] For a succinct and excellent account of Mendoza's family background and his personal accomplishments, see C. Pérez Bustamante, *Don Antonio de Mendoza: Primer virrey de la Nueva España* (1535-1550), (Santiago de Galicia, Spain, 1928), chap. I, pp. 1-10. For salary and allowances, see *ibid.,* pp. 19-20. It is likewise given in chapter I of Arthur Scott Aiton, *Antonio de Mendoza: First Viceroy of New Spain* (Durham, N.C., 1927).

[7] Pérez Bustamante, *loc. cit.*

Cortés knew this at the time he first met Mendoza is a matter of conjecture, but it seems reasonable to assume that he did not know it when his marked propensity to defend his rights is taken into account. One should remember, too, that Cortés appeared to accept the viceroy with good grace; he soon came to an agreement with Mendoza upon the protocol they would observe when in company, either publicly or privately.

Cortés, moreover, apparently acting on the principle, "if you can't beat him, join him," proposed to Mendoza that they become partners in exploration, share and share alike in costs and gains. The viceroy became very much interested in Cortés' proposals as soon became evident to his suite. One of the gentlemen of his household, observing how closely he had become engaged with the conquistador, warned the viceroy against it much as Velázquez was importuned against Cortés in Cuba many years before. In fact, Cortés' case with Velázquez was cited against him; Mendoza was reminded that Cortés did not make any return at all to the governor of Cuba for what the latter had invested in their Mexican venture, but kept it all for himself. The viceroy was assured that he would fare likewise if he should become Cortés' partner, and was urged to engage in exploration on his sole account. As Mendoza was convinced by this argument, he decided not to accept what the Marqués had proposed.[8] Again Cortés' Cuban chickens came home to roost. Afterward, in 1537, Mendoza asked the emperor's permission to take part in discovery "and for the same favors granted to others in like cases."[9]

---

[8] Pérez Bustamante, *op. cit.*, footnote on p. 59, quoting Juan Suárez de Peralta, *Noticias históricas de Nueva España* (Madrid, 1878), chap. XXI.

[9] Bancroft, *History of Mexico*, vol. II, p. 424, and footnote 48.

As Bancroft has stated accurately, little is known about Cortés' seafaring activities during the next two or three years after his return from Baja California in 1535. It is reasonable to assume, however, that he did not neglect ship construction for, in September 1538, he wrote the Council of the Indies that he had nine good ships built but not launched because of the scarcity of sailors. In the light of Cortés' later statements, however, one cannot agree with Bancroft that, in 1539, the conquistador's enthusiasm for exploration "was raised by the marvellous reports brought by Marcos de Niza of the cities of Cíbola." [10]

Friar Marcos de Niza had been sent in 1539 by Viceroy Mendoza to investigate the truth of stories which Alvar Núñez Cabeza de Vaca and some companions had brought to Mexico. Núñez was a survivor of an expedition which Pánfilo de Narváez, the same man whom Velázquez had sent to Mexico to seize Cortés, led to the Florida coast in 1428 and lost there. After years of almost incredible experiences and wanderings, Núñez arrived in Sinaloa in 1536. He and his companions had heard tales of the great kingdom of Quivira and the Seven Cities of Cíbola, they said, and these were not far beyond the areas through which they had passed. They had not seen these marvels; they had merely heard of them from the Indians; but, Friar Marcos returned and reported that he had seen but not entered a city of Cíbola. "To him it looked larger than Mexico City, though reputed to be the smallest city of the famous seven." [11] If it ever occurred to Mendoza that the friar really had not seen anything even faintly resembling these fabled cities replete with gold and silver, he has not left any records of his doubts.

[10] *Loc. cit.*   [11] Chapman, *History of California,* pp. 52-53.

One may wonder, withal, why so capable a man as Antonio de Mendoza did not go thoroughly into Friar Marcos de Niza's background. Cortés, it seems, had done so, although, at the time he wrote about the friar, he was very likely looking upon everything with a jaundiced eye. Cortés said Friar Marcos was always fabricating and relating accounts of where he had gone and what he had seen, whereas, in fact, he had never been there and had never seen anything new. For this very thing, Cortés wrote, the friar was notorious in the provinces of Perú and Guatemala. Cortés said also, that, upon his return from Santa Cruz, he gave Friar Marcos some accounts of the lands which he and his captains had discovered and of what his Indian interpreters had told him; because, as he understood that the friar had some knowledge of navigation, he planned to include that religious in his next expedition. Cortés insisted that, as far as the geography and topography of the northerly provinces were concerned, Friar Marcos de Niza merely related what the great captain had told him.[12]

Thus, it hardly seems logical that Cortés could have become enthusiastic over accounts from Friar Marcos, one already notorious for fabrications as Cortés stated. On the other hand, Cortés, by every previous indication, was vehemently bent upon asserting his rights and keeping the lead in nautical exploration.

From Acapulco, on July 8, 1539, Cortés dispatched three ships under the command of Francisco de Ulloa. These were the "Santa Agueda," the "Trinidad," and the "Santo Tomás"; of 120, 35, and 20 tons respectively. The "Santo Tomás" was soon lost on the coast of

[12] Ms, Patronato 21, no. 2, ramo 4, AGI.

Culiacán.[13] By Cortés' own statement, Ulloa's mission was to seek the land which had been described to the captain-general, the same area of which the latter, in turn, had informed Friar Marcos de Niza.[14]

In this same document, Cortés made bitter accusations against Antonio de Mendoza. He said that the viceroy, overly stimulated by Friar Marcos' account, sent detachments to every port where he suspected Ulloa might put in with intent to learn what Ulloa had discovered, to detain him, and to prevent his going farther. When Ulloa went into Puerto Santiago de Buena Esperanza, Colima, where he put a sailor ashore to give Cortés a report on the voyage, the sailor was seized by the viceroy's orders and tortured in a vain effort to extract information from him. A mounted detachment was sent to seize the ship, but Ulloa had sailed before the detachment arrived, whereupon it followed him more than one hundred twenty leagues up the coast. As Ulloa was afraid to enter port, he was caught in a storm in which he lost his anchors and a small boat, so he was forced into Guatulco where the pilot and the ship were seized, and the ship was lost.

According to Cortés, the viceroy next ordered that none would leave Nueva España without his permission. Then, in order to make sure that Cortés could not move, he ordered Gómez de Villafaña, governor of Guamalula, to Tehuantepec to seize all of Cortés' ships, his stores of sails, shrouds, rudders, and other gear, and to put all his yard workmen under injunction against further work there.

---

[13] Hubert Howe Bancroft, *History of the North Mexican States and Texas* (San Francisco, 1884), vol. I, pp. 78-80.
[14] Ms, Patronato 21, no. 2, ramo 4, AGI.

Francisco de Ulloa, nevertheless, was well away on his nautical exploration. His 1539-1540 voyage has contributed features of importance geographically, for he was the first to sail around the greater portion of Baja California's perimeter. It has been alleged also that he went along all of that peninsula's coastline, probably reaching the latitude of San Diego, California. Apart from speculation, however, it seems certain that he did reach Cabo del Engaño or Cape Deceit in approximately thirty degrees north latitude.

Bancroft, while disclaiming the geographical importance of Ulloa's voyage, "as but few of the points mentioned can be identified," gave it, nevertheless, "a certain degree of historic value" because it was the first expedition to explore the Gulf of California to its head. The great historian condensed the details into a footnote, and gave credit for the record to Preciado's account in Ramusio.[15]

One feature of Ulloa's cruise is most noteworthy; he used long reaches against the prevailing northwesterly winds as he clawed his way to the northern limit of the gulf. For example, he stood across that body of water from Guayabal to La Paz; thence, he crossed back to the Mexican side at the mouth of the San Pedro and San Pablo River. As the gulf narrowed with his northward advance, Ulloa clung more to the Mexican side until he reached its head. From his farthest north, he ran down the east coast of Baja California. This should have been easy sailing with the wind abaft his starboard beam, if not on his starboard quarter, most of

---

[15] Bancroft, *North Mexican States,* vol. I, p. 79, and note 13. He cited Giovanni Battista Ramusio, *Navegatione et Viaggi* (Venetia: tom. I, 1554; tom. II, 1565; tom. III, 1583), no volume nor pages specified. Francisco Preciado, of whom more later, kept a diary of this voyage as long as the two ships were in company and of the "Santa Agueda's" cruise to its completion.

the time. At any rate, he was back at La Paz on October 18, just one month and twenty-five days after his departure from that place. This, certainly was not bad time, taking into account delays due to reconnaissances, head winds and currents to buck, and plowing through uncharted waters.

From La Paz, Francisco de Ulloa went around Cape San Lucas onto the broad Pacific Ocean. His step-by-step progress will not be traced, yet it is significant that he most probably went into Magdalena Bay on his way up to Cedros Island. On January 20, 1540,

> wee sailed with scarse and contrary windes, and at length came to the cape of the point of the Island, which we called Isla de los Cedros or the Ile of Cedars, because that on the tops of the mountaines therein, there growes a wood of these Cedars being very tall, as the nature of them is to be.[16]

At Cedros Island, the two ships parted company; Ulloa dispatched the "Santa Agueda" to Acapulco, carrying off the infirm of both ships' companies and a report of his cruise up to that point. Ulloa, in the "Trinidad," then stood away to the north to carry on his nautical exploration. As stated earlier, speculation has been indulged regarding the upper limits Ulloa may have reached after he started north alone, because no specific record of this part of the voyage has been discovered.

In this connection, it is especially interesting to note a development by the late Henry Raup Wagner, a great California historian who devoted a great deal of research to early nautical exploration along the coasts of

---

[16] Richard Hakluyt, *The Third and Last Volume of the Principal Navigations, Voyages, Traffiques, and Discoveries of the English Nation . . . any time within the compasse of these 1600 yeres* . . . (London, 1600), p. 418. Cited hereafter as *Third and Last Volume*.

the Californias and also on the northwest coast of the
United States. Wagner brought up the point that some
of Ulloa's place names north of Cedros Island appear
on a chart made in 1568 by Diego de Homem. This led
Wagner to think that this chart may furnish traces of
the return voyage, and that Ulloa may have gone as
far as thirty-three degrees north latitude. Wagner
made a worthwhile suggestion also with regard to what
the writer feels must have been a Homeric nod on the
part of Antonio de Herrera in his *Décadas,* often cited
herein. Herrera said that Ulloa never returned to New
Spain. Wagner suggested that Herrera may have inter-
preted incorrectly a remark by Preciado, "that he had
not heard any more of the "Santa Agueda," and thought
that this referred to Ulloa." [17]

The matter of a Homeric nod on Herrera's part
seems cogent on account of the following statements by
Preciado:

> After this ship the Santa Agueda departed from the Generall
> Ulloa, and returned backe the 5 of April, she arrived in the port
> of Sant Iago de buena esperança the 18 of the said moneth, and
> after she had stayed there foure or fiue dayes, she departed for
> Acapulco: howbeit until this present seuenteenth of May in the
> yeere 1540, I have heard no tidings nor newes of her. . .

> Moreouer after the departure of the Santa Agueda for Nueua
> Espanna, the General Francis Ulloa in the ship called the
> Trinitie proceeding on his discouery coasted the land untill he
> came to a point called Cabo del Enganno standing in thirty
> degrees and a halfe of Northerly latitude, and then returned
> backe to Newspaine, because he found the winds very contrary,
> and his victuals failed him.[18]

Thus, Preciado did not say that he never heard of

[17] Henry R. Wagner, *Spanish Voyages to the Northwest Coast of America
in the Sixteenth Century* (San Francisco, 1929), p. 14.
[18] Hakluyt, *The Third and Last Volume,* p. 424.

AN ARTIST'S CONCEPTION OF ULLOA'S SHIP, THE "TRINIDAD"
Courtesy of San Luis Rey Historical Society, Oceanside, California.
Photo by Markey-Herbster, Oceanside.

the "Santa Agueda" again; he merely hadn't heard of her up to May 17, 1540, quite a different matter. As for not hearing of Ulloa again, Preciado certainly stated that he returned and gave the reason why. Hakluyt said categorically on this same page that "This relation was taken out of that which Francis Preciado brought with him."

Bernal Díaz said that Ulloa's voyage lasted seven months going and coming; that Ulloa did nothing worth relating, and returned to

> the port of Jalisco. And a few days afterward, while Ulloa was ashore resting, one of the soldiers among those who had been aboard his flagship, waylaid him and killed him there by sword thrusts.[19]

Neither of these accounts of Ulloa's return to New Spain, apparently, satisfied Dr. Wagner. Pursuing his researches further, he found excellent evidence that Ulloa not only returned to Mexico but also that he went on to Spain and served again with his great chief, Cortés. Wagner found his evidence in the record of a lawsuit which Juan Castellón brought against Hernán Cortés for seventeen hundred pesos before the Audiencia of Mexico on February 17, 1541. This record, according to Wagner, had been part of the Cortés papers stored in the Hospital de Jesús until these were transferred to the Archivo General in Mexico City.

As Francisco de Ulloa, by Cortés' order, had superseded Juan Castellón in command of the "Trinidad" in 1539, Castellón listed Ulloa as a witness in his behalf to support his claim for payment of services rendered Cortés. About the end of December 1539, Cortés left Mexico to go to Spain. In May 1541, Licentiate Juan

---

[19] Díaz del Castillo, *Historia verdadera*, vol. II, p. 485.

Altamirano stated in Mexico that Francisco de Ulloa and Gonzalo Hidalgo had gone to Spain after Cortés' departure, accompanying Cortés' son to that country. As others involved in the suit had gone to Spain also, the audiencia appointed a commission to take testimony in the homeland.

In May 1542, Iñigo López de Mondragón presented depositions in Valladolid.

> Only two witnesses were examined in Valladolid (at least that is all that are named in the documents), namely, Alonso de Ulloa and Francisco de Ulloa. The testimony of Alonso de Ulloa does not concern us, but Francisco de Ulloa said that he was more than twenty-five years old and in answer to one of the questions replied that the reference to Francisco de Ulloa was to himself. This settles for all time whether Ulloa returned or not. . .
>
> I recently saw a notice of Ulloa in the *Vita dell' in vittissimo e sacratissimo imperator Carlo V,* printed in Venetia in 1562. The author, Alfonso Ulloa, in speaking of the Argel expedition in 1541, tells the story of Cortés' losing his famous emeralds and states that he was accompanied by his great friend, the author's father, Francisco de Ulloa.[20]

While Wagner, apparently, felt that he had clinched his point and, therefore, did not find it necessary to cite any additional evidence, he might have added an interesting item which seems to corroborate Alfonso de Ulloa's position. In a biography of this man, one finds the following statement in literal translation: "Son of an officer who was in Africa with Charles V, he followed the paternal career. . ." The same biography states that, in later years, he began to devote himself to writing and, among several works he published, it lists *"Vida del invictísimo y sacratísimo emperador Carlos*

---

[20] Henry Raup Wagner, "Francisco de Ulloa Returned," *California Historical Society Quarterly,* vol. XIX, September 1940, pp. 241-243.

V [*Life of the Most Invincible and Most Venerable Emperor Charles V*] (Venecia, 1566; 3a edición, 1606)." [21]

Despite the evidence cited herein, J. J. Markey, M.D., of Oceanside, California, has been publishing claims that Ulloa and most of the "Trinidad" personnel died in the San Luis Rey Valley near that place. Markey has said that the first evidence of this was found in a diary which one Pablo Salvador Hernández had kept. Hernández was "an official reporter who accompanied Ulloa on his voyage," one among a few who survived disease in the San Luis Rey Valley and made their way back to Mexico. Markey implied that he found this diary among old papers in vaults underneath the Biblioteca Nacional in Madrid. He has said that "its meticulous record" enabled him and a party to find Ulloa's grave.[22]

Reverting now to the period between Cortés' return to Mexico from Lower California and the beginning of Ulloa's voyage just under discussion, one should note that, among the letters Ulloa delivered to Cortés

[21] Espasa-Calpe, S.A., *Enciclopedia universal ilustrada europeo-americana* (Madrid, Barcelona, Bilbao: no date), vol. LXV. One might note in the renderings of this title the striking similarity between the Italian and the Spanish languages.

[22] From an article in *The Southern California Rancher*, (Oceanside), February 1952, p. 7, and from letters, Markey to writer, February 5, 13, and 18, 1957. By letters from Madrid, the writer has been informed that the papers formerly stored in the basement of the Biblioteca Nacional were those belonging to the Archivo Histórico Nacional which was later established on the second floor of that edifice, facing El Paseo de la Castellana, where the writer found it in 1955-1956. It was moved sometime after May 1956 to Calle de Serrano, 115, Madrid. Search by archivists in the Sección de Manuscritos, Biblioteca Nacional, in the Archivo Histórico Nacional, and in the Archivo General de Indias, Sevilla, has revealed that there is no documentation whatever connected with any Pablo Salvador Hernández. – Letters to writer, Luis Morales Oliver, March 1; Tomás Magallón, April 2; Benito Díaz de Villafranca, May 10 and July 13; all, 1957.

at Santa Cruz, there were dispatches from the Audiencia of Mexico and Viceroy Mendoza begging and even
ordering Cortés to return to New Spain. His presence
was necessary, they explained, not only for maintaining
peace and good government there, but also to provide
support to Francisco Pizarro in Perú. Pizarro was in
dire need of assistance in the land he had invaded because a general Indian uprising was threatening the
liquidation of all the Spaniards in that country. This,
Pizarro wrote, would represent a grave disservice to
the emperor.

Cortés acted at once in Pizarro's behalf, and forthwith dispatched two ships to Callao under the command of Hernando de Grijalva. These ships carried
many troops, horses, munitions, arms, subsistence stores,
and gifts of clothing, trappings, and, on the part of
Cortés' wife, dresses.[23]

According to Gómara, Cortés never received any
recompense for his princely contribution to Pizarro's
cause because the conqueror of Perú was assassinated a
little while after the ships arrived. Pizarro, however,
did send "many and rich things to the Marchioness,
Doña Juana de Zúñiga, but Grijalva ran away with
them." [24] As nothing more was ever heard of Hernando
de Grijalva and the two ships he commanded after
their departure from Perú, events in that land had
again influenced the course of movements toward California.[25]

---

23 Miguel Venegas, *Noticia de la California y de su Conquista Temporal
y Espiritual Hasta el Tiempo Presente* (Mexico City, 1943), vol. I, pp. 123-
124. This work hereinafter will be designated *Noticia*.

24 López de Gómara, *Conquista de Méjico*, vol. II, p. 183.

25 From the points of view of historical interest and verisimilitude, it is
regrettable that Markey's investigations did not point to Grijalba instead of
Ulloa as the discoverer of Alta California. Markey, according to the *Daily
Blade-Tribune* of February 3, 1957, said "Ulloa wasn't broadcasting his ac-

As far as movements toward California were concerned, Antonio de Mendoza was not only bent upon circumventing Cortés as has been seen in his efforts to thwart the activities of the captain-general's ships; he was also determined to project exploring expeditions on his own account. According to Venegas, the viceroy believed that he had at hand the opportunity to make a conquest which would enable him to become as famous and as rich as Cortés had become through his conquest of Mexico.[26] So, against Cortés' vigorous protests that such was an unwarranted invasion of his sole rights, as he termed it, Mendoza began preparing expeditions by land and by sea for projections into the great stretches northwest and north of Mexico.

The expedition by water was entrusted to Hernando de Alarcón who had served Mendoza many years as *maestresala,* a post probably much higher socially than understood by the English terms butler and chief wine-taster.[27] Just where or how Alarcón developed qualifications for a sea command has not come into the writer's view; perhaps it is reasonable to assume that he was chosen more for administrative skill than for qualities as a seaman. Probably all matters pertaining to navigation and seamanship were entrusted to sailing masters anyway; just as that practice prevailed even on men-of-war down through Nelson's day.

At any rate, two vessels were fitted out at Acapulco;

tivities because he was running off with a quantity of loot belonging to his superior, Hernando Cortés," and that this gold, "stolen from Cortés," was estimated to be worth millions. Markey was quoted to much the same effect by the *Los Angeles Times,* February 11, 1957, part III. How, and under what circumstances, Ulloa accomplished such theft was not explained. On the other hand, a ready explanation would have been available in case Grijalba should have been the protagonist in this drama.

[26] Venegas, *op. cit.,* p. 130.

[27] Pérez Bustamante, *Don Antonio de Mendoza,* p. 65.

the "San Pedro," under Alarcón, and the "Santa Catalina," commanded by Marcos Ruiz. Domingo del Castillo was in this expedition also, sailing up the gulf again, for he had been with Ulloa in 1539 as cartographer.[28]

Mendoza's purpose in setting Alarcón forth was well conceived and entirely sound; it was maritime logistic support for the land expedition which the viceroy was forming under the leadership of Francisco Vázquez de Coronado. With all the passion for detail, however, which is manifest in the written instructions that Spanish authorities issued in the sixteenth century, these planners appear to have been blandly unaware of the extreme importance time and space factors assume in good planning. It doesn't seem reasonable to presume that they could have been ignorant of the space factors involved, for the Cabeza de Vaca party had provided a written description of the route it had followed into Culiacán, and this had been verified, presumably, by Friar Marcos de Niza. As far as the coastline was concerned, surely Domingo del Castillo, who had charted it, could have given expert advice as to its extent and configuration.

The complete absurdity of Mendoza's planning is readily apparent as Bolton tells the story of the two expeditions' initial movements.

> The expedition did not leave Acapulco until May 9 [1540]. This was more than two months after Coronado said goodbye to Compostela, seventeen days after he left Culiacán with his advance guard, and about the same time that Arellano started north from there with the rest of the army. So the vessels were far behind the land forces.[29]

---

[28] Herbert Eugene Bolton, *Coronado, Knight of Pueblos and Plains* (Albuquerque, 1949), p. 153.

[29] Bolton, *Coronado,* pp. 153-154.

The approximate distance, headland to headland, along the coast from Acapulco to Compostela, is 540 statute miles; from Compostela to Culiacán, likewise, 280 land miles. From these figures and the dates which Bolton has given, Coronado was averaging better than ten miles a day, probably appreciably more when the necessarily circuitous route he followed is taken into account. This was certainly not a poor accomplishment when it is considered that he was encumbered by pack animals, flocks, and herds. In Alarcón's case, on the other hand, there were undoubtedly days when he couldn't make any northings at all against head winds, and Coronado was 820 land miles ahead when Alarcón started.

Some suggestion of coordination might have been expected as Alarcón put into Santiago near Manzanillo Bay where he repaired storm damages, and took aboard additional personnel and supplies. He fared thence to the port of Culiacán where he found the "San Gabriel" loaded with supplies for Coronado, and took her into company with his other two ships.

As Alarcón fared on northward, he hugged the shore as he was looking for "markers" erected by Coronado and for Indians who might give him information regarding the land expedition. He looked in vain, however, and to Bolton this seemed "a little strange" because, when Alarcón went along the Sonora coast, Arellano was founding San Gerónimo on the Sonora River.[30] Also, Arellano sent patrols to the gulf to look for Alarcón's ships.[31]

As one may have suspected from what has been in-

---

[30] This was Captain Tristán de Luna y Arellano who commanded Coronado's main body from Culiacán northward and later was to be identified as a conqueror in Alabama. *Ibid.*, p. 70.

[31] Bolton, *Coronado*, pp. 154 *et seq.*

dicated as poor planning, Alarcón and Coronado never established contact with each other. This failure has been ascribed to Coronado's indifference which, in turn, was attributed to his overweening desire to reach the fabled cities of Cíbola.[32] As partially indicated already, this is neither accurate nor fair to Coronado. He passed through "the provinces of Cametla, Culiacan, and Sinaloa," and went on north and northwest, following the courses which had been provided in writing by Cabeza de Vaca's party, yet veering to the west and to the coast to inquire about Alarcón. From the Indians, he got an account of "two houses in the sea," sighted on northerly courses, while they were in one of the nations of Yaquimi.[33]

Coronado continued marching, north and northwest, then sent a thirty-man patrol toward the gulf from a town named Vacapa. This detachment marched forty leagues toward the coast in thirty-one degrees north latitude, and, from the Otan or Pima nation, they learned that one ship had been sighted offshore in the gulf. The patrol rejoined and reported and Coronado fared northward beyond thirty-four degrees, where, in a very lush valley near the Mosqui [sic] nations, he encamped to recuperate forces for further advance.

From this encampment, Coronado dispatched a forty-man patrol, mounted on the best of his horses, in search of Alarcón whom he believed nearby. The patrol made ten marches northwest and west, and struck the shore in thirty-nine degrees.[34] The author did not say

---

32 Alvaro del Portillo y Diez de Sollano, *Descubrimientos y exploraciones en las costas de California* (Madrid, 1947), p. 152.

33 Ms, "California, historia y viajes," Museo Naval, Madrid, tomo I, doc. no. I, fols. 6v.-7v.

34 Ms, "California, . . ." Museo Naval, Madrid, tomo I, doc. no. I, fol. 8. ". . . fueron caminando al Norueste, y Poniente diez Jornadas, y con bastante travajo llegaron á sus Playas en altura de 39/ grados. . ."

how they determined this latitude, obviously far in error, as the Gulf of California would thus have extended up to Lake County, California!

According to this same account, the patrol went northward along the coast without finding positive traces of Alarcón although they again got the quaint native report of having sighted "houses in the sea" with this significant variation, "and many on shore." Sure enough, they did strike a port where two small vessels lay at anchor and they found some "pavillions" set up ashore. Around these were a few kinky-haired men and some others with long straight hair, brunettes, who indicated that their country lay to the west beyond the ocean sea, perhaps toward Asia or China.[35]

The cases cited already seem sufficient evidence that Coronado, instead of being indifferent toward contact with Alarcón, was, from the outset, anxious to get in touch with him. While his searches never led to sighting Alarcón's ships, they did uncover positive evidence as to the scope of that seafarer's movements.

According to Juan Jaramillo, Coronado sent Mel-

---

[35] One may wonder why these foreigners' presence did not set off an alarm as great as that raised on Spain's Mediterranean shores by the ancient cry, *hay moros en la costa!* – "there are Moors along the coast!" Contrary to his usual practice, Navarrete did not cite the source nor the authorship of this manuscript. The writer believes that it has been extracted from the original which now appears in print in Juan Matheo Mange, *Luz de Tierra Incógnita en la América Septentrional y Diario de las Exploraciones en Sonora* (Mexico, 1926). The original manuscript was printed in this publication according to statements on p. 172. The writer's clue to the author of "California, historia y viajes" appears in Tomo I, doc. 1, fols. 2-2v., in "according to what I saw from a hill during the entry I made in 1701 with the Reverend Fathers Juan María Salvatierra and Eusebio Kino, Jesuits." Fols. 6-7v. and 8, cited herein, appear verbatim on pp. 93-94 of the printed work. Venegas, referring to this entry and its establishing Lower California as a peninsula, said: "to the same effect, they cite Captain Mateo Mangé's narratives, printed in French, although I haven't been able to lay hands upon them either in that language or in Castilian." – Venegas, *Noticia*, vol. II, p. 70. One may wonder why Mange's work went out of circulation.

chior Díaz with about forty mounted troops, one hundred fifty leagues westward to the river Alarcón ascended and named Buena Guía or Good Guide (now the Colorado). Díaz reached it "thirty leagues from the coast," meaning, one must assume, from the gulf coast. Alarcón had gone upstream as many leagues more, about two months before Díaz arrived.[36]

In this area, the Indians undoubtedly had accurate information as to Alarcón's movements for they had towed his two launches upstream almost from the beginning of his river trip. He thought that, except for this, he could not have gone so far inland.

> Wherefore if we had not had this helpe, the current of the river being exceeding great, and our men that drew the rope being not well acquainted with that occupation, it would haue beene impossible for us to haue gotten up the riuer so against the streame.[37]

Díaz learned from the Indians that Alarcón and his launches had been downstream from the point where he struck the river, so he marched three days in that direction and reached a spot about midway between the gulf and Yuma. There, he found a large tree which Alarcón had marked, a ceiba, according to Obregón; and, at the foot of it, he dug up an earthenware jug which contained letters, a copy of Alarcón's instructions, and a record of the nautical expedition's discoveries up to that point.

Díaz thence retraced his steps along the river, and went on northward, looking for a ford, because he wanted to see what was on the other side. After marching to the vicinity of Yuma, he crossed over on rafts; made five or six marches westward; then, he returned

[36] Ms, Patronato 20, no. 5(8), AGI.
[37] Hakluyt, *The Third and Last Volume*, p. 428.

because he found only sand dunes instead of grass and water. He had to fight upon his return because the natives decided to take advantage of his vulnerability while recrossing the river. He circumvented them very cleverly, however, and fared on his way to rejoin Coronado.

Soon thereafter, Melchior Díaz gave himself a mortal wound by heaving a lance at a dog which was chasing the sheep the patrol had herded along its march. According to Bolton, the lance missed the dog; stuck in the ground; and, Díaz, overriding the lance, received the butt of it in his groin where it penetrated his bladder. About a month later, Díaz died.[38]

In the meantime, Alarcón had carried out his orders; he had been instructed to sail up to thirty-six degrees north latitude and to wait there for Coronado's arrival. If contact with Coronado were not established within a certain period, Alarcón was to return to New Spain.[39] So, early November 1540 found Alarcón and the three ships he had taken to the head of the Gulf entering the port of Colima.

And whom should Alarcón find at anchor there but that nautical impresario, Pedro de Alvarado, who again had sailed away from Guatemala in order to fish once more in troubled waters. Alvarado "ordered Alarcón

---

[38] Based upon Bolton, *Coronado,* pp. 171-175, and upon Baltasar de Obregón, *Historia de los descubrimientos antiguos y modernos de la Nueva España* (Mexico, 1924), p. 202. Printed from MS transmitted to Felipe II, April 17, 1584, and retrieved from AGI for publication.

With reference to Díaz' wound from his lance butt, the writer considers such penetration entirely feasible. He has observed in the cases of many sixteenth century lances on exhibition in the Royal Armory, Madrid, and in several lesser museums in Spain, that the shafts tapered acutely toward the butt or were cone shaped there. Díaz' lance shaft could very well have been one of this type.

[39] Venegas, *Noticia,* vol. I, p. 132.

to lower his sails, for Tonatiuh himself had ambitions regarding northern explorations." Alarcón said he prepared to disobey and defend himself but that Castillo persuaded him to use discretion instead. So, Alarcón sailed away that night and avoided bloodshed.[40]

As the career of Alarcón, the first to show that Lower California was a peninsula, drew to a close, Bolton left him in what, apparently, was a fair state of grace. Viceroy Mendoza prepared to send him out again with ships to cooperate with Coronado; he was to seek Coronado and Díaz and to establish a settlement on the Colorado River among the Quícamas and Coanas tribes. Mendoza said that Alarcón was to deliver dispatches to Coronado

> For I am writing to him that since you were the discoverer of that river, and since its people liked you, and you have served his Majesty by exploring that region, he should place you in charge of it, and since you have information of the country beyond, he shall, if necessary, furnish you more men with whom to go farther up that river.

By the time the ships assigned to Alarcón for his second voyage to the Colorado were ready to sail, however, the Mixtón War had reached such proportions as to endanger all of Nueva Galicia. Sailing orders, consequently, were cancelled, and Alarcón was sent to defend the town of Autlán against the revolting Indians.[41]

While Bolton left Alarcón in Autlán, Venegas and Pérez Bustamante took him directly from the end of his cruise into self-imposed exile from the capital and a spell of mortal sickness. Venegas stated that, as a result of Alarcón's cruise, the viceroy became dis-

---

[40] Bolton, *Coronado,* p. 176.
[41] Bolton, *Coronado,* pp. 177-178.

gusted with his erstwhile favorite who then retired from Mexico City to Cortés' estates where he died very soon of sorrow and sickness.[42]

Pérez has been under reference earlier with respect to the great favor with the viceroy which Alarcón had gained during many years' service as Mendoza's *maestresala*. He said, however, that Mendoza's affection for Alarcón turned into abhorrence when the viceroy learned that his sea captain had sent the emperor a more ample and finished account of his expedition than he had furnished his immediate superior in command and benefactor. According to Pérez, also, Alarcón's end came as Venegas described it.[43]

As noted earlier with respect to Alarcón's nautical expedition and Coronado's northward incursion by land, Cortés had protested vehemently but vainly that, in dispatching these forces, Mendoza had usurped his rights based upon capitulations with the emperor and his authority as captain-general. Apparently, Cortés had not learned yet about the clause in the viceroy's instructions which authorized him to bypass the conquistador as far as functions of the captain-generalcy were concerned. In addition to these grievances, Cortés charged Mendoza with further malfeasance in office by exposing the crown to dire risk of losing Mexico, Nueva Galicia, and other provinces, for lack of fighting men during Coronado's lengthy absence. In view of the proportions the Mixtón War assumed, this should have been a telling point.[44]

As far as matters in New Spain stood, however,

---

[42] Venegas, *Noticia*, vol. I, p. 132.

[43] Pérez Bustamante, *Don Antonio de Mendoza*, p. 65, citing Torquemada, *Monarchía Indiana*, Lib. v, chap. XI, p. 609, and *Cartas de Indias*, vol. I, pp. 253-255.

[44] Ms, Patronato 21, no. 2, ramo 4, AGI.

Cortés realized that he could not get justice there. Once before, withal, he had vindicated his rights to a large degree by appearing before the throne in Spain; he decided to take that step again. So, toward the end of 1540, he sailed from Vera Cruz with a brilliant suite, never to return to New Spain alive. He would not believe, apparently, that, as the cards were stacked against him in Mexico, so were they in Madrid also; and, that in the Spanish peninsula, his style, long since, had been outmoded.

In view of the fact that late 1540 found Pedro de Alvarado again in Mexican waters, it is appropriate now to see what his major activities had been since April 1539. It may be recalled that he was then transporting from the Gulf of Honduras to Acajutla on the Pacific the immense loads of ship equipment he had brought from Spain. This heavy freighting, incidentally, worked hundreds of *tamemes* to death; but, if their demise gave Alvarado any grave concern, the writer has not found it so recorded.

IV

Alvarado Joins Mendoza

In the chapter which treats of Pedro de Alvarado's
development as a maritime impresario, reference was
made to his second trip to Spain and to his spectacular
return to Guatemala with his second wife and their
suite of marriageable young ladies. He had just begun
his voyage to Spain when two letters were delivered to
Bishop Marroquín in Guatemala. One of these was for
the Bishop; the other was for Alvarado; both were
from Francisco Pizarro, asking for help because of the
general Indian uprising in Perú.[1] In fact, the plea upon
which Cortés acted in Pizarro's behalf was contained
in a copy of the letter which the latter had written
Alvarado.[2]

Thus it was that Alvarado missed a chance to fish by
invitation in those intensely roiled Peruvian waters.
Under these circumstances, he could seek new realms
only to the northward, and, in order to provide himself
the means necessary to maritime exploration, he had
brought from Spain the *tameme*-killing loads of ship
chandlery to which reference has been made.

As Alvarado's ship materials arrived at Acajutla,
construction of his second flotilla went on apace under
the supervision of Juan Rodríguez Cabrillo. With
respect to these ships, thirteen in all, Fuentes y Guz-

---

[1] Rodolfo Baron Castro, *Pedro de Alvarado* (Madrid, 1943), p. 145.
[2] López de Gómara, *Conquista de Méjico,* vol. II, p. 183.

mán wrote in 1690 that "so great was the cost of construction, equipment, and soldiery, that eighty ships
could have been built in Sevilla for the same amount." [3]
This sounds as if Fuentes were borrowing from his
ancestor, Bernal Díaz del Castillo, who said the same
thing more than a hundred years earlier at page 501 of
volume II of his *Historia verdadera*. At any rate, part
of this cost might have been due to the pains Cabrillo
took to insure craft of high quality.

While Alvarado's flotilla reached the strength of
thirteen vessels, all of these were not built at his expense. Cabrillo built one, the "San Salvador," on his
personal account with no investment in her whatever
by Alvarado or his stewards. When all the ships were
ready for sea, Alvarado begged Cabrillo persistently to
sail in the "San Salvador" as admiral of the entire
force. Cabrillo finally acquiesced in this and, about
mid-1540, the fleet sailed north.

When they arrived at Santiago, Colima, Alvarado
went on to Michoacán to see the viceroy and there
entered into partnership with him, throwing in Cabrillo's ship although Alvarado owned no interest in
her at all. This sounds rather highhanded and un-
scrupulous on Tonatiuh's part, yet, he had granted or
was to grant Cabrillo generous compensation.[4] While
in Colima, Bishop Marroquín, who had sailed from
Acajutla with Alvarado, interceded with him in Cabrillo's behalf and procured for the admiral the
encomiendas of Tacuba and Jumaitepeque. According
to their assessments, these towns paid a tribute valued

3 Francisco Antonio de Fuentes y Guzmán, *Historia de Guatemala o
Recordación Florida* (MS in 1690. Madrid, 1882), vol. I, p. 152.

4 Except where specified otherwise, this account will have been based upon
Ms. Justicia 280, folios unnumbered, AGI.

at six hundred *pesos de oro* or between twenty-four hundred and three thousand dollars per annum.[5]

Cabrillo, forthwith, sent a duly authorized agent to Guatemala to take possession of these towns in his name, but he was frustrated. Alvarado had left his brother-in-law and son-in-law, Francisco de la Cueva, as acting governor and that young nobleman decided to award himself these juicy *encomiendas*. As soon as Cabrillo learned what Cueva had done, he entered suit before Licentiate Maldonado. Although the record of proceedings of this suit provides a great deal of very valuable data regarding Guatemalan society of that day, its major treatment will be left to the appendix hereto.[6]

With reference to the pact between Viceroy Mendoza and Pedro de Alvarado which included the use of Cabrillo's ship, both partners have been criticized unfavorably with particular denunciation of Alvarado's part in the transaction. Venegas, for example, contended that the viceroy was not contented with employing just his authority and treasure in discovery, so enchanting until disillusion arrived; but, by a master-stroke of policy, he engrossed his power and supporters, and took from Cortés support which should have been staunchly his. He referred, of course, to Alvarado who, he said, was not very scrupulous about preserving the sacred rights of friendship and gratitude but, on the contrary, was very anxious to compete with his old chieftain. Along with these strictures, Venegas maintained that everybody abominated Alvarado's procedure against Cortés, to whom he owed all that he was and had.[7]

---

[5] Ms, Justicia 286, fols. 20 and 21v., AGI.

[6] Ms, Justicia 286, fols. 1-2v., AGI.

[7] Venegas, *Noticia*, vol. I, pp. 132-134.

Whether these aspersions against Alvarado's character are entirely justifiable is a matter certainly open to contention. There is some reason to believe that more than mere greed could have motivated Alvarado to ally himself with Cortés' great rival, Mendoza, and thus eliminate the captain-general from competition in sea movements toward California and also toward the Spice Islands. As indicated previously in this paper, Cortés affronted and humiliated Alvarado severely at Cozumel Island on the way into Mexico in 1519. He did likewise in Mexico City in 1520 when he returned there to find that Alvarado had provoked the Aztecs into revolt. Alvarado certainly had some reason to harbor a grudge against his former commanding officer. He might have believed, too, that Cortés was an obstacle in his pathway; indeed, as noted earlier, he complained that Cortés had intervened in the Audiencia of Mexico in order to prevent his making the expedition to Quito where "he went for wool and came back sheared."

In addition to this, Alvarado, in company with many of the conquistadores, could feel that Cortés had got more than his due from the conquest of Mexico. From the outset, Cortés took a fifth, an emperor's share, from the loot which they sacked from the Aztecs' hoards of gold, jewels, and handicrafts. Initially, without doubt, Cortés deserved this for he had invested all he was worth in the expedition organized in Cuba. After he had more than adequate compensation for his forty thousand peso investment, however, he continued to take just as much as they allocated His Majesty. Then, when His Majesty made him a marquis and authorized him a marquisate which embodied twenty-three thousand Indian vassals – Cortés claimed that meant families, not individuals – it indeed seemed time to let someone else get a share in the spoils. Bernal Díaz said he was impelled to write his *True History* because too much credit had been given Cortés at the expense of his followers. Alvarado could have felt very sincerely that it was time for Cortés to step aside and let others have a chance to conquer another realm like the Aztec or the Inca Empire.

Be that as it may, events were moving swiftly by March 28, 1541 when Alvarado wrote the emperor from Jalisco with regard to plans concerted between him and Viceroy Mendoza. They had agreed to divide the fleet into two parts; for, according to Alvarado, it was sufficient for everything. One task group was to go to the *"Islas de Poniente"* or western islands, circumnavigate them and see what might be there; the other was to run along the North American Pacific coast "until its end and secret" were sighted.

Three big ships and a galley, very well stocked with subsistence stores and three hundred very fit men aboard, were to sail for the "western islands" under Ruy López de Villalobos; five ships and a lighter under Juan de Alvarado, Pedro's nephew, with a like complement of personnel, were coastwise bound. The latter group was to sail during the following month of April while the former was to sail within three months.[8] According to Pedro, this organization still left two big ships and another under construction which would be available to sail in support of the task groups if circumstances should so require.

Just as the Mixtón War, however, upset Mendoza's plans for pushing Alarcón up the Gulf of California and the Colorado River again, so it checked execu-

---

[8] *Documentos inéditos,* Ser. II, vol. 2, pp. I *et seq.*

tion of the plans he and Alvarado had formed for cruises to the Spice Islands and along the Pacific coast northward of New Spain, toward Alta California. In view of the gravity of the situation in the vicinity of Guadalajara, the viceroy advised Alvarado to postpone his voyage and to march with all the force he could muster to support the Spaniards under Cristóbal de Oñate, acting governor of Nueva Galicia.

Although Alvarado was about to put to sea, he complied at once with Mendoza's wishes, and marched rapidly to Guadalajara where he arrived June 12, 1541. The cabildo and residents of that place welcomed him as if he were their saviour and explained the situation to him in detail. He expressed his desire to march at once against the Indians although he was urged to wait for the reinforcements which the viceroy had ordered to Guadalajara. They urged him also to wait until the rains stopped in view of the fact that mud had made the terrain almost impassable; that the Spaniards' most effective arm, their cavalry, was practically useless at the time.

Alvarado persisted in his stand upon instant action despite the wise counsel those on the spot gave him; he even chided them for inaction, attributing the increasing strength of the uprising to lack of energy on the part of Oñate and the Guadalajarans. Furthermore, he prohibited their joining forces with him, and marched forthwith upon the *Peñol,* or Big Rock, of Nochistlán where the Indians in huge force had fortified themselves intensively.

The details of the action which ensued there are not germane to this paper. Suffice it to say that the Indians repulsed the Spaniards with heavy losses, then counterattacked furiously, driving them more than three leagues to the rear. Alvarado, fighting on foot, established a rear guard to cover the retreat as best he might. He had very probably reached terrain favorable for a stand as his troops filed along a narrow path leading up a steep hill.Baltasar de Montoya, Alvarado's scribe, was driving his jaded horse up a sharp slope ahead of Tonatiuh; the animal lost its footing and rolled back, catching Alvarado in its descent. The crushing he received was mortal, and, on July 4, 1541, he died.[9] Reference has been made in the course of this work to three instances of rashness or impetuousity on Pedro de Alvarado's part which cost him the displeasure of his superiors and severe reprimands; the fourth case cost him his life.

When Alvarado departed from Colima to take part in the Mixtón War, he left the flotilla in charge of Juan Rodríguez Cabrillo. After Alvarado's death, the ships, for all practical purposes, became the viceroy's property and he, manifestly, shared Alvarado's high regard for Cabrillo because he confirmed the latter's prior assignment.

One of the first special tasks which fell to Cabrillo, according to his heirs, was to dispatch a portion of the fleet to the Moluccas under the command of Ruy López de Villalobos. Cabrillo might have allocated the ships for this purpose, but he could not have sent them out because the viceroy dispatched Cabrillo to sea about five months before Villalobos sailed.[10]

In the meantime, Cabrillo probably had gained a very good idea that Alvarado had overextended his financial means before the great impresario died for he lost little time in filing claim against the Alvarado

---

[9] Pérez Bustamante, *Don Antonio de Mendoza,* pp. 78-80.
[10] Ms, Justicia 290, fols. 45-47v., AGI.

legacy for what Don Pedro owed him. Less than two months had elapsed after Alvarado's death when, on September 1, 1541, Cabrillo delivered personally to "the very magnificent señor don luis de castilla chief justice etc.," in La Navidad, proof, *ad perpetua rey memoriam,*[11] setting forth his claims. There were ten questions to be asked each of seven witnesses, testifying under oath. One of these witnesses, incidentally, had gone twice to the head of the Gulf of California and had produced a complete chart of that body of water; he was Domingo del Castillo, a pilot, and, as he styled himself, "pilot of the Viceroy's ships." Another notable Cabrillo witness was also a pilot, Ginés de Mafra.[12] He was to sail in Villalobos' flotilla as pilot of the "San Juan," one of five named in the same account.[13] It is highly probable that he was the same man who piloted the "Trinidad" in Magellan's flotilla, and the author of *Declaración que dió en Valladolid á 2 de Agosto de 1527, sobre los acontecimientos de la nao Trinidad en las Malucas* (*Declaration Which He Made in Valladolid on August 2, 1527, Concerning the Happenings to the Ship Trinidad in the Moluccas*).[14] His experience in the Spice Islands must have given his services especial appeal to the partners Alvarado and Mendoza. Cabrillo, manifestly, travelled in high class company.

In this classification, also, was Bishop Marroquín

---

11 The scribe really meant *ad perpetuam rei memoriam* (for the perpetual remembrance of the thing).

12 Ms, Justicia 280, folios unnumbered, AGI.

13 Pérez Bustamante, *Don Antonio de Mendoza*, p. 68.

14 Espasa-Calpe, *Enciclopedia universal ilustrada*, vol. XXXII. "In this work he narrates the aggression committed by the Portuguese, who captured him, the imprisonment he suffered upon arrival at Lisbon, where they robbed him of his books and sailing directions, among which there were two composed by Andrés de San Martín, one of His Majesty's pilots."

who, undoubtedly, was aware that Francisco de la
Cueva had prevented Cabrillo from taking possession
of the Tacuba and Jumaitepeque encomiendas. As a
result of this, Cabrillo had not been paid for the "San
Salvador," and the good bishop appeared determined
that he should be. Marroquín had been named with
Juan de Alvarado as coexecutor of Pedro de Alvarado's
estate and, as such, he ordered that Cabrillo be com-
pensated for his ship from Don Pedro's legacy. Her
value at the time she was seized was to be fixed by
persons who knew it. Cabrillo, furthermore, was to be
paid for the services he had rendered Alvarado according to the proofs thereof which he should submit.[15]

In the meantime, the latter half of 1541 and the first
two or three months of 1542, Viceroy Mendoza had
been bringing the Mixtón War to a successful conclusion. With these Nueva Galicia Indians again sub-
dued, the viceroy became free to resume maritime
exploration; and, on June 27, 1542, he dispatched Juan
Rodríguez Cabrillo to sea in command of the "San
Salvador" and the "Victoria."

All the details of this voyage, the first known definitely to have reached Alta California, will not be
treated in this book although some features of it will
be cited later for purposes of comparison or criticism.
Detailed treatment of it is considered unnecessary
because several eminent California historians have
devoted themselves to Cabrillo's cruise, providing excellent studies as far as its essentials are concerned.
These writers form a galaxy which includes Bancroft,
Bolton, Chapman, George Davidson, and Wagner. All
of them have used basically, however, the account

---

[15] Remesal, *Historia general de las Indias Occidentales*, p. 267.

whose authorship has been ascribed to Juan Páez as of July 1543.[16] As there are some discrepancies between this narrative and evidence recorded later in lawsuits, it seems appropriate to indicate some of these variants.

Cabrillo has been identified in detail with his nautical services to Pedro de Alvarado and Viceroy Mendoza by Ms, Justicia 290, fols. 45-47v., AGI, part of a *probanza* of his merits and services. It refers particularly to his having supervised construction of Alvarado's armada and serving in the meantime as magistrate of the port, and to his post as admiral of the ships which sailed from Guatemala to La Navidad, Colima, in early 1541. This, and his subsequent commission by Viceroy Antonio de Mendoza to command the expedition to Alta California, are amply substantiated by eyewitnesses in the folios following those cited above.

These witnesses stated, moreover, that Cabrillo was bound ultimately to Especiería and the Moluccas. Francisco de Vargas testified that Cabrillo went more than five hundred leagues beyond the furthest points reached by the Marqués del Valle, Don Hernán Cortés. He knew that Cabrillo discovered the island named Capitana and, according to the pilots who measured the latitude, they were very close to "Maluco" and "Especiería." Bartolomé Ferrer and "The Corsican," Lorenzo Hernández, were the most positive of all in that opinion. Some of them had been to the Moluccas. He stated further that, at Capitana Island, the Indians made constant war on the Spaniards.

One day, when some soldiers had "jumped ashore"

---

16 This report has been published in *Documentos inéditos,* Ser. I, vol. 14, pp. 165 *et seq.* It is headed: "Relación del descubrimiento que hizo Juan Rodríguez, navegando por la contracosta del mar del Sur al Norte, hecha por Juan Paez – (Julio de 1543)." It is also in manuscript in the AGI and likewise in the Colección Navarrete, Museo Naval, Madrid.

to take on water, a number of Indians attacked and so maltreated them that they soon found themselves in a perilous situation. "General" Juan Rodríguez saw this from his ship, noting the speed and outcry the Indians were putting into their attack. He quickly assembled a group of soldiers and hurried to the rescue in person. Upon reaching the beach, and starting his jump ashore, a foot slipped away from him and he shattered the shin bones of one leg against a rock. He went on, nevertheless, to rescue eleven soldiers and, ten or twelve days later, he died on board his ship. "And the witness knows this because he was there."

De Vargas was certain that, if Cabrillo had lived, he would have reached the lands of Especiería and the Moluccas and beyond. For one thing, he carried more than three years' supplies and, besides that, he showed the will always to explore in the service of God and His Majesty. He wanted to excel other captains and discoverers and, as a person who knew and understood seagoing matters better than anyone who had preceded him, he would have performed a great service. Vargas also pointed out that Cabrillo's report to the viceroy prompted the latter to order more armadas built to carry on exploration and, when in Mexico about a year before, he learned that Viceroy Velasco had given orders to like effect for building and fitting out at La Navidad. It is lamentable that Vargas did not state how and under what circumstances Cabrillo's report had reached Viceroy Mendoza.

Lázaro de Cárdenas testified to the same effect with regard to Cabrillo's manner and place of death. He said, however, that Cabrillo sailed up the coast to forty-five degrees and decided to winter at an island he named La Capitana, the same island where he was buried.

Before Cabrillo died, he called Captain Ferrer to his deathbed and "prayed him to carry on. . ." Cárdenas had so testified, he said, because he was there and saw everything.

One of the most perplexing features in accounts of Cabrillo's career is the discrepancy as to the cause of his death. In the court records, the shattered shin bones caused it; in the cruise report attributed to Juan Páez, his death resulted from a fall in which he broke an arm next to the shoulder.

There is a discrepancy, too, as to how long he lived after the injury. The court records show that he lived ten or twelve days after he was injured. In the Páez account, he died January 3, 1543 at Posesión Island from the injury he received "the other time they were there," November 23, 1542. So, according to this account, he lived about a month and ten days after his fall. It is possible, of course, that the first arrival was on December 23, yet the account does not indicate any lapse which might justify such an assumption although, indeed, there is no day by day recording between November 23 and January 3.[17]

In the preceding chapters, close relationship between Cabrillo and Juan Páez has been shown. As far as available positive evidence indicates, they were together initially in the force which Pánfilo de Narváez led from Cuba to Mexico in 1520. As members of the Narváez contingent who went over to Cortés, they served through the conquest of Mexico and went thence

---

[17] From the Páez account in Instituto Histórico de Marina, *Colección de diarios y relaciones para la historia de los viajes y descubrimientos,* Luis Cabreiro Blanco, editor (Madrid, 1943), vol. I, pp. 39, 42. The account is well edited and there is a plate which shows the tracks of Cabrillo's ships on both legs of his cruise.

to Guatemala under Pedro de Alvarado, and became residents of Santiago de Guatemala when Alvarado founded that capital. The authorship of Cabrillo's cruise report, however, has been attributed to another Páez. As this Páez has not been indicated as one of the conquistadores, it seems appropriate now to examine some circumstantial evidence which seems to weight the pan on the warrior's side of the scales.

V
Who was Juan Paez?

The distinguished California historian, Wagner, in discussing the authorship of the log covering Cabrillo's Alta California voyage, said:

> Juan Páez was undoubtedly Juan Páez de Castro, who was appointed *cronista mayor* [chief chronicler] in 1555 and continued in active research on the history of the Indies until his death in 1570.[1]

The writer is not inclined to agree with this conclusion, despite the respect he bears toward the eminent scholar who reached it. At the same time, the writer admits that he cannot cite definitive evidence to the contrary. To him, it merely seems more logical that one of Cabrillo's close associates, especially one who was an *escribano público* or notary public or public scribe as well, should have fallen heir to this task. Up to this moment, the writer has not been able to find Juan Páez de Castro's name in any connection with the conquest of Mexico and Guatemala or their settlement; plain Juan Páez, conquistador, and the same, escribano público, has appeared in numerous cases in this book already and will appear in some more cases yet.

With respect to Juan Páez de Castro, that gentleman's early life is also obscure, at least as far as one

---

[1] Henry R. Wagner, *Juan Rodríguez Cabrillo, Discoverer of the Coast of California* (San Francisco, 1941), p. 14.

biography of him is concerned. While it became known that Quer, Guadalajara, Spain, was his birthplace, no records of his birth or baptism could be found there. As to the date of his birth, 1515 has been conjectured because, in 1545, he appeared as a man about thirty years old. He was supposed to have studied at the University of Alcalá de Henares, yet no record of his enrollment there could be found. A little while prior to 1541, he was in Salamanca, and, during the early 1540's, he travelled quite widely over Spain.

In 1545, this Páez went to Trento, Italy, in the suite of Cardinal Diego Hurtado de Mendoza, and he also accompanied that prelate to Rome in 1547. He was near the emperor in the Low Countries in 1555 when, on account of an incorrect report that Ocampo, the chief chronicler, had died, he was appointed to that post with a salary of eighty thousand *maravedises,* possibly eight hundred dollars per annum today.

In 1560, Juan Páez de Castro returned to Quer and remained in Spain the rest of his life. There is no mention of his having visited any countries beyond continental Europe during his lifetime. Surely, if any travel as prosaic as journeying in his homeland were worthy of mention, a trip to the fabulous New World would have been stressed indeed. With respect to his stature, one finds that,

> according to a modern critic, Páez de Castro, through his assiduity in study and his eagerness to communicate his learning to others, represents the most finished type of Spanish humanist in the sixteenth century.[2]

From the foregoing points, it seems reasonable to presume that Juan Páez de Castro was in Spain during

---

[2] Espasa-Calpe, *Enciclopedia Universal Ilustrada,* vol. XL.

1543. The endorsements on Cabrillo's cruise report indicate that it was submitted in July of that year, and the report states that his two ships returned to La Navidad on April 14, 1543.[3] Even if predilection toward Páez de Castro had existed in New Spain at the time – the writer has been unable thus far to find anything of the sort at all – let time and space factors determine the possibility of this Páez' authorship of Cabrillo's smooth log. There would have been an over-all period of three months and sixteen days for the basic papers to be sent to Spain, to overtake Juan Páez de Castro on his travels, to be incorporated by him into a smooth draft; and, to be returned to Mexico City before midnight, July 31, 1543, in order to be noted for filing as the report was recorded. Obviously, such would have been an utter impossibility prior to the day of air mail.

Juan Páez de Castro was a careful investigator, but he never attained eminence as a writer. In the many years after Felipe II had assigned him the task of writing Spain's history, he never finished any more than its prologue.[4] Even if he had been pre-eminent throughout the Spanish Empire as a scribe, it is extremely doubtful whether Antonio de Mendoza would have authorized Cabrillo's papers to be transferred to Spain before a smooth copy had been placed on the viceroy's desk. As indicated previously in this work, Mendoza was not one to brook being by-passed by a subordinate's report; the case of Alarcón's disgrace bears eloquent testimony to the viceroy's stern aversion to such practice.

So, the writer believes it highly improbable and well-

[3] *Documentos inéditos,* Ser. I, vol. 14, pp. 165, 191.
[4] Espasa-Calpe, *loc. cit.*

nigh impossible for Juan Páez de Castro to have written Cabrillo's cruise report. He believes, on the other hand, that the weight of circumstantial evidence bears heavily in favor of plain Juan Páez, conquistador, and in company with Cabrillo, one of the earliest residents in Santiago de Guatemala.

Although Juan Páez was presented among dramatis personae in the Cortés Mexican cast of 1520, a slightly earlier bit of information regarding him has been found under the date February 23, of that year. At this time, "Xoan Paez" was signed as witness to a *poder* or power of attorney which a large group of Pánfilo de Narváez' followers gave one Cristóbal Morante. On the same date, he also witnessed an accompanying *rrequery-miento* or written demand which the same men submitted upon Lucas Vázquez de Ayllón. These documents were drawn up then in Puerto de Guanyguanico, Cuba, a place on the north side of Cape San Antonio.

Juan Páez' manifest ability to read and write led him into clerical work in the cabildo of Santiago de Guatemala in December 1524 as noted in a preceding chapter. On January 4, 1526, the records show that one Rodrigo Díaz was appointed by the cabildo as Páez' relief

> inasmuch as Juan Páez escribano público of this city is gone to Mexico City to negotiate things in accordance with his obligations, and this city is without an escribano. . .

He was back in Guatemala on September 4, 1526, however, for on that date he attested another cabildo act. On November 21, 1527, he rose in a cabildo session to express his opinion regarding the location of a town which that body proposed to found.

Then, on November 26, 1527, Juan Páez requested his share in the lots of Santiago de Guatemala, "sus

solares é caballerias." On March 18, 1528, the members
of Santiago's cabildo

> received as residents of this said city the following persons, with-
> out prejudice to the residences which have been formed in this
> city, after those founded in this province in Pedro de Alvarado's
> time.

Juan Páez' name appeared on this list and, on September 25, 1528, the cabildo gave him title to his "solar y
tierra" or town lot and outlying land. Juan Rodríguez
Cabrillo's name appeared also on this same list. In fact,
Páez' and Cabrillo's names appeared nearby in almost
all the foregoing instances where residence and property were concerned; likewise, also, in witnessing
proclamations by the cabildo. That they must have been
closely associated appears well-nigh inescapable under
the circumstances.

To specify all the instances where Juan Páez appeared in the cabildo records would serve no useful
purpose. Perhaps one more entry should be cited,
however, to show that he wanted to keep his cabildo
employment. That body, on August 23, 1529, granted
Páez' petition to be reappointed escribano público, a
job from which he had been ousted by Francisco de
Orduña when that worthy, as noted earlier, came to
Santiago de Guatemala to conduct the *residencia* of
Jorge de Alvarado, acting governor, and assumed the
governorship itself.[5]

One cannot but wonder, however, if there was only
one Juan Páez in Mexico and Guatemala from 1520
into the later 1540's. From one particular point of view,
it seems indeed that only one was there, that is; where
the same paternal surname was widespread, the usual

---

[5] *Libro viejo*, pp. 9, 15, 22, 24, 30, 32, 43, and 83, corresponding in order
with the dates cited.

practice was to identify individuals by adding the maternal surname, a proceeding which, of course, the individuals originated in order to identify themselves and also to manifest legitimate birth. Thus, one need not confuse Juan Páez with Juan Páez de Castro nor Juan Rodríguez Cabrillo with Juan Rodríguez Villafuerte. As plain Juan Páez appeared so consistently, one may assume with probable accuracy that only one individual was known by that name.

It seems very likely, too, that Juan Páez' pen was in demand beyond his functions as escribano público in Guatemala. Another conquistador must have wanted his services because "by Jun Páez" appears on the cover sheets of two documents which constitute "Report made by Captain Juan Jarmillo . . . con . . . Francisco Vázquez Coronado . . . 1537." [6] The distance from Guatemala to the general area of Jaramillo's activities cannot be accepted as an obvious reason against his writing that report, for at least one trip to Mexico City in connection with his obligations has been recorded already.

Juan Páez' family was involved in the cataclysm which, in early September 1541, practically destroyed the capital city Pedro de Alvarado had founded in Guatemala. The elements of tragedy, among which Alvarado had moved so long and had his being, appeared to have been stalking him and his. His first wife, Francisca de la Cueva, died as they were arriving in Vera Cruz from Spain in 1530. As noted previously, Pedro received a mortal injury ignominiously in Guadalajara Province, Mexico, in June 1541. His widow, the former Beatriz de la Cueva, was killed

---

[6] Ms, Patronato 20, no. 5(8), AGI.

when the Volcán de Agua flooded Santiago de Guatemala with a wall of water charged with débris.

As Bishop Marroquín expressed it, these events were

> something, certainly, in our opinion, as mysterious as may ever have happened in our time, and worthy of wonder, that a house like this should have passed out of existence in such a short time and two persons of so much esteem have died.

The Bishop went on to say that Doña Beatriz had not yet dried the tears she was shedding over the death of her husband when she perished underneath a dwelling.[7]

One may note in passing that Pedro de Alvarado, at least, was spared the pain over his wife's demise which Lummis has depicted, as Pedro died more than two months before Doña Beatriz was killed. Speaking of the effect her death had upon Pedro, Lummis said: "Her death broke the brave soldier's spirit for he loved her very dearly." [8]

And the family of Juan Páez, Alvarado's faithful follower, was also stricken by this stark tragedy. Under date, September 10, 1541, it was recorded that "Alonso Martín Granado's wife died and also his grandsons, Juan Páez' sons, and likewise his daughter, who lived in Colima, embraced with four children." [9]

From 1541 to 1548, there is a gap in the records as far as any data referring to Juan Páez are concerned. To be sure, Soares mentions a João Pais among Cabrillo's Portuguese companions on his famous voyage to Alta California. He said:

> Bartolomeu Ferrer, Ferrel or Ferrelo, who succeeded him in the

[7] Letter, Bishop Marroquín and officials to the Emperor, Santiago de Guatemala, November 25, 1541 in *Cartas de Indias*, pp. 432-433.
[8] Charles F. Lummis, *The Spanish Pioneers* (Chicago, 1899), p. 178.
[9] *Documentos inéditos*, Ser. I, vol. 14, p. 165.

command, Antonio Correia and Joao Pais, as a tribute to his memory gave his name to the Island before called de La Posesión.[10]

Soares, unfortunately, did not give the source supporting that statement nor anything to identify Pais with the Páez who has been credited with writing Cabrillo's cruise report.

Thus far, neither date nor place of the death of Juan Páez, the Guatemalan resident, has been fixed. Perhaps one might assume reasonably that it occurred sometime between 1543 and 1549 because, in the record of *tasaciones* upon Guatemalan encomiendas for the period, 1548-1551, appeared, "Ystapalatengo y Aguacatlan el menor hijo de Juan paez," dated February 20, 1549. All such entries show an ellipsis between the latter or the last name of the encomienda and the owner's name. "Menor hijo de Juan paez" is believed to mean Juan Páez' heir, minor in age, because the Cabrillo court records of that period designate Juan Rodríguez Cabrillo, junior, the same way.[11]

---

10 Celestino Soares, *California and the Portuguese* (Lisbon, 1939), p. 43.

11 These *tasaciones* seem quaint, by the way, to those accustomed to tax levies in so many cents or, more often, dollars and cents, per $100 valuation. On April 4, 1549, when young Páez' encomienda, Zacapula, was assessed, the Indians thereon were to provide the encomendero nine dozen Castilian hens a year, four *fanegas* of salt a month, and eight Indians of ordinary intelligence whom he would feed and instruct in church doctrine. — Ms, Audiencia de Guatemala 128, fol. 54v., AGI. This meant, of course, that young Páez got a hen about every three days and 6.32 bushels of salt every month. — Haggard, *Handbook for Translators,* p. 76, gives the fanega in Guatemala at 1.58 bushels. If that seems an excessive amount of salt, one may assume that Páez marketed what he didn't use. As for the eight Indians he had to feed, he very probably decided that he had to inculcate habits of steady work into them in order to school them properly in church doctrine.

Although Ms, Audiencia de Guatemala 128, fol. 112v. showed that young Páez was entitled as of May 6, 1549, to half of the Miguetlan encomienda, its assessment was not stated. At any rate, all the encomiendas in his father's legacy were not sufficient to keep him from suffering "extreme necessity"

For current purposes, however, the most important item in connection with Juan Páez' minor son is a *probanza* he submitted in connection with a petition for assistance from the crown. This *probanza* set forth the merits and services of Juan Páez, his father. The son, Alonso Páez, craved the rewards due conquerors' heirs, so, he proceeded to show himself not only a conquistador's son but also one's grandson as well. His maternal grandfather was the Alonso Martín Granado to whom reference has been made above. As if this weren't enough, Alonso Páez showed further that his wife, Catalina de Ardón, was a conqueror's granddaughter; that her maternal grandfather, Juan Pérez de Ardón, "was one of the first conquistadores of these provinces, a very illustrious gentleman, hidalgo and captain and deputy governor in this city and in the provinces." [12]

Folios 7v.-32v. of this manuscript recorded the testimony bearing on Juan Páez which Diego López de Villanueva, Juan de Aragón, Pero González Nájara, Gonzalo de Alvarado [Pedro's brother], Alvaro de Paz, Alvaro de Loarca, Diego de Vivar, and Antonio Ortiz de Leyva gave in response to thirteen questions which composed Alonso Páez' deposition. Of these witnesses, Diego de Vivar, the youngest at more than fifty years old, had known Juan Páez the shortest time,

about nineteen years later. On July 9, 1568, one finds, "Alonso Páez, resident and native born in the city of Santiago de Guatemala," petitioning the crown for such an allocation of Indians as would provide him 1,000 pesos annual rental from the first encomiendas to be vacated and, in the meantime, to help him make both ends meet, with a governorship. There is an endorsement on the back of this petition, recommending that Alonso Páez be "entertained in jobs and governorships in conformity with his quality and ability." It is dated, Madrid, February 22, 1570, and signed "Licentiate Vaños."–Ms, Patronato 68, no. 2, ramo 3, fols. 1-1v., AGI.

[12] Ms, Patronato 68, no. 2, ramo 3, fols. 4-7, AGI.

more than thirty years; Juan de Aragón, more than
sixty-five, had known him more than forty-five years.
These were the extremes; in between, Alvaro de Loarca
and Antonio Ortiz de Leyva each had known Juan
Páez more than forty-four years. With the exceptions
of Diego de Vivar and Alvaro de Paz who, apparently,
had not served in either conquest, Mexico or Guatemala, all testified as eyewitnesses to Juan Páez' service
in Guatemala and several of them said they had
observed him serving in both conquests.

Although this *probanza* did provide much supple-
mentary material with reference to the conquerors of
Mexico and Guatemala, it left much to be desired as
far as the authorship of Cabrillo's cruise report is concerned. Why Alonso Páez might not have identified his
father in more detail is hard to understand. He took
pains to establish the fact that Juan Páez served in the
Mexican conquest and came to Guatemala with Pedro
de Alvarado in that country's conquest. He proved,
too, that Alvarado gave his father in encomienda half
of Zacapula, all of Aguacatlan, Ysla Palatengo, and
half of Miaguatlan as remuneration for his expenses
and his services. Of his functions with the Cabildo,
Santiago de Guatemala, not a word; of his services to
Cabrillo, if he performed any, Alonso was likewise
silent.

Who was the Juan Páez that wrote Cabrillo's cruise
report? That yet remains to be answered definitively.
One is struck, however, by the close association which
the conquistadores – first, under Narváez and Cortés
in Mexico; then, in Guatemala under Alvarado –
maintained among themselves. Some of their names,
Bernal Díaz del Castillo, Diego Holguín, Gonzalo de
Alvarado, Pero González de Nájara, Juan de Aragón,

Ginés de Mafra, Pedro de Avilés, Alonso Barrios, Cristóbal Rodríguez Picón, Alonso Pérez, Sancho de Barahona, are among the witnesses who testified in the Cabrillo and Páez suits or *probanzas*. Several of these are mentioned by Bernal Díaz del Castillo in his account of "the valiant captains and enterprising soldiers" whom Cortés led from Cuba to conquer Mexico.[13]

The lengthy association of the conquistadores is emphasized by their youth at the outset of the conquest. On August 20, 1520, Juan Ochoa de Elexalde, testifying under oath as a Cortés witness, gave the ages of many of the great leader's followers. The following appeared to be a representative sampling among them: "Juan Jaramillo, 25; Alonso Davila, 28; Antonio de Quiñones, 23; Bernadino Vázquez de Tapia, 27 or 28; Juan Rodríguez de Villafuerte, 22."[14]

If Viceroy Antonio de Mendoza's edicts had been carried faithfully into execution, possibly a complete list of Cabrillo's expeditionary personnel would be available today. On August 24, 1539, the viceroy ordered that every ship sailing from a Pacific port in New Spain would submit to port authorities, prior to departure, a list of cargo, passengers, and other personnel aboard. One might reasonably think there were teeth in this decree because non-compliance was to be punished by confiscation of the offending ship and half of its owner's estate. The oldest of such inventories which the writer has seen, however, have been those connected with the voyages by Francisco de Ortega, beginning in 1632. It is believed that their inclusion, withal, was incidental to Ortega's attempt to prove that

---

[13] *Historia verdadera*, vol. II, pp. 517-543.
[14] Ms 19,243, Biblioteca Nacional, Madrid.

he had met the terms of his concessions from the crown because, according to officials in the AGI in January 1956, such lists were matters of local record [15] and, normally, would not have been forwarded to national archives in Spain. Possibly Cabrillo's personnel roll may yet emerge into light from some obscure storage place in Colima or Jalisco.

Be that as it may, one is yet confronted by the question, who was Juan Páez? From these pages, the following could be postulants for the authorship of Cabrillo's cruise report: Juan Páez de Castro, the Spanish chief chronicler; the Portuguese, João Pais; and, Juan Páez of Guatemala.

As for Juan Páez de Castro, the time and space factors involved must eliminate him unless evidence, yet to come to light, should establish his presence in Mexico during the first half of 1543. Along with this, too, it would have to be established that he had gained Viceroy Mendoza's favor and confidence because such information as Cabrillo had gained, positive or negative, was not to be shared freely with others.

In the case of João Pais – if, indeed, he was in Cabrillo's expedition – surely some nuances of Portuguese expression must have crept into the cruise report if he had been its author. As far as the writer has been able to determine, there is nothing in the diction or style of Cabrillo's smooth log which sets it apart to any degree from reports in Castilian of the sixteenth and early seventeenth centuries.

So, the weight of circumstantial evidence must bear the most favorably on the side of Juan Páez of Guate-

---

[15] Francisco del Paso y Troncoso, *Epistolario de Nueva España* (Mexico, D.F., 1939), vol. III, pp. 260-261.

mala, Cabrillo's old companion at arms and neighbor for many years in Santiago de Guatemala. His competency for such authorship may be inferred from his functioning as escribano público for the Cabildo of Santiago; certainly, he was the senior scribe in Guatemala for nearly all of the period from 1524 to 1545, the year in which the Audiencia *de los Confines* (of the boundaries) held its first meeting in Central America. Thus, the writer casts his ballot in favor of the old conquistador.

In the course of this chapter and those preceding it, some idea has been expressed regarding Mendoza's efforts to learn what Cortés' sea captains had discovered, notably in the case of Ulloa. Cortés, manifestly, was just as anxious to safeguard his information for his own benefit. It has been indicated also that, when Alarcón sent the emperor a more ample and finished report of his 1540 cruise than he had furnished Mendoza, he lost the viceroy's favor completely. Possibly, Alarcón's report could have incited a rival faction in Spain to vie with Mendoza for the emperor's favor and perhaps supplant the viceroy in maritime discovery.

Just as Spain's representatives in the New World wanted the sole benefit from what they learned, so the Spanish crown strived to exclude its rivals in Europe from the benefits of Spain's discoveries. The need for Spanish safeguards, the nature of some of them, and some of the means of circumventing them will be discussed in the following chapter.

VI
Spanish Information Security

Writers, too numerous to mention more than a few, Spanish and otherwise, have written at length about Spanish carelessness or indifference in filing or exaggerated and needless security measures as responsible for their having deprived themselves of the benefits of original reports or narratives. Perhaps Clavigero expressed the consensus as to carelessness or indifference sufficiently to illustrate its burden. Speaking of the orders which the Viceroy of Mexico, Marqués de Villena, issued in 1640 to Luis Cestin de Cañas, Governor of Sinaloa, to reconnoiter the Baja California coast and neighboring islands, Clavigero said:

> The reason why so many voyages at such cost should be repeated was that instead of publishing the journals and the geographic charts of the first discoverers, they were sent to Spain where they were buried in some archive, and thus those who found themselves entrusted with such missions could not profit by previous enlightenment.[1]

Discussing Friar Antonio de la Ascensión's account of Vizcaíno's 1602-1603 expedition along the Californias, an American historian, Brebner, said:

> Father Antonio's conversational narrative, with its good maps and profiles of the coastline, is an interesting report, which was

[1] Francisco Javier Clavigero, *Historia de la Antigua o Baja California.* Translation from Italian by Nicolás Garcia de San Vicente (Mexico City, 1852), p. 35.

the more important to Spain because of the disappearance of the records of the Cabrillo-Ferrelo expeditions.[2]

Brebner's work had been placed on the writer's desk in the Museo Naval, Madrid, by some member of the staff shortly after its arrival there. When the writer encountered the quotation just used, he remarked to one of the director's principal assistants that it was a shame that Cabrillo's records had disappeared. He replied that such was not necessarily the case precisely. He explained that, during most of the sixteenth century, new data as received from such expeditions were entered upon the *Padrón,* or master chart, maintained in the Casa de Contratación, Sevilla. The charts used in bringing the master chart up-to-date were then torn up, mainly for security reasons, but also because they had no further utility. Only European charts were lithographed; American charts were made by hand because discoveries there were so frequent that lithographing these would have been inordinately expensive. Copies of portions of the master chart were taken by hand in case of ships bound for the Americas.[3]

With respect to the *Padrón,* the Spanish procedure seems to have been entirely logical as far as security was concerned, for control against leaks from one

[2] John Bartlett Brebner, *The Explorers of North America,* 1492-1806 (Garden City, N.Y., 1955), p. 338.

[3] Conversation with Lieutenant Roberto Barreiro y Miera, Spanish Navy, Museo Naval, Madrid, May 17, 1956. The writer, recently, about fifteen months after the above conversation, has encountered Harold Lamb, *New Found World: How North America Was Found & Explored* (Garden City, N.Y., 1955). On page 90 of this work, one finds that "The master chart, or *Padrón Real,* was kept under lock probably at Seville, with two keys, one being given to the Pilot Major, the other to the Cosmographer Major." Again, p. 109, Lamb said: "Locked behind the two keys . . . , the master map, the Padrón Real, was presently to become the Padrón General of 'all the islands and continent already discovered, or to be discovered.'"

master chart could certainly be exercised more effectively than it could be maintained over files of basic papers. Reports, then as today, might easily have been "mislaid" until copies should have been taken. On the other hand, copies from the master chart could have been subjected to constant scrutiny while a draftsman made them; and, the responsibility for unauthorized drafts could be fixed definitely. That sound reasons for taut security measures existed in Spain can be demonstrated amply from writings of the era.

Reverting to Cabrillo's records for the moment, one is inclined to agree with Wagner that

> the most cruel thing that happened to Cabrillo, however, was that he was deprived of all evidence on the maps of California of his visit to this coast. This was due to Sebastián Vizcaíno, who, in 1602 and 1603, covered much the same ground as did Cabrillo.[4]

While Wagner might have made exceptions of Cape Mendocino, Point Arenas, and Sierra Nevada, he went on to show that Vizcaíno, better equipped than Cabrillo for more accurate fixes, arbitrarily changed the latter's toponomy, pretending that he couldn't locate Cabrillo's terrain features. There is a great deal more, definitely unfavorable, which can be said regarding Vizcaíno and, of that, additional strictures later. Even so, within sight of the writer's desk, there is a monument to Juan Rodríguez Cabrillo on Point Loma, San Diego, which more than eight hundred thousand people visited in 1956 – who hears anything at all about Sebastián Vizcaíno?

Be the final disposition of Cabrillo's charts what it may have been, the information they provided was not

---

[4] Wagner, *Juan Rodríguez Cabrillo*, p. 30.

lost by any means. Long before Vizcaíno used it, Friar Andrés de Urdaneta, "monk-mariner," as he has been styled, but chronologically, "mariner-monk," as he was actually, showed himself to be familiar with Cabrillo's discoveries prior to his 1564-1565 voyage when he established the round trip route for the Manila Galleon between Acapulco and the Philippines, sailing westward across the Pacific with Miguel López de Legaspi. Urdaneta referred to Cabrillo's discoveries in a letter he wrote to the king in 1561. According to the monk, Legaspi's expedition was to sail along the coast of Nueva España

> which runs westnorthwest, and, weather permitting, we shall sail, albeit somewhat distant from the beach, up to thirty-four degrees or more, where we will try to reconnoiter the land along the coast which Juan Rodríguez Cabrillo discovered.

They were to go ashore to pick up what they should require from whatever were available there – presumably, water, firewood, spars, and foodstuffs – and converse with the Indians, by signs, at least, about a "great water they reported to Juan Rodríguez Cabrillo which lay beyond there toward the interior. . ." Urdaneta said furthermore that he would follow the coast to see what this water was, fresh or salt, and go thence to land's end where he would turn southwest. He then would run down to thirty-seven or thirty-five degrees whence he would head due west.[5]

From the fact that Urdaneta could mention specific features of Cabrillo's report eighteen years after the latter's death, and that Vizcaíno could be familiar with it sixty years after Cabrillo died, one may surmise that,

---

[5] *Documentos inéditos,* "Expedición de Legaspi," Document 17, 1561. "Derrotero muy especial para dirigir a s.m., hecho por Fr. Andrés de Urdaneta," Ser. II, vol. I, pp. 132-134.

while his reports were not published, they were not buried in some archive either. Indeed, it appears feasible to establish a rather good case for Spain's security measures; possibly poignant need for safeguards has been expressed adequately by an Englishman, one definitely partisan to his land which harbored inveterate enmity to Spain through most of the 1600's, who said, smugly, boastfully, or gloatingly, as the reader may choose:

> Moreouer, because since our warres with *Spaine,* by the taking of their ships, and sacking of their townes and cities, most of all their secrets of the *West Indies,* and euery part thereof are fallen into our peoples hands (which in former time were for the most part unknowen unto us,) I have used the uttermost of my best endeavour, to get, and hauing gotten, to translate out of Spanish, and here in this present volume to publish such secrets of theirs, as may any way auaile us or annoy them, if they driue and urge us by their sullen insolences, to cõtinue our courses of hostilitie against them, and shall cease to seeke a good and Christian peace upon indifferent and equal conditions.[6]

From an unbiased point of view, this would seem to indicate that it was incumbent upon "Spaine" to be careful.

Yet, an eminent Spaniard of the nineteenth century, Fernández Duro, took a scornful view of security measures in the case where Felipe II refused permission to publish a work by Juan Escalante de Mendoza, finished in 1575, which "could be considered the sum total of maritime knowledge of that age." Mendoza had spent many years composing his opus, putting into it the fruit of nearly a lifetime as a sea captain. When he requested permission to publish his manuscript, the king submitted it to the judgment of the outstanding

---

[6] Hakluyt, *The Third and Last Volume,* "The Epistle Dedicatorie," p. A2v.

astronomers, cosmographers, and navigators of that era in Spain. These, and also the Council of the Indies approved it; but, Felipe would not authorize its publication ". . . because the Government was afraid to make it ostensible to foreigners. . ." Fernández, with manifest scorn, asked how it could have been dangerous to Spain to publish something already known by the English and the Dutch. As a final dig at the king, he stated that Escalante de Mendoza claimed he had spent ten thousand ducats on his work – all he got from the crown was his manuscript's return.[7]

Perhaps Fernández Duro had not read Hakluyt's work prior to writing *A la mar madera*. Surely, he must otherwise have pricked up his ears at this:

And for an appendix unto the ende of my worke, I haue thought it not impertinent, to exhibite to the graue and discreet judgements of those which haue the chiefe places in the Admiraltie and marine causes of *England,* Certaine briefe extracts of the orders of the Contraction house of *Siuil* in Spaine, touching their gouernment in sea-matters; together with The streight and seuere examinations of Pilots and Masters before they be admitted to take charge of ships, aswell [*sic*] by the *Pilot mayor,* and brotherhood of ancient Masters, as by the Kings reader of *The lecture of the art of Nauigation,* with the time that they be enioyned to bee his auditors, and some part of the questions that they are to answere unto. Which if they finde good and beneficial for our seamen, I hope they wil gladly imbrace and imitate, or finding out some fitter course of their owne, will seeke to bring such as are of that calling into better gouernment and more perfection in that most laudable and needfull vocation.[8]

Along this line of effort, Hakluyt would have found

[7] Fernández Duro, *A la mar madera*, pp. 35 *et seq.* A copy of Mendoza's treatise is in Colección Navarrete, Museo Naval, Madrid, as MS 523, Captain Jhoan Escalante de Mendoça, *Ytenerario de Navegación de los Mares, y tierra Oçidentales,* 1575. Original is in the Biblioteca de Palacio, Madrid.

[8] Hakluyt, *op. cit.,* p. A3.

Escalante de Mendoza's *Ytenerario* a veritable windfall if he could have laid hands upon it. If it had been published in 1575, he could have translated it – and he was no mean translator – and provided the "Admiraltie" with copies of it, possibly in time for Sir Francis Drake to use on his epochal voyage into the Pacific, thence around the world, in 1577-1580. And history records cases where Drake sought Spanish charts and Spanish and Portuguese pilots to help him along the way from Cape Horn to Drake's Bay, California, and across the Pacific Ocean.

A vivid instance of this proclivity on Drake's part, has been cited by Rumeu de Armas:

> In March 1579, the Golden Hind anchored at Isla del Caña, off the south coast of Costa Rica, for damage repair and the pirate rested several days ashore while his men captured by chance, with a skiff, a Spanish ship which was taking to Panamá two renowned pilots, Alonso Sánchez Colchero and Martín de Aguirre. In order to show the outstanding importance of the acquisition, it will suffice merely to indicate that these two were pilots of the famous Acapulco ship by whose means communication was established across the Pacific with the Philippines; and, when Drake had despoiled them of their sailing directions and their navigating charts, he held in his hands all of the means for attempting the transit over the great marine fosse.[9]

In early April 1579, Drake captured Francisco de Zárate in his own ship but, after sacking her, he returned the ship and freed Zárate and the pilot Sánchez Colchero. At Huatulco, he put Nuño da Silva ashore.[10] It is regretted that Rumeu did not state anything regarding Silva's seizure. He might possibly have thrown light upon Silva's employment.

---

[9] Antonio Rumeu de Armas, *Los viajes de John Hawkins a América* (1562-1595). (Sevilla, 1947), pp. 351-352.
[10] *Ibid.*, p. 352.

With respect to Silva, Mason has stated that Drake departed from Mayo, one of the Cape Verde Islands, on January 30, 1578. Shortly thereafter, Sir Francis captured a fine Portuguese ship, heavily laden with very rich goods; but, according to Mason,

> there was, however, one commodity upon that Portuguese caravel of more value to Drake than all the rest put together – a Portuguese pilot, Nuño da Silva, who had travelled far and wide in Brazil and in the land to the south of Brazil, and this pilot, being told that Drake was voyaging to the South Sea, volunteered eagerly to go with him.[11]

With respect to Drake's usual practice with foreign pilots, however, a striking discrepancy appears in Mason's account. After stating that Drake had put Nuño da Silva ashore at Huatulco, Mason averred that

> What use he served, why Drake kept him so continually on the 'Golden Hind," it is impossible even to conjecture. He was far from any waters of which he had expert knowledge. There is not a hint to be found that Drake ever made the slightest call upon his services.[12]

As far as "conjecture" is concerned, it is not farfetched, perhaps, to surmise that Drake, with his passion for charts and cartography, kept Silva busy in charting the areas which became new to both of them. Also, Silva might have instructed the young gentlemen aboard the "Golden Hind" in navigation and Portuguese.

Zárate threw some sidelights upon Drake which

---

[11] A. E. W. Mason, *The Life of Francis Drake* (Garden City, N.Y., 1942), p. 66. Mason's treatment of Drake's voyage around the world appears to be based principally upon Hakluyt's *Third and Last Volume* and the Hakluyt Society's edition of *The World Encompassed by Sir Francis Drake* (London, 1854).

[12] *Ibid.*, p. 140.

should be recorded in justice to Spanish security. He wrote that he had been cruising until Saturday, April 4, 1579, when, a little before dawn, they made out a ship in the moonlight, very close aboard, which proved to be Drake's galleon. A small boat took Zárate off and delivered him aboard the "Golden Hind," "a very good galleon, fitted out and gunned as I've never seen such in my life." She was about a 400-tonner with an extreme spread of sail, as Zárate described her, with a hundred men on board who were ripe in age and fitness for war, and as well exercised in it as old veterans of the Italian campaigns. Every one of them took particular pains to keep his arquebus clean. Drake was kind to them, and they treated him with great respect. Among them, Drake had nine or ten gentlemen, second sons of leading Englishmen; these, the writer fancies, were very likely forerunners of the "gentlemen adventurers of Bristol" who figured so prominently in later clashes between the English and the Spaniards at sea.

As for Drake, personally, Zárate bespoke admiration. "Francisco Drac" was his name, a man thirty-five years old. He was small, blonde bearded, "one of the best mariners there are at sea, as well in celestial navigation as in ability to command his ship."

Drake also had artists aboard who painted all the coast for him in its own colors. "This was what it grieved me to see," said Zárate, "because everything looks so natural that anyone who followed the paintings could by no means get lost." [13]

According to Ricardo Cappa, that priest had to go to "the dusty reports in our Archivo de Indias," or to

---

[13] Letter, Francisco de Zárate to the Viceroy of New Spain from Realejo, Nicaragua, April 16, 1579, quoted in Cappa, *Estudios críticos acerca de la dominación española en América*, vol. x, pp. 185-186, 190-192.

copies of them, in order to pass with reasonable certainty of accuracy between Scylla and Charybdis. Perhaps many researchers in Spanish American history today feel as Father Cappa did on this matter. At any rate, Cappa appeared to have gone thoroughly into the activities of English and Dutch sea captains who went freebooting into the Pacific during the last quarter of the sixteenth century and the first half of the seventeenth. He gave a seemingly thorough account of one of the English sea captains who entered the South Sea via the Strait of Magellan about eight years after Drake plowed those waters. This refers to Thomas Cavendish whose procedure was strikingly similar to Drake's; like the latter, the former seized Spanish charts and captured their pilots; and, in so doing, he gained for his country much of the data over which Hakluyt rejoiced.

When Cavendish was sailing from Piura, Perú, to Panamá in 1587, he captured a 120-ton vessel and took out of her one Miguel Sánchez, a native of Marseilles, highly skilled in navigating the Americas' Pacific Coast. According to Cappa, it was Sánchez who gave Cavendish timely information about the Manila Galleon. "On November 4, the Englishman, being on the parallel which the "Santa Ana" should run down, captured her." And what a prize! "She was a 700-tonner, and carried 122,000 pesos in gold, many silk-stuffs, damasks, etc. . ." From her also, Cavendish took two pilots; one, a Spaniard, and the other, a Portuguese. He then disembarked the rest of the "Santa Ana's" personnel and, on November 19, 1587 he set course toward California.[14] He was sailing, no doubt, in very bright circumstances.

The type of his luck is indicated further by some

---

[14] Cappa, *op. cit.*, p. 217.

items about these pilots which Hakluyt has furnished from Cavendish's report, stating that he took aboard

> one Nicholas Roderigo a Portugall, who hath not onely bene in Canton and other parts of China, but also in the islands of Iapon . . . and hath also bene in the Philippinas.
>
> Wee tooke also from them a Spaniard whose name was Thomas de Ersola, which was a very good Pilote from Acapulco and the coast of Nueua Espanna unto the islands of Ladrones. . .[15]

Spain not only felt poignant need to maintain security regarding her geographical and hydrographical knowledge but also her advances in naval construction as well. Some idea concerning her measures to protect her geographic and hydrographic discoveries has been given. Let it suffice for the moment with respect to security measures in the case of naval construction, to state that practically every royal cédula concerning shipbuilding which was issued between the fifteenth and seventeenth centuries prohibited sale of Spanish-built ships to foreigners. Spain's international commitments during the sixteenth century were indeed formidable. As one Spaniard has expressed the situation:

> Good monarchs as those of the House of Austria were, they weren't able to ignore their imperial and religious engagements and, actually, it was miraculous that Spain could advance in Europe against so many enemies and attend to her colonial empire in the rest of the world. It was an empire which reached its maximum greatness with Felipe II. . . It was a dizzy steep with a sharp vertex, extremely difficult to flatetn off and make stable.[16]

---

[15] Hakluyt, *The Third and Last Volume*, p. 817.

[16] Rafael Estrada y Arnaiz, *La influencia del mar en la historia de España* (Zaragoza, 1950), pp. 18-19. Estrada was then Admiral-Captain General of the Maritime Department of Cádiz and a member of the Royal Academy of History.

Spain's hegemony over more of the world than any other nation exercised in the sixteenth century is too well known to justify any exposition here. Perhaps one may say correctly that its apogee was reached in 1581, when Portugal was annexed to Spain; that its decline began just seven years afterward, when England defeated Felipe II's Invincible Armada.

> The defeat of the Armada marked the end of the great days of Spain. For the greater part of a century she had imposed herself on the world to an extent unwarranted by her population and resources. She had relied on the bullion from the American mines and, latterly, on the spices from the East. Under the Emperor Charles V she united the greater part of Italy and the wealth of Burgundy with the Empire, but after his death and the outbreak of revolt in the Netherlands, Spain's strength was fictitious. This was hidden at the time and was only slowly understood by England or Spain, or, indeed, by any part of Europe. . .[17]

The Armada's defeat, however, may be considered as due to widely different employment of means rather than to Spanish ships' inferiority in staunchness and sea-keeping qualities. The English used their main batteries to destroy the enemy; the Spaniards used theirs to reduce English speed in order to be able to grapple and board. They taunted the English as cowards because these would not come to grips with them. As Rodgers has said, "The tactical development of this war was the substitution of great-gun fire for hand-to-hand fighting of boarders as the chief effort." [18]

---

[17] William Ledyard Rodgers, *Naval Warfare Under Oars, 4th to 16th Centuries: A Study of Strategy, Tactics and Ship Design* (Annapolis, Md., 1939), pp. 328-329. The author was placed on the retired list of the U.S. Navy in 1924 with the rank of vice admiral after fifty years' service.

[18] *Ibid.*, p. 333. Yet, two hundred seventeen years later, at Trafalgar, Lord Nelson advocated grappling and boarding. Possibly, this was not due entirely to retrogression in tactics – the English fleet was inferior in numbers to the Invincible Armada; it was numerically superior at Trafalgar. Oddly

Reverting, however, to Spanish shipbuilding in the sixteenth century, they had manifestly wanted to be ahead in this field even before that century began. A royal edict of March 21, 1492 was devised to stimulate ship construction. This was followed by another, dated March 20, 1498, which offered rewards for building ships ranging from six hundred to a thousand tons. That they had been building well seemed to be indicated by a 1501 edict which prohibited sales of ships, or lesser vessels, to foreigners, even in cases of those naturalized as Spaniards. While this was an undesirable prohibition, Fernández Duro thought, it still manifested the prosperous state of Spanish shipbuilding since their product was desired by foreigners. The Cantabrians, Vizcayans, and Guipuzcoans enjoyed unrivalled prestige in every respect of constructing and fitting out ships.[19]

While Spanish royal policy restricted other industrial development in Spanish America to an almost prohibitive degree, shipbuilding there was an inescapable concomitant of two factors: one, the destruction in New World waters which the *broma* or marine borer inflicted upon hulls built in Spain; two, the extreme difficulty in sailing Spanish-built craft around Cape Horn to supply needs in the Pacific. For these reasons, one finds that all early Spanish maritime exploration along the coasts of the Californias was undertaken in vessels built on the Pacific seaboard of the New World.

The right to build ships in Spanish America was

---

enough, 325 years after the Armada's defeat, the writer noted on his first battleship cruise that the USS "Illinois" carried a long underwater projection beyond her bows for ramming. As for the Americans toward the turn of the century, perhaps the havoc of the CSS "Virginia" in ramming, wrought in Hampton Roads in 1862, before the USS "Monitor" arrived there, was still fresh in our naval constructors' memory.

[19] Fernández Duro, *A la mar madera*, p. 11.

first granted by Fernando el Católico about mid-1514 when he ordered Pedrarias de Avila, governor of Tierra Firme, to build three or four caravels for exploration along the coast of the South Sea. As the king had been informed that the broma, worm-eating the ships Pedrarias sailed there, had made them unserviceable, he ordered the House of *Contratación* (often termed "House of Trade") to send shipwrights to Darién. These were to use *madera amarga* or bitterwood, which was found in Tierra Firme, for shipbuilding, as he believed it might not be eaten by the broma.[20]

While the writer has not seen any evidence that this particular suggestion proved efficacious, several indigenous woods were found along the Pacific coasts of the Americas which proved highly resistant to *teredo navalis.* Only a few of these woods will be mentioned as the list of them is very extensive. All their collateral qualities such as lightness, strength, propensity to "suck in the nail," non-splintering attributes, ease of bending to curves in hull design, etc. are also too numerous to cite in detail. Cappa chose those which abounded in the vicinity of Realejo, Nicaragua, as representative of the varieties which were to be found along the Pacific littoral between the Tropics.

One favorite wood was *cedro* or cedar, *cedrela glassiovii,* because of its lightness. Ships built of it wouldn't sink if capsized but would "lie between two waters"! *(quedan entre dos aguas, por ser madera ligera).* Other favorites were *guachapelí,* no known English equivalent, *acacia guachapele;* and, *bálsamo* or balsam, *myrospermum salvatoriensis.*[21]

---

[20] Cappa, *Estudios críticos,* vol. x, p. 20.

[21] Cappa, *op. cit.,* pp. 55, 100-101. The Latin equivalents are from Malaret, *Diccionario de americanismos.*

At this time, the writer does not intend to dwell upon the course of shipbuilding in Spanish America. That it flourished, can be demonstrated amply; that the Spaniards had reasons to safeguard their methods, can likewise be shown. Perhaps Cappa had an observation, unexpected as it may be, which might lead some Americans to take stock of their concepts regarding Spanish ships and shipbuilding. Cappa supposed that the vessels which the English and the Dutch pilots sailed into the Pacific would not have been the poorest constructed in their countries. They should have been sturdy and fast. Yet, ships constructed by the Spaniards along the Pacific in the New World frequently outsailed the "pirates" even when tacking.[22]

So, one must assume that ships built in Tehuantepec, Iztapa, Acajutla, or Realejo, carried the first Spaniards to reach the Californias through the vicissitudes of head winds and seas, adverse currents and storms. One may assume, too, that, in the cases of Alarcón, Ulloa, and Cabrillo, they were rather staunch craft on account of the fact that, if for no other reason, all which stood away on these voyages sailed back into their ports of departure.

While Spanish-built craft carried the first Spaniards to the two Californias, this is not to say, however, that the Spaniards were the first foreigners to reach those lands. Men of other nationalities may have preceded them there, and some evidence to show that such might really have been the case will be presented in the next chapter.

---

[22] Cappa, *op. cit.*, pp. 124-125.

VII
First Aliens in California?

Chapman has devoted a chapter to "The Chinese along the Pacific Coast in Ancient Times." [1] In this splendid portion of his work, he presented a great deal of circumstantial evidence to show that either the Chinese or other Orientals visited the California or Mexican coast many centuries before the Spaniards reached the New World. However conclusive his evidence may appear to others, it appeared definitely so to Chapman.

One of the most interesting facets, if not the burden of this chapter, is his identification of Fusang with an area in California or in Mexico. Fusang was the name which Hwui Shan, a Buddhist priest, gave a land that he described after his arrival in China in 458 A.D. and, into which, he had introduced Buddhism and various other reforms. Chapman considered the description of the flora Hwui Shan encountered in Fusang overwhelming evidence that he had been in Mexico or some other land along the Pacific Ocean where the century plant was indigenous.

Finally, the story of Hwui Shan agrees strangely with the Mexican legend of the pious Quetzalcoatl, who came from across the seas and introduced many religious practices into the country. The likenesses of the old Mexican religion to early Buddhism are many and striking. There is record of a high priest of

[1] Chapman, *A History of California,* chapter III.

Mixteca who was called "Taysacaa," or "the man of Sacaa." It is at least a curious parallel that Buddha was called "Sakya-muni," or "the man (hermit) of Sakya." The root "Zaca" (Sakya), it may be noticed, occurs frequently in Mexican place names, e.g. Zacatula, Zacatecas.[2]

Chapman did not state how "Zaca" had been identified with "Sakya." While the writer is not proposing any argument whatever as to the etymological points involved, he finds it interesting, nevertheless, to note that "zaca" is defined as a large "zaque," or a wineskin, for drawing water out of wells in mines. The etymon of zaque is given as Arabic "zac." One finds that the term, "zacate," grass, pasturage, or forage, has for its etymon the Mexican "çacatl." "Zacateca" is a Cuban term meaning undertaker, especially one who accompanies corpses in livery.[3] Possibly the "çaca" of "çacatl" does hark back to "sakya"?

Chapman very logically went on toward the end of this chapter to point out why the Chinese might not have followed Hwui Shan's discovery by establishing themselves on the Pacific Coast in North America. He alleged that, by the fifth century A.D., "the day had already come when they were too contented with the greatness of their past, and stratification had set in." Confucius influenced them "to turn inward upon themselves," with the result that they abandoned natural science and began memorizing ancient books in order to absorb the solutions of life's problems.

One wonders if, in fact, the Chinese or other Orientals really abandoned contact with Fusang, if established. How, on the contrary, can the alleged

---

[2] Ibid., p. 28.
[3] Real Academia Española, Diccionario de la lengua española, (Madrid, 1947).

presence in 1540 of foreign ships near the mouth of the Colorado River be explained? Such has been noted already in this work in connection with Melchor Díaz' patrol in Coronado's effort to make contact with Francisco de Alarcón as set down in *California historia y viajes,* Colección Navarrete, undated, of which, the writer believes, Captain Juan Matheo Mange was the author. While Mange did not state the source of his account, he might have taken it from Gómara or Torquemada or he might have had access to an original source in private hands. It seems a very well established fact that much source material resides yet among family collections in Spain, for example, which has not appeared in any of the national archives.[4]

Be his source what it might have been, Mange said that the foreigners encountered by the Díaz patrol indicated, as their signs appeared to the Spaniards, that their homeland lay toward the west, beyond the Ocean Sea, perhaps toward Asia or China. According to piles of slag which the Spaniards noticed there, the foreigners were working mines and extracting metals. Their ore seemed to have been brought from some high sierras opposite this position on the coast by Indians from nations nearby.

When one considers the difficult sailing conditions which obtained and yet persist in the Gulf of California, head winds prevailing against northerly bound craft, one is impelled to look for a motivation. Perhaps

[4] An outstanding instance of this can be noted in the legacy of the Marqués de Santa Cruz which has been willed to the Spanish Navy together with a vast depository in a former family castle at Visos del Marqués, about 110 miles generally south of Madrid. According to Captain Julio Guillén, Spanish Navy, Director of the Museo Naval, documents which hitherto were property of the Santa Cruz family have been assembled in that castle *por toneladas* — by tons.

these mining activities lured the Orientals up to the gulf's northern limits; possibly there were pockets of precious metals in northwest Sonora even if the greater deposits have been found generally in the northeastern part of that state. At any rate, the exotic vessels with golden pelicans as figureheads may have been there, whatever their motivations were.

And, if so, it appears within the bounds of possibility that they, or some of their compatriots, might have been returning there about thirty-three years later. In 1573, a report of eight sail, sighted off the coast of Jalisco or Tepic, led to an official investigation by order of the king of Spain. The testimony received in this inquiry was recorded in Ms, Justicia 1041, AGI, entitled:

Guadalaxara Year of 1574
Investigation made by the Audiencia of Nueva Galicia *about* certain Ships which arrived on that coast which it was said were turks and Moors.

(Signed) Secretary Valmaseda.

The hearings began in Tepique (Tepic), Compostela Province, Nueva Galicia, on December 2, 1573, before Diego de Bolaños, alcalde mayor of Compostela City and some mining areas in that vicinity. The first witness called was Friar Juan de Luco, a Franciscan, who stated under oath that he was about thirty-eight years old, a native of Alava Province, Vizcaya, Spain, and, that about ten years previously he had come to those parts in Pedro de las Roela's fleet. Several next ensuing questions were manifestly designed to test his credibility.

He was asked if he knew the South Sea coast and what part of it and how long he had resided there — yes, all of that in one question. The Friar answered that he did know it because he had been along it and had swum at its beaches, and, for ten years up to that time, he had lived in Sinaloa, Tepic, and on down to Puerto de Matanchel which was on the South Sea coast where it was called Tecomatlan.

Then, he was asked if he knew what ships were, their form, and if he had sailed in them or had seen them sailing. Yes, he knew what ships were because he had sailed in them; he had lived in the port of Laredo (about thirty miles east of Santander, Spain) three years and a half, and a year and a half in Santander, where he had seen many vessels, ships as well as caravels and other types. Ships had high freeboard and topsails; caravels did not have as much freeboard and did not carry topsails. He had seen them under sail and with bare poles and, as he had said, he had sailed in them and that he came to these parts in a transport (*urca*) belonging to Juan Gallego.

Friar Luco was next asked whether he had seen any ships along the Pacific Coast, around Compostela, La Purificación, Puerto de Chamela, and elsewhere, and how many there were and in what part and place and time he saw them and how many and at what hour of the day it was and what people were with him when he saw the ships and at what distance they were from land.

He replied that, about two months before, he, Mateo Pasqual y Napolitano, Juan Rodrigues, and Francisco Ponçe, who were Spaniards and mestizos, met in the town of Tecomatlan which is on the South Sea shore. They were near the church in that town and the sea breaks on the beach behind it. About an hour after sunset, one of them yelled, "Look at that ship there!" They looked, and the friar saw a very large bulk about, as he judged, four leagues offshore. Presently, they saw the large mass divide in two and made out two ships, one following in the wake of the other. They came from the direction of the point at Puerto de Matanchel and were headed toward the three unpopulated islands which lay to seaward in range with the ships.

And, while they were watching, they next saw three or four others, small ships like Galician caravels, which were sailing toward the first-mentioned, on the same course, and a league or a league and a half astern of them. Then, as this witness looked, it appeared that they were spreading sail. In order to determine better whether these objects were ships, Francisco de Orozco marked them by a fig tree which stood on the beach and all sighted the objects in range with it. At first, these were behind it; then, after a little while, they passed ahead of the tree. As darkness came on, the ships disappeared in the same direction aforesaid.

This happened on a Monday evening, and the next day, Tuesday, about half past two in the afternoon, all of them met again at the same church. This witness and the others saw a very large ship with all its sails spread in the same place where they had seen the first two vessels. The other men began insisting that what they saw was a rock but Luco maintained that it was a ship and a very big one. While arguing still, they turned to look at it again but it had disappeared completely and, as it didn't appear again, they understood that it was a ship. At the time they sighted it, the ship again appeared to be about four leagues offshore.

The next day, about three or four in the afternoon, this witness, Mateo Pasqual, and Francisco Ponçe were at the door of the church mentioned previously. The others had gone to Luis Berdejo's farm, a league away from the town. In the same place and in the same way as on Tuesday, another very large ship came into view and, to the friar, it seemed from its size to be the same vessel. He couldn't see whether it was moving or not. Pasqual and Ponçe went to Berdejo's farm in order to get a better view because the farm and farmhouse were on high ground. When they got there, however, it was out of sight.

It was public and notorious in all the province that the aforesaid ships had been sighted because this witness had talked to many persons who said they had seen them, besides those who were with him when he saw them. He didn't recall their names but some had told him that, in the direction of the islands, they had seen a lot of fire at night which appeared as if the savannas were burning.

Luco was next asked if the light was good at the times he saw the ships in order that he could be certain as to what he saw and not be deceived by rocks or cloud effects which were usual in that sea. He replied that when he saw them, there was sunlight, a cloudless sky, and that the sea was gentle and undisturbed. He saw the ships very well and was not deceived by what he saw. They were not rocks nor cloud effects of the sort usually found in the sea. In the case of rocks, these ordinarily remain fixed and do not disappear; the ships disappeared. Moreover, in the locality where they sighted the ships, there is only one white rock which, even in a storm, the sea does not cover and is visible as usual. He reaffirmed his statement that he saw ships.

One might think at this stage in the proceedings that the examiner might have eased up somewhat on Friar Juan de Luco but such was not to be the case. When asked if the ships were dead in the water or moving and in what direction or if their sails were spread or furled, he stood on his previous testimony which, if necessary, he said, he would restate. He was then asked what were the size and build of the vessels, how many masts each had, and how many topsails they carried. The reply was that the first two he saw appeared to him as ships and so did the two he saw on Tuesday and Wednesday. The others, as he had stated, appeared like Galician craft to him, under sail and moving, and they were not large vessels. He saw them with their sails spread, and these were square sails, but he did not see whether they carried topsails nor how many masts each one of them had.

The security element began to assume emphasis although it had been implicit from the outset. Luco was asked next if he knew or had heard it said that any of the people aboard the ships had jumped ashore and in what places and if they had taken off water or other supplies and if they had harmed anyone and if they had dealt or communicated with anybody in the country. He answered that he didn't know and had not heard anyone say anything of the sort.

Then he was asked if he knew whether the people aboard the ships were Turks, Moors, French, or English Lutherans, or to what nation they belonged; if they were vassals or friends of the King, Our Lord, or if they were operating in disservice to him and attempting to do harm in those parts. The witness didn't know who they were but surmised that probably they were French or English who were likely journeying, wrought up by fear of their princes on account of being Lutherans and, consequently, not authorized to stay in their realms. They probably came to those parts to settle on some island or on the mainland.

While this, of course, was opinion, conjecture, and hearsay, almost valueless as evidence; it showed, nevertheless, royal concern over the reported presence of unidentified vessels in the far-off Pacific. Apparently, no stone was to be left unturned in the effort to find out the origin of these ships; nothing was adduced to prove them nonexistent – quite the contrary.

When the Friar was asked if he knew the bays and ports on the coast of the South Sea where the ships could anchor, from Puerto de la Natividad to Culiacán, he said that he wasn't cognizant of any port besides that of Matanchel and he didn't know whether the ships could anchor there or not. The questions indicated indeed that no pains were to have been spared in testing Friar Juan de Luco's credibility.

In continuation, he was asked if he knew what islands and mainland lay in that part of the country toward the west, how far away they were, what land they were, and whether they were inhabited or uninhabited. He replied that, from the towns Xalpocotlan and Santa Cruz, he had seen three islands which he had heard were uninhabited; and, that a long time ago, there were Indians who went there on rafts and in canoes to make sacrifices. These islands [apparently, the Tres Marías] lay to the west; one of them appeared to be large; and, to this witness, it appeared that they were more than fourteen leagues from the aforesaid towns. The province of Sinaloa lay in range with these islands generally, set a little toward the north, where there was a great number of native Indians and, previously, it had been inhabited by Spaniards. Perhaps about three years prior, when this witness was there, the Indians rose against the Spaniards and killed two friars and other people. When Diego de Bolaños, the alcalde presiding this investigation, heard about it, he sent in reinforcements to withdraw the settlers from that province and, from that day to this, it had not been inhabited by Spaniards. It was more than one hundred and thirty leagues from the islands in reference; its land was very rich in many high grade mines as well as in a great production of maize, kidney beans, squash, and fish, and many herds of mares, horses, and cattle.

This witness had heard that thirty-six or forty leagues beyond Sinaloa there was a port called Valle de Yaquimi. He had been told that here, in a stretch of ten leagues, there were twenty thousand "bow and arrow" Indian inhabitants. The Valle de Mayo lay between Sinaloa and Yaquimi where he had been and had counted there fifty-five hundred Indians armed with bows and arrows.

By order of Francisco de Ibarra, governor of Nueva Vizcaya, Esteban Martín, captain by the governor's appointment, had allotted those Indians into encomiendas. The province was very rich in mines and subsistence supplies for it had a quantity of cattle, mares, and horses, and maize, beans, poultry, and other foodstuffs. The people in the aforesaid ships could easily settle that province and fortify themselves in it.

The friar was then asked if he knew or had heard where the ships were then; where, it appeared to him, they could be; if he knew what they were doing or what they could do; what their direct destination was; and, if they had settled on some island or mainland. The witness responded that he did not know any more than what he had stated already.

This statement did not deter his examiner, however, who seemed obsessed by a conviction that he must extract something worthy of the king's ears. Martín Vélez, *escribano receptor,* a scribe commissioned to take evidence – possibly "receiver notary" might serve? – went on, relentlessly squeezing, as if by prolonged pressure even a turnip must ultimately provide him the drops of blood he wanted so avidly. Perhaps, too, he was convinced that the friar was the best witness of all those available; that he couldn't have again as good an opportunity to develop something worth sending to Spain. At any rate, he next asked the friar if he knew where the ships could provide themselves with supplies and other necessary items. Luco replied that they could get those things in Sinaloa, Mayo, and Yaquimi.

Did Luco know if there was a strait called the Englishman's Strait, from the North Sea to the South, through which the said ships could pass, or, did he know of any other strait or way through which ships could go from the North to the South Sea? The friar said he didn't know anything at all about that. Then he was asked if he knew whether the ships had come through any of the said straits and through what parts and places they had passed and whence they had come. He replied that he said what he had said and didn't know anything about the rest.

These questions did indicate indeed that the Northwest mystery, the Strait of Anián, or the Englishman's Strait *(el estrecho del yngles),* was an international obsession in those days, an incursion passage to which Spain was supersensitive. The obvious route of ingress across the Pacific, known to them since 1521, did not seem to occur to the Spanish in connection with these ships. Possibly, they were little concerned over incursions by Orientals for these were subjects of evangelization. English, Dutch, and Huguenots were a different matter; heretics, they could not be tolerated within Spain's domains.

In fairness to the examiner who, no doubt, had been

oriented by the Audiencia of Nueva Galicia, one should say that an important purpose of this investigation may have been to impress upon His Majesty the vulnerability of New Spain to occupation by foreigners. These eight ships, obviously, could have carried a force sufficiently substantial for a serious reckoning; especially so, in case it should have become allied with five thousand to twenty thousand Indians already hostile to the Spaniards. The final question asked Friar Juan de Luco appeared definitely pointed to such a purpose.

Did he know whether all the South Sea coast from the Villa de Culiacán to Puerto de la Natividad and beyond was uninhabited by both Spaniards and Indians and what the length of the shoreline was from Culiacán to Natividad? He answered that Sinaloa and the other provinces he had named were along that coast and that they were populated by natives; from Culiacán to Yaquimi, there was no Spanish population at all. From Yaquimi to Natividad, this witness couldn't say what the situation was for the reason that he had not been there nor seen it,

and he said that this is the truth upon the oath that he swore and he signed it with his name and likewise the said chief alcalde signed it friar juan de luco, diego de bolaños Paniagua before me martin velez receiver notary ——

So, on with the investigation.

Pedro sanchez. – On this said day month and year aforesaid being in the said Town and present the said diego de bolaños chief alcalde he ordered to appear before him Pero sanchez yzquierdo from losa and leones near llerena in the Kingdoms of Castille a resident of tecomatlan in the province of conpostela from whom oath was received in legal form by God and by Saint Mary and being asked about the foregoing the following questions were put to him and he answered and deposed concerning it ——

He was then asked his name, age, and occupation, where he was born, and how long it had been since he came to those parts. Well, his name was Pedro Sánchez Yzquierdo; he was twenty-five years old, a tailor, and he was managing a cacao planting on the coast of this province. He was a native of Los Ayleones near Llerena in Castille and it could be fifteen years, a little more or less, when he came to those parts but he couldn't remember the name of the general commanding the ships. Sánchez had "been around," for he said he had resided in Guadalajara, Zacatecas, Mexico City, San Martín, Compostela Province, and along the South Sea coast. Perhaps he was a "journeyman" tailor!

When asked if he knew the South Sea coast and where and how long he had resided along it, this witness replied that he had lived the last four months on it in a cacao orchard. Did he know what ships were, their types, and had he sailed in them or seen them sailing? He said he knew what they were because he had seen them while coming to those parts. They were made of lumber; were big and wide; they had a prow and a poop, a galley, masts, mastheads, sails, decks, yards, a rudder, and shrouds. He had seen them put the rudder over and bring the ship about and had sailed there from Spain and, although he was ten years old when he came there, he remembered ships very well.

As, apparently, he had now established his competency as a witness, he was asked an extremely long-winded and multiple-jointed question which today, in courts-martial certainly, would be simply, "If you have seen ships on this coast recently, state all the circumstances." Sánchez' reply indicated the detailed and varied scope of the question.

What happened was, according to the witness, that

about two months ago, he was in company with Luis Verdejo, Francisco Ponçe, and Juan Rodrigues, all of whom were Spaniards except Luis Verdejo who was a mestizo. They were at Verdejo's house which was near Tecomatlan, about a league from the coast, on a Wednesday evening just after sunset. Francisco Ponçe told this witness and the others to see what a white rock there was out there in the ocean. Luis Verdejo said there was no such thing; that in all the fifteen years he had been living in that house, he had never seen a rock there. Then, all of them got up and walked toward the sea a little while, looking toward the place where Ponçe said he had seen the rock. Soon, they saw a large bulk which divided in two and one part passed on ahead of the other. In a little while, they made out these masses as two very big ships and all saw them move out with sails spread, one in the wake of the other, standing toward Culiacán. While all of them were watching these two ships sail away, they saw an equally big ship, standing up from the direction of Matanchel, which joined the first two. While all were saying that these were ships, they saw five more coming under sail from the direction of Culiacán which joined the other three and all stood away toward the three islands fifteen or sixteen leagues offshore. Of these last five, three were large and two were small vessels. They lost sight of the eight ships as these drew near the three islands. He judged the distance offshore to these ships where first sighted at about a league and a half. They went then to report what they had seen to the alcalde.

Three or four days after they had sighted the eight ships, Sánchez said that he and Juan Rodrigues went to Luis Verdejo's house for supper. About two hours and a half after dark, while eating under an arbor there,

Juan Rodrigues told this witness to look out to seaward and he would spot a light. They put out their own light and saw one at sea which appeared like a bundle of fodder burning. They watched it as long as about half the time to say the Apostles' Creed when it disappeared, an even clearer indication to them that ships were along the coast.

This blaze, incidentally, could have been indeed a special signal between ships offshore near that place. Changes in course and other maneuvers were generally indicated at night by rigging lanterns in particular positions in addition to the usual running lights or *faroles;* but, some emergencies were signalled by their equivalent to the modern flare or pyrotechnic signal. This, of course, was to set fire to some material, ready to hand, which would blaze quickly and burn long enough to catch the eyes of lookouts aboard ships in company. For example, in the conference between Juan Sebastián Vizcaíno and the principal officers in his armada, held aboard his flagship, the "San Diego," in La Navidad on May 20, 1602, it was agreed that, if any vessel should get into shoaling water at night, she would lie to. Then, she would signal the rest by burning a section of esparto rope until the others acknowledged the signal (. . . *con un estrenque enzendido hasta que les respondan* . . .).[5]

The receiver notary went on questioning Sánchez just as he had examined Friar Luco and he got almost identical replies. One variation was that Sánchez had heard from some Indians, whose names he couldn't remember, that a lot of men with many horses had gone ashore from these ships in Chiamela. There, they had cut a lot of fodder and taken a mulatto prisoner. Since

---

[5] Ms, Audencia de Méjico 372, fol. iv., AGI.

then, however, he had learned that all of this was a hoax and that no one had landed from the ships. Another variation was that Sánchez had heard it said publicly that the personnel aboard the ships might have been Juan de Achis' (John Hawkins) men; that they, probably, had come to get satisfaction for the damages inflicted upon them in the port of San Juan de Ulloa.

To this manuscript, under the heading "Ynformación," is appended testimony which very likely was part of the preliminary questioning which led to the formal investigation that has been under consideration because it was dated August 11, 1573. One may recall that the formal hearings began on December 2 of that year.

On the earlier date, one witness was examined in the Valle de Xaltenba where Diego de Bolaños Paniagua said the Audiencia of Nueva Galicia had ordered him to go to see the place where the ships had been sighted. There, he called a colored slave, Pedro Analço, before him to testify. All Pedro could say was that, about sunset on Saturday evening after the Feast of the Visitation of Our Lady, being near the seashore, he saw a large number of ships. He didn't count them but saw that one big ship headed out to sea and the rest followed it. He watched until he lost sight of them and never saw them any more.

The paucity of examination in this instance astonished the writer until he read the certification. Instead of Martín Vélez, escribano receptor, it was certified by Pedro de Villareal, escribano nombrado, or appointed notary. He was undoubtedly a mere amateur.

At any rate, there seems to be no doubt at all that eight ships, mostly large ones, for which Spain could not account, were sighted off the coast of Jalisco in September or October of 1573. The answer, which naturally suggests itself, is that the ships were pirate craft. To be sure, they could replenish water, firewood, grain, and meat there; whenever they chose, they could stand over to the vicinity of Cape San Lucas with the view to waylaying a rich prize bound from the Philippines to New Spain. As there is no record, however, that anything of the sort was attempted or done, that answer must be dismissed as inconclusive.

The writer has not found any record of pirates on the North American Pacific coast prior to 1579, the year Sir Francis Drake was there with his "Golden Hind" in ballast of Spanish bullion. Father Cappa, in a manifestly careful study of pirates in the Pacific, has cited none, north of the Gulf of Panamá, prior to that year.[6]

As noted above, ships, which might have come from Asia, were reported as near the head of the Gulf of California in 1540, and it seems entirely possible that other foreign ships were bound there in 1573. This, of course, may lead one to speculate over the type of approaches which might have been the most feasible for vessels which had not necessarily entered the Pacific via the Strait of Magellan. Some additional data bearing upon this point, therefore, will be included in the next chapter which is to treat of some sidelights on voyages to Alta California.

---

[6] Cappa, *Estudios críticos,* vol. X, p. 185; vol. XI, pp. 93 *et seq.*

VIII

Some Sidelights on Voyages to Alta California

At first glance, the Spaniards appear to have made their principal maritime expeditions to Alta California by sailing the hard way; that is, they began their surveys along the Baja California Pacific coast upon departure from Cape San Lucas and so continued along the Alta California coast as far as physical endurance would allow them to go. Thus, it is obvious to anyone at all familiar with this coast, that they had to surge against prevailing northwesterly winds all the way, constantly tacking in ships which, as noted previously, probably had a length-to-beam ratio of three to one. Such ships, very likely, made about as much leeway as they gained to windward. As part of the hard way, it seems almost unnecessary to mention the physical demands upon the crews which every change of course or tack required while the multifarious lines were slackened and hauled taut as the yards were braced to catch the wind on the new course. Possibly, also, they frequently had to break out sweeps as the old tubs got caught in irons while attempting to come about, a back-breaking job indeed.

Along with all this, too, is the time factor involved while cruising between the coves and bays really worth charting, for these were and are relatively few and far apart on the west coast of both Californias. One might ask what lost time mattered when, since there was no competition with any other nation, the Spaniards had no reason to hurry. True enough, but that isn't the point: the matter was that all hands had to eat. Bread and meat could not last indefinitely, neither could they remain edible even while they lasted. Remember, too, that there was no train to follow with replacement stores nor any refrigeration to preserve what they carried.

Perhaps one might not be impressed particularly by the slow advance during the outbound voyage unless one noted for contrast the swifter return to a given point of departure. For example, Juan Rodríguez Cabrillo spent seventy days' cruising to reach Pinos (Monterey) Bay from La Navidad. Bartolomé Ferrelo, Cabrillo's successor in command, went from the Monterey entrance to La Navidad in twenty days. In both cases, the days spent at anchor or lying to have been excluded from elapsed time.[1] Juan Sebastián Vizcaíno, likewise, took 118 days from the Islas de Mazatlán to Monterey Bay. From abreast Monterey, he made the return to these same islands in twenty days.

Drake's account of his 1579 voyage in the Pacific emphasized, perhaps more than anything else could, how, in 1542, his predecessor, Cabrillo, had gone to Alta California the hard way; how, in 1602, his successor, Vizcaíno, had found that way even harder. Drake related that he departed Huatulco, Oaxaca, on April 16, 1579,

---

[1] Instituto Histórico de Marina, *Colección de diarios y relaciones para la historia de los viajes y descubrimientos,* vol. I, pp. 29-42. In this series of five volumes, the original reports of Cabrillo's, Vizcaíno's, and other voyages have been published. This work will be designated hereinafter, *Colección de diarios.*

setting our course directly into the sea, whereon we sayled 500 leagues in longitude, to get a winde: and betweene that and *June* 3, 1400 leagues in all, till we came into 42 deg. of North latitude, . . .

If we accept his league as three nautical miles, Drake covered 4,200 miles in forty-eight days, an average of 87.5 miles per day or three and six-tenths miles per hour; certainly, not a fantastic speed. One may wonder, though, how his average speed on that five hundred-league reach compared with what he logged after he got "a winde." Even so, one may fancy that he didn't have to tack often before he fetched the northwesterlies abaft his port beam.

A glance at the forty-two degrees north, he said he reached on June 3, shows that he had come within one degree of Cabrillo's farthest north; more than a degree and a half above Vizcaíno's highest latitude. Whether he ever got as far up as forty-eight degrees is a matter of unconcern in this study; what does concern it, however, is that he reached Drake's Bay sixty-two days out of Huatulco, whereas Vizcaíno took one hundred twenty-nine cruising days to reach the same place from La Navidad, more than five hundred miles nearer. No time in port can be deducted from Drake's elapsed time because he did not state how long he lay in the bay he reached on June 5 where they "were not without some danger by reason of the many extreme gusts and flawes that beate upon vs. . ."

Drake did not mention any hardships at all in connection with his cruise until he had passed forty-two north,

where in the night following we found such alteration of heate, into extreame and nipping cold, that our men in generall did grieuously complaine thereof, some of them feeling their health much impaired thereby. . .

Furthermore, they did not escape the cold even by sailing south for

> in 38 deg. 30 min. we fell with a conuenient and fit harborough, and *June* 17 came to anchor therein, where we continued until the 23 day of *July* following. During all this time, notwithstanding it was in the height of summer and so neere the sunne, yet were wee continually visited with like nipping colds as we had felt before; . . .

With respect to this cold weather, Drake appeared to be anticipating Chapman for, against the idea that he and his men felt it worse than it really was because they were thin-blooded from their sojourn between the Tropics, he wrote that the Indians, never resident outside that area in California,

> vsed to come shivering to vs in their warme furres, crowding close together, body to body, to receive heate one of another, and sheltring themselues under a lee bancke, if it were possible, and as often as they could labouring to shroude themselues under our garments also to keepe them warme.[2]

Chapman, rather airily, pooh-poohed the cold weather Drake reported, saying:

> . . . It is, of course, clear to Californians how these statements came to be made. The fogs of the summer along the northern coast do indeed seem cold to one who is not acclimated; many a man from the east of the United States will shiver through his first summer, but rarely afterward. It may well have seemed worse to Drake and his men who had for a long time been in the tropics. . .[3]

The writer is inclined to believe that Drake's account of the cold he encountered was based more in fact than fancy. While the photograph following this page is not

[2] Francis Drake, *The World Encompassed by Sir Francis Drake.* (London, 1628), pp. 113 *et seq.*

[3] Chapman, *A History of California,* p. 103.

The Plaza Fountain, San Diego, California, January 6, 1913
Courtesy of Union Title Insurance and Trust Company, San Diego.

considered proof by any means that the weather at Drake's Bay in June-July 1579 was as severe as we've been told, it does show, nevertheless, that some rather low temperatures have been encountered in much more unlikely spots in California; viz., San Diego, more than five degrees of latitude south of that "conuenient and fit harborough."

Drake gave the high snow-covered mountains of the Asian and American continents as the source of this cold which north and northwest winds swept southward. These continents, he thought, "if they be not fully ioyned, yet seeme they to come very neere one to the other." He conjectured the absence of a passage through the northerly coast of North America and that, even if there were, it would be unnavigable.[4] In the light of current knowledge, one must admit that Drake's conjectures were rather accurate.

And, before quitting Alta California's cold weather, let another account of it be considered:

> . . . and we remained there [Monterey Harbor], dispatching matters necessary toward our Cape Mendocino voyage, the crew working hard in taking aboard water and firewood. With respect to the great cold which prevailed, it was so extreme that Wednesday, New Year's Day of 1603, dawned with all the sierras so snow-covered that they looked like the Mexico volcano. The well where we were drawing water was frozen over to a depth of more than eight inches and the jugs, which had remained overnight full of water, were all so frozen that, although they were sent rolling, they did not spill a drop. . .[5]

So, such was Monterey Bay on New Year's 1603. Many learned men have alleged in recent years that our planet's climate has been growing warmer – perhaps North America may yet have one or more Straits of

---

[4] Hakluyt Society, *op. cit.*, pp. 113 *et seq.*
[5] *Colección de diarios*, vol. IV, p. 63 [Vizcaíno's voyage].

Anián – but the writer will share little concern about that during this incarnation.

As for approaching Alta California the hard way, one finds a great deal about scurvy, rotten or wormy meat, and weevil-infested hardtack in Vizcaíno's account. There was no mention of scurvy in the Cabrillo-Ferrelo log and the writer has searched in vain for any reference to it in any account relating to Drake while he was along the Pacific side of the Americas. One wonders how he prevented it; possibly he discovered some specifics against it, some antiscorbutics, a hundred and thirty years before Woodes Rogers did. Rogers, speaking about Juan Fernández Island as he found it in 1709, said:

> In the first Plain we found store of Turnip-Greens, and Water-Cresses in the Brooks, which mightily refresh'd our Men, and cleans'd 'em from the Scurvy: the Turnips, Mr. *Selkirk* told us, are good in our Summer Months which is Winter here; . . .[6]

One can only speculate over the possibilities of Drake's having picked up turnip greens or water cress along the courses he sailed from England through the Strait of Magellan, into the Pacific, and on to California, and how he could have preserved them if he did.

On the other hand, Rogers mentioned another antiscorbutic which, from the writer's personal observation, could have been available to Drake along the coastwise run from at least the Gulf of Panamá to Cape San Lucas – how far offshore it may have been available, the writer has not observed. Let Rogers state what this was.

Tho' our Men have their Fill of Land and Sea Turtle, which

---

[6] Woodes Rogers, *A Cruising Voyage Around the World* (London, 1712), p. 135.

keeps them from the Scurvy, yet I find them weak, it being but faintly Food, except they had sufficient Bread or Flower with it, they having but a Pound and a Quarter of Bread or Flower, for five Men a Day, to prolong our Stock of Bread against we come to live wholly on our salt Provisions, and then must be forced to allow more.[7]

This observation was made off Mexico in twenty degrees forty-five minutes north, October 4, 1709.

One cannot but feel that a sea captain, ingenious, imaginative, and enterprising as Drake's record shows him to have been, could very well have discovered the antiscorbutic qualities of fresh sea turtle meat as indicated by Woodes Rogers. That he could have netted sea turtles in any quantity he fancied and kept them "on the hoof" in canvas tanks aboard the "Golden Hind" requires no stretch of the imagination whatever.

Well, if Drake's and Cabrillo's personnel, respectively, kept free of scurvy as negative evidence seems to indicate, such indeed was not the case with Juan Sebastián Vizcaíno. Recalling that the latter sailed out of La Navidad May 22, 1602, December 16 that year found his crews in such bad shape that the leaders' council decided in Monterey Harbor to send the *almiranta,* flagship of the second in command, back to New Spain direct with all of the most seriously ill aboard and to ask the viceroy for replenishment of victuals and personnel. Vizcaíno, then, fared on northerly and it was recorded that, by January 12, 1603, when abreast of Cape Mendocino, there were only two sailors aboard his *capitana* who were able to climb to the masthead.

After weather vicissitudes which carried them northwest then swept them southeast again, January 25,

---

[7] *Ibid.,* p. 267.

found them off Monterey Harbor the second time.
Although the Indians made many welcoming smoke
signals to them, they didn't dare to run inside because
the demands of health were too imperious and

> the sick were clamoring while we couldn't furnish them a doctor
> nor medicine, nor any treat besides rotten jerked beef, hardtack
> soup or mush, beans and chick peas riddled by weevils. The
> mouths of all were afflicted; the gums were bigger than the teeth
> so they could scarcely drink water. The vessel appeared like a
> hospital instead of a seagoing ship and matters were in such an
> extreme state that men who had never taken the helm in their
> lives steered, climbed to the masthead, and performed the rest
> of the tasks. Others, who could just get around, gathered in the
> galley to make mush and other stuff for the sick.[8]

Now, this decision to by-pass Monterey Harbor
might not have seemed blameworthy if that opening
and its environs had not been praised so highly previously. Of course, its mere advantages as a port could
hardly have invited Vizcaíno's re-entry there but the
lush surroundings should surely have appealed to an
able leader as a fit site for recuperation. Just to cite a
few of its resources: there was a great deal of game;
stags, the size of cattle two to three years old, deer,
bison, very big bear, rabbits and hares, geese, partridge,
quail, ducks, fish, and shellfish. The Indians were
gentle and affable; they collected an edible acorn available there and, besides, they had another edible product
bigger than a chestnut. Needless to add, they had
reported fresh water, firewood, and timber in abundance around that harbor.[9]

But Vizcaíno was having none of this. He ran down
before the wind, not daring even to anchor at Catalina

8 *Colección de diarios,* vol. IV, p. 65.
9 *Ibid.,* p. 62.

Island where the Indians wanted to trade him fish and other items, because he was afraid that his crew was too weak to weigh anchor afterward. On February 6, 1603, he did anchor at Cedros Island because, without fresh water and firewood, he simply couldn't carry on. So, here he dropped a small anchor with the view of cutting its cable in case his men should be too weak to weigh.

Enough of these vicissitudes – Vizcaíno was persuaded against stopping at Cape San Lucas despite the fact that he would have to abandon a longboat he had left there the year before.[10] The *junta,* or leaders' council, it seemed, always made decisions for him. But, in spite of the good press he has enjoyed, largely due no doubt to Friar Antonio de la Ascensión's facile pen and the chartings along the Californias which his cartographers have left to posterity, he really missed a wide-open opportunity to become an immortal; to forestall the fame the little lime came to enjoy and be perpetuated by the "limeys" or "limejuicers" as British Royal Navy personnel are styled today in the United States Navy.

You see, shortly after Vizcaíno arrived in the Mazatlán Islands, February 18, 1603, most of his men, after suffering as related already, had reached a stage where they could hardly eat or even talk. As Venegas depicted the situation, all despaired of recovering their health except at the cost of much treatment and a great deal of medicine.

Aboard the ship when she arrived, nothing was heard except cries and appeals to Our Lady who was the Patroness and protectress of this voyage; and She, as a merciful mother who

---

[10] *Ibid.,* pp. 65-66.

sympathized with so many people, came to their rescue so that
during the nineteen days the ship was here, all recovered health
and strength and got out of bed . . . and in order that it
may be known better how health proceeded from such hands as
those of Our Lady, the Virgin Mary of Monte Carmelo, those
who read this account shall know that there were no medicines,
nor pharmacy drugs, nor prescriptions, nor doctors' medica-
ments, nor other human remedy known to be effective against
this disease: and if any human remedy did exist, one was the
restorative of fresh and substantial food given them from the
things the General had provided (as has been said) and in eating
a small fruit, found in abundance in these islands, which the
natives there call *Xocohuistles*.

Apparently, the good padre let his timing get out of
order momentarily for the scurvy-stricken, by his
description, could scarcely drink water, much less eat
"fresh and substantial food," until their gum swelling
should be reduced and their teeth tightened in their
sockets. This was the xocohuistles' prime function for

God gave this small fruit such virtue that it shrank the gums;
tightened and cleaned the teeth; and made one spit out all the
bad, filthy blood which had collected in the swollen gums.

He gave this small fruit a detailed description which
furnished, perhaps, a more precise picture of it than
Sir Walter Scott provided in his portrayal of the Lady
Rowena. The writer fancies that it was somewhat
similar to a cactus pear with a yellow skin.

The way the virtue of this fruit became known was that, among
some soldiers going to the island with the Father Commissary
to say Mass and to bury some dead men, a corporal named
Antonio Luis saw the small fruit and, desirous of trying out
things ashore, began to split it and eat some of it with the greatest
labor and pain in his mouth, teeth, and gums. As it tasted good
to him, he ate one as well as he could and then began to spit out

a lot of rotten blood. When he put another one in his mouth, he noted that his teeth didn't hurt as much and that he could chew better and so, the more he ate the better he got. He took some of the fruit along and when he came on board the ship, he told what it had done for him and divided what he had among his friends who tried it and found themselves bettered as their friend had been improved. So, they went ashore to get more of it and everyone ate it. When the General [Vizcaíno] came back on board, he found that some could eat food already and thus could benefit by the fresh rations which were brought to them every day.[11]

Here, then, was the general's glorious opportunity. Surely God would not have withdrawn from the xo-cohuistles – *jucoistles,* in Vizcaíno's cruise report – the healing virtue He had bestowed upon it, so Vizcaíno could have tried preserving a lot of them in wine, brandy, or tequila and selling them as a sure shot scurvy specific. If the English, about a century and a half later, could carry bottled lime juice to sea without losing all its antiscorbutic properties, surely a promoter like Vizcaíno could have exploited the xocohuistles. If he had removed this scourge of sailors and soldiers in the seventeenth, eighteenth, and nineteenth cen-turies,[12] he might have been honored as Jenner, Pasteur, Gorgas, and Fleming have been.

But Vizcaíno seemed beset by ineptitude. He got a running start, as it were, on his 1602-1603 expedition to the Californias for, with the expectation of long,

[11] Venegas, *Noticia de la California,* vol. III, pp. 83-85.

[12] The nineteenth century still found scurvy existent, even in the present United States. The writer's grandfathers were discharged from Lee's army in Virginia in November 1864 by medical survey on account of scurvy, to return to their homes in Pontotoc and Lee Counties, Mississippi. They had been serving continuously in Virginia forces since the First Battle of Bull Run.

favorable weather ahead, he shoved off from La Navidad on May 22 – Cabrillo's sailing date had been June 27. Vizcaíno, however, shilly-shallied; he did not clear Cape San Lucas until July 5; Cabrillo had cleared that port on July 6, 1542. Vizcaíno, thus, wasted thirty-five of the thirty-six days' advantage which, initially, he had held over Cabrillo in prospects of favorable cruising. And what did the Cape San Lucas area have to offer which had not been discovered already by Ulloa, Cortés, and others, and even by himself when he visited it six years previously? Well, perhaps he was similar to an old Spanish grandee's concept of Felipe II, *siempre meando en vado* – always urinating in fords which he should have crossed without delay.

Withal, it must be said in fairness to Vizcaíno that his council had decided to sail on June 19, and at four o'clock p.m. that day, they weighed anchor and stood out to sea. A strong northwest wind forced them back, however, so they waited two days for more favorable weather. They got underway the second time; the same type of wind blew them back again; and, this time, they waited three days for a good wind. They couldn't get out on the third effort although they spent five days struggling with all their might. So, they were again blown back "with great force into the said bay and cape." This time, they waited until July 5 when an offshore wind took them out of port and on their way. Just how a *viento norueste* or northwest wind [13] could have handled them in such fashion is extremely hard to understand.

It seemed that this wind designation must have been a scribal or a typographical error, yet, in the record of

[13] *Colección de diarios,* vol. IV, p. 44.

proceedings of the council convened on June 27, 1602, Vizcaíno himself stated that the winds had been *Huestes, Hues-Noruestes* or wests, westnorthwests.[14] Possibly there was some shoal, hook, or point to leeward which does not show on charts today? If there was, it doesn't appear either on Vizcaíno's chart of the Cape San Lucas anchorage.[15] (See map at page 185).

A study of the U.S. Hydrographic Office chart no. 1666, entitled San Lucas Bay, indicates that the longitudinal axis of Cape San Lucas lies almost east-west. In fact, it lies nearly in prolongation of the entire coastline from Cabo Falso eastward, merely jogging a little northward at its southern union with the mainland. From the Cape's northern union with the mainland, the shoreline trends northeasterly to Cabeza Ballena, approximately four nautical miles away. The ten-fathom curve is nowhere more than a quarter of a mile offshore in the entire stretch between these points and no shoal water whatever is indicated except at a spot about a half-mile southwest of Cabeza Ballena and even that carries four and a half fathoms of water. So, no reason beyond inefficiency for not getting out against westerly winds seems possible in this case on the basis of conditions in 1896 when the data for this chart were collected. (See map at page 185).

In order to convey graphically an idea of the type of work Vizcaíno's cartographers produced, the writer has inserted in continuation a reproduction of the chart of San Diego harbor which was made from data obtained during the period November 10-20, 1602. One may wonder why no evidence of San Diego River

---

[14] Ms, Audiencia de Méjico 372, fol. 3, AGI.
[15] *Ibid.*, fol. 6ov.

appears – why Point Loma is shown as a peninsula –
why Mission Bay had only two fathoms of water in its
entrance and as much as five inside. For purposes of
then-and-later comparison, a chart made in 1859 under
United States' auspices has been inserted following the
Vizcaíno product. (See maps at page 187).

Reverting to Vizcaíno's personal qualities, however,
the writer could cite much in a category definitely
derogatory to him. The Conde del Valle, for example,
made a statement in Mexico City, December 22, 1631,
that Vizcaíno did not have the capacity to justify his
being entrusted with such grave matters as maritime
exploration. The Count thought, too, that it was unjust
to let agreements with him close the door to others who,
gifted with better intelligence and leadership, would
be able to accomplish what they might be ordered to
do.[16]

Perhaps Boatswain Gonzalo de Francia was the most
damaging witness against Vizcaíno of all those whose
statements are yet available. Under date, May 27, 1629,
he stated that he had served in both of the latter's expeditions to the Californias; that he had thirty-two years'
sea duty behind him then. Francia cited a number of
errors or omissions on Vizcaíno's part during his California voyages which could not serve any very useful
end by repetition here. In short and in substance, his
former commanding officer could neither plan nor
execute.[17]

More unfavorable criticism could be cited, including his report on Monterey Harbor which has been
considered a shameless fabrication designed to indicate

---

16 Ms, Colección Navarrete, vol. xix, Doc. 20, fols. 228-230.
17 *Ibid.*, Doc. 15, fols. 208v.-210.

that his mission had been accomplished and also to flatter the Viceroy of Mexico, Conde de Monterrey, by naming that haven in his honor. After he had quoted extracts from Vizcaíno's and Friar Antonio de la Ascensión's reports on Monterey Harbor, Chapman, for example, said:

> The curious feature about these reports (and much more might be added to them, including references to the vast wealth in gold and silver that the Indians said was to be found in the interior) is that nearly all they had to say was true, save for the yarn about the excellence of Monterey as a sheltered port, but it was precisely this departure from strict accuracy that had the most effect; the legend of the port of Monterey became one of the moving factors for a century and a half in Spanish expansion to the northwest.[18]

In fairness to Vizcaíno, it seems appropriate to examine what was stated about Monterey Harbor, not only by him but also by the officials who had been charged with composing the sailing directions from Acapulco to Cape Mendocino. Friar Antonio de la Ascensión was present when these were adopted.

> . . . the said port [Monterey] is ample for any class of ships whatever, sheltered from all winds. Its least depth is seven fathoms. Within it, there is much fresh water and a great deal of timber for building and equipping any type ship. There is also a great deal of game; geese, ducks, quail, deer, bear, and other classes of animals. There are Indians who, although reticent about dealings with us . . . came up peaceably . . . and brought us shellfish. . . (Signed, 29 December 1602) Sebastian Vizcayno=Geronimo Martin=Francisco de Bolaños =Juan Pasqual=Esteban Rodriguez=Before me Diego de Santiago. Chief Notary.[19]

---

[18] Chapman, *A History of California*, p. 135.
[19] Ms, Audiencia de Méjico 372, fol. 57v., AGI.

The writer is inclined to believe that this was a sincere statement although it isn't obvious from their chart (refer to the map at page 189) that all of the port was sheltered from due north winds. By the same token, a due northwest wind must have agitated a goodly portion east of the anchorage indicated on it by an anchor. It is regretted that the cartographers did not indicate the character of terrain in this port's immediate surroundings for, possibly, high ground and forests might have provided lees which this plan doesn't indicate. With respect to Vizcaíno's minimum depth of seven fathoms, U.S.H.O. chart no. 5403 shows that the ten-fathom curve lies, except in one area at the southernmost part of the harbor, within a half-mile offshore.

As for the coastline changes, the writer might suggest erosion, a quite common occurrence, or possibly, sinkings and upheavals due to earthquakes, not such a common occurrence; although, heretofore, earthquakes in Alta California have been entirely too common. Great changes could have occurred in all manner of terrain features between December 1602 and December 1956. Where today, for example, is that cleat-shaped projection which Vizcaíno's chart shows as about three and a half leagues northeast of Punta de Pinos? On Vizcaíno's chart also, Punta de Pinos flares sharply from its neck outboard. The shoreline between its northwest and northeast tips is approximately double the width of its neck. Today's chart shows the entire point as almost a cone with its base against the mainland.

The strongest element in the situation, however, which has inclined the writer to believe that the Puerto de Monterey was charted and reported as the Spaniards found it in December 1602 is that five of them signed the statement about it. If that statement had been untrue, a "yarn" as Chapman expressed it, someone in that expedition would have been only too eager to expose the deceit. How could Boatswain Gonzalo de Francia have abstained from using such a telling blow at his former chief? How could Friar Antonio de la Ascensión have been party to such a hoax?

Insofar as Alta California was concerned, there was only negation, apparently, as sequel to the discovery of Monterey, the harbor fit in all respects to support the Manila Galleon on her return run to Acapulco. In 1606, to be sure, Felipe III did order the Viceroy of Mexico, the Marqués de Montesclaros, to found a settlement there; but, as far as history in general has recorded events of that period, Montesclaros found one means or another to enable him to evade compliance with His Majesty's directions.[20]

So, an investigator's surprise upon reading an historical statement that a settlement actually was made at Monterey, presumably in 1606, can be imagined better than the writer can depict it. The alleged settlement was abandoned for several reasons of which, perhaps, the Viceroy's failure to follow up with support within two months, as he had promised, was really the key.

The writer might not have given this item a second glance except for the fact that Martín Fernández de Navarrete had left it incorporated with his manuscript, "California, historia y viajes." Surely, so eminent and so painstaking an historian must have had cogent reasons for leaving this in his records. If he ever chal-

---

[20] See Chapman, *A History of California,* pp. 138-139, for splendid treatment of this subject.

lenged its authenticity, the writer has not been able to find any trace of his action. The original is transcribed verbatim below.[21]

The question naturally arises as to why no traces of this settlement have been found. One might just as well ask the same thing regarding the lost colony of Roanoke.

Be that all as it may, the writer yet thinks that Drake's approach to high latitudes on the Alta California coast was the easy way – Cabrillo and Vizcaíno made it the hard way. How much better it would have been for either the Portuguese or the Spaniard to have run parallel to Drake's tracks and to have arrived above Cape Blanco by the end of August, for instance, thence to run with the California Current and before the wind all the way back with the climate growing ever balmier as they dropped leisurely from cape to cove in the course of reconnaissance and charting.

---

21 Ms, "California, historia y viajes," vol. I, Doc. I, sect. 4, fol. I, Museo Naval.

"Amas de los quatro Viajes, que quedan expresados en los capitulos precedentes, que fueron al descubrimiento de California, quedamos en el último, que hizo el General Sebastián Vizcayno el año de 1602, ahora digo, que el dho General en virtud de relaciones, que fueron a la Magestad de Felipe III Vino el año de 1606 Real cedula del señor Virey Conde de Montesclaros para fuese á poblar al Puerto de Monterey, que está en 37/ grados de latitud boreal, y aunque se efectuo con alguna Gente, y abio comestible, armas y Municiones, ofrecieronle, qe dentro de dos meses se le despacharia dos Naves cargadas de Gente y bastimentos, y con la ocasion de promover al dicho Virey, no se le remitio el socorro, y la necesidad obligó, a que no subsistiera el pueble con otras intenciones, y motines, que entre la Gente huvo, con que precediendo algunas muertes, despoblaron luego, pudiendo ser antemural asi lo amparo, y refugio de la Nao de China para renovar Bastimentos, Maderas, y otros adminiculos trato, y comercio mediterraneo a las Provincias de Sonora reduccion de muchas Naciones a nuestra Santa Fee, y descubrieran las Minas, y Gente blanca, que dicen las travajan, que si acaso no son Extrangeros, puede ser la Gente Española, que se perdio con las Naos en varios tiempos."

It has been claimed that, in 1564, "Juan Fernandes discovered the mode of navigating between places on the west coast of South America by standing out obliquely to a distance from the continent; . . ."[22] May one suppose that Drake picked up this idea from the Pacific Coast pilots he seized and put into his service? After all, he was a very resourceful sea captain. One couldn't expect anything so apt from Juan Sebastián Vizcaíno, however; he was too inept even to exploit the xocohuistles despite evidence of its antiscorbutic properties which was demonstrated before his very eyes. The efficacy of such courses for the ancient sailing ship will be demonstrated further as attention is given to some other sixteenth century approaches to Alta California.

[22] Robert Greenhow, *The History of Oregon and California and the Other Territories on the North-West Coast of North America; from Their Discovery to the Present Day* (Boston, 1847), p. 65.

IX

Other Early Approaches to Alta California

As far as any record known to the writer now indicates, Ulloa and Cabrillo were the only sea captains in the sixteenth century whose approaches to Alta California had been staged in New Spain for sailing directly there. This is not to say, however, that other approaches weren't made; quite the contrary. Perhaps the easier way, pointed out in the preceding chapter, had gained a foothold in the Spanish impresarios' minds; possibly, what had occurred to Juan Fernandes in 1564 and to Sir Francis Drake in 1579 was glimmering fitfully in the ideas current among those who were projecting Spain's maritime expeditions northward.

As a matter of fact, Friar Andrés de Urdaneta gave a striking demonstration in 1564-1565 of the relative ease which sailing westward from New Spain afforded.

The start was made from Navidad in New Spain, on November 21, 1564. Urdaneta ran south to about 10° north of the equator, and then sailed due west to Guam, over which today the American flag is raised. On February 13, 1565, the expedition reached the Philippines, after a voyage of less than three months, – in quicker time than Juan Rodríguez had taken to go from the same port of Navidad to San Diego in Alta California! Indeed, the route westward across the Pacific offered comparatively few problems to the navigator. . .[1]

[1] Chapman, *A History of California*, p. 85.

Now, the writer is completely in accord with Chapman insofar as easy sailing westward into the Pacific was concerned; still, the writer must say that the great historian used an unfortunate illustration. To be sure, Urdaneta's voyage required only eighty-four days – Cabrillo spent ninety-four days on his run, La Navidad to San Diego. But, Cabrillo was reconnoitering the Pacific Coast of both Californias; and, in so doing, he spent fifty-three of those ninety-four days either at anchor or lying to. His actual cruising time between those two ports was only forty-one days![2]

Many writers, including Chapman, have accorded Urdaneta the honor of having been the first to trace a route across the Pacific to North America from the Philippines even if, indeed, he was not actually the first to make that crossing.

He was somewhat chagrined, no doubt, to find that another ship of his original fleet had preceded him across the Pacific. This was the forty-ton tender, commanded by one Arellano. Nine days out from Navidad on the westward voyage, Arellano had deserted, eager to find "rich islands" for his own advantage. . . Arellano had started the return voyage on April 22. He ran most of the time between 40° and 43°, and is said to have reached the American shore about at Cape Mendocino, being possibly the discoverer of that point. On August 9 he came to anchor at Navidad, having thus completed the eastward voyage two months earlier and in twenty days less time than Urdaneta. Nevertheless, Urdaneta got the credit. As commander of the expedition and sponsor for the ideas which the deserter Arellano followed, Urdaneta was clearly entitled to the honor.[3]

What's wrong with this picture? Nothing, perhaps; yet, didn't Cabrillo's expedition discover and name Cape Mendocino?

With respect to credit due Urdaneta, Father Mariano

---

[2] Recapitulated by the writer from *Colección de diarios*, vol. I, pp. 29-34.
[3] Chapman, *op. cit.*, pp. 85-86.

Cuevas has taken up the cudgels very energetically in the mariner monk's behalf. He initiated his defense by attacking Henry R. Wagner's stand regarding Urdaneta in *Spanish Voyages to the Northwest Coast of America in the Sixteenth Century.* It would seem idle to trace the discussion, pro and con, through the several personalities involved in establishing the probable paternity of the cruising pattern Urdaneta followed even if such were germane to the purpose of this work which it is not.

Toward the end of Cuevas' argument, however, he struck at Wagner's point that Urdaneta's selection of courses from Baja California to Acapulco could have been due to Cabrillo's observations. "We do not know," said Cuevas, "how Mr. Wagner might prove that Urdaneta actually availed himself of Rodríguez Cabrillo's notes." Well, as for proof that he actually did use them, the writer doesn't know either. That Urdaneta was familiar with them and once had implied an intent to use them, however, is another matter. Such has been demonstrated already in footnote 6, chapter V of this work. Cuevas went on to say that Urdaneta didn't need any help from Cabrillo because he knew that route from his own experience. He did not state, nevertheless, when and how Urdaneta got that experience.

Wagner had reinforced his doubt that Urdaneta had fathered the route he established by citing the earlier voyage Alonso de Arellano made. Cuevas agreed as to the point in fact but said that Arellano's return trip in the *patache* "San Lucas" was not made with acceptable and praiseworthy sailing directions. It was foolhardy; "it was not a sensible and safe voyage," which was all the Crown wanted.[4]

---

[4] P. Mariano Cuevas, *Monje y marino: La vida y los tiempos de Fray Andrés de Urdaneta* (Mexico City, 1943), pp. 271-278.

After all, one may wonder why Chapman did not follow Urdaneta's *tornaviaje,* return trip, more carefully because his statements about it are not only incomplete but also inaccurate.

So Urdaneta, who left Cebú on June 1, 1565, on his five-hundred-ton ship, went north to about 39° 30', and then crossed over, reaching the Baja California coast in 27° 12'.[5]

According to the logs kept by Chief Pilot Esteban Rodríguez and by his assistant, Rodrigo de Espinosa, on Urdaneta's *tornaviaje,* they steered east by north on June 11, just ten days out of Cebú. Bear in mind, if you please, that this was just eleven degrees fifteen minutes north of due east, a course of seventy-eight degrees forty-five minutes in today's usage. Although the logs did not state whether the courses steered were true or magnetic, they did mention sometimes a compass correction for variation. On June 12, they reached fourteen degrees north latitude, a little more than three degrees north of Cebú.[6] As a matter of fact, according to Rodríguez, thirty-nine degrees thirty minutes was the highest latitude they reached; he determined this by solar observation on September 2, 1565, then ninety-three days out of Cebú.[7] Their courses had been easterly in general until September 4 when Espinosa shot the sun in thirty-nine degrees twenty minutes and they began sailing southeasterly and southerly.[8]

On September 15, Espinosa found himself about eight leagues off Point Conception and, on the eighteenth, he sighted San Miguel Island, giving it about five leagues' berth as they sheered to the west, standing clear of the rest of the Santa Bárbara Islands. This was

5 Chapman, *op. cit.,* p. 85.
6 *Colección de diarios,* vol. v, pp. 115-116.
7 *Ibid.,* p. 119.
8 *Ibid.,* p. 129.

their last view of Alta California and their last landfall until September 23 when they made out Punta Eugenia [9] just south of Cedros Island on the Baja California coast.

After widespread reference by historians to Urdaneta's voyage from New Spain to the Philippines and to his having established the return route which the Manila Galleon was to follow more than two centuries thereafter, it was rather surprising to find no official status prescribed for him in the ships he rode. He was consulted frequently, yes, during the outbound voyage with regard to fixes, courses, and land ahead; yet, he served apparently in only an advisory capacity on board and, on shore, he appeared merely as Legaspi's representative in negotiations with the natives. His name arose casually in connection with a chart which Pilot Rodrigo de Espinosa consulted on the *tornaviaje* executed by the galleon "San Pedro," Captain Felipe de Salcedo, but that was all.

Yet, it became obvious very soon that the mariner monk occupied a high place with the powers that were after letters between him and His Majesty had been read. This was accentuated upon noting that Urdaneta was sailing in the "San Pedro" in accordance with written orders which the Audiencia of Mexico had given Miguel López de Legaspi on September 1, 1564. This monk was to be aboard the ship or the flagship, if two or more were sent back, because, on account of his experience and ability, "he will be the principal factor toward success in navigating the return to New Spain." Legaspi had even to send back the ship and the captain of it that Urdaneta should indicate and request! [10] No wonder that this became Urdaneta's cruise.

[9] *Ibid.*, pp. 130-131.
[10] *Ibid.*, p. 167.

Lieutenant Commander Manuel Valdemoro, Spanish Navy, editor of Volume V, *Colección de diarios,* has thrown a very interesting sidelight upon the mariner monk. According to Valdemoro, Urdaneta had not been able to arouse any interest at court toward new settlements in the Moluccas after his return from those islands to Spain in 1536. So, he went to New Spain, either because he supposed it would be easier to accomplish his purpose there or, probably, because he had reached already an agreement with Pedro de Alvarado in connection with the latter's capitulation with the emperor to explore the Western Islands. At any rate, Urdaneta embarked with Alvarado for New Spain in 1538.[11]

Apart from the fact, as far as known at present, that the mariner monk was among the first to sight Point Concepción after Cabrillo and Ferrelo had located it, his contribution to Alta California exploration consisted only in his having traced a feasible set of sailing directions for the Manila Galleon's *tornaviaje.* One might say too that, indirectly, he made a negative contribution to Alta California exploration in the light of later developments. Specifically, he was cited as source of the legend regarding the Armenian's Islands which, together with Rica de Oro and Rica de Plata, actually served in part to divert interest from Alta California ports as appropriate supporting harbors for the Manila ship.

In 1583, Friar Andrés de Aguirre gave the "Archbishop, Governor, and Captain General" of New Spain an account of the Armenian's Islands. Aguirre related from memory an account which he said Friar Andrés de Urdaneta had set down in writing and of which he

---

11 *Ibid.,* p. 11.

gave the relater a copy. According to Aguirre, Urdaneta had the story from a Portuguese sea captain. Its
burden was that a Portuguese ship, sailing out of
Malacca laden with trade goods, had been running
before a storm nine days. When the weather cleared,
she found herself close by two big islands which lay
between thirty-five and forty degrees north latitude,
longitude unknown, yet east of Japan.

These islands, according to Friar Aguirre, proved
to be almost incredibly rich in everything imaginable.
By great good fortune, a very personable and astute
Armenian trader, embarked in this Portuguese ship,
was able to insinuate himself very quickly into the good
graces of the ruling elements of these two islands to
the unsurpassed enjoyment and profit of all aboard the
Lusitanian vessel. In deference and in gratitude to that
trader, these islands thenceforth were called *Islas del
Armenio* or the Armenian's Islands.[12] In the light of
later developments, one might observe at this point,
how much could hang on so little!

In strict adherence to chronological sequence of
events regarding Alta California, however, it would
seem that Francisco de Gali's name should be mentioned for, as commander of the 1584 Manila Galleon,
he did run along its coast from about thirty-seven
degrees thirty minutes southward. Perhaps his greatest
claim to fame rests upon the opinion which Archbishop Moya, viceroy of Mexico, expressed to the king
about him in 1585. The archbishop had chosen Gali to
lead further exploration

because he was the most excelling man and had the highest standing of any there are here and, in these matters, he could compete
with the very select in Spain, and so, I trust that he will succeed

---

[12] *Documentos inéditos,* Ser. I, vol. 13, p. 545.

in serving Your Majesty to the great benefit of this New World
and its commerce. . .[13]

An unsung seafarer followed the way to America
across the vast Pacific in 1587, one to whom the Spanish
world should have listened but, apparently, did not.
He, too, saw more of Alta California than any other
Spaniard had seen since the Cabrillo-Ferrelo exploration. He had orders to investigate the fabled islands,
Rich-in-Gold, Rich-in-Silver; one can almost hear
disgust dripping from his quill as he related his vain
search for them and this should have remained loud in
the Spaniards' auditory memory.

The reason, possibly, why he has gone unsung is that
he pricked bubbles which the Spaniards wanted to
keep flying. They must have been extremely loath to
believe that there simply weren't any more Aztec or
Inca realms to sack; no more vast gold and silver troves
to be won by sword, lance, crossbow, and arquebus.

At any rate, Captain Pedro de Unamuno,[14] frigate
"Nuestra Señora de la Buena Esperanza" – "Our Lady
of Good Hope" – sailed away from the Babuyanes
Islands on July 16, 1587 where he had shot the sun and
had found them to be in a "scanty twenty degrees and
a half." That day, he set out for Rica de Oro, four
hundred fifty leagues from the Babuyanes, on course,
"Les Nordeste Oeste Sudueste." While literally, this
course expresses "eastnortheast westsouthwest," the
writer believes that, in current usage, Captain Unamuno was sailing eastnortheast or on course or azimuth,
sixty-seven degrees thirty minutes. Rica de Oro was

13 Ms, Colección Navarrete, vol. XIX, fols. 20-21.

14 Ms, Colección Navarrete, "Historia y viajes," vol. XVIII, Doc. 41, fols.
231 *et seq.* All the following references to Unamuno are based upon this
manuscript.

supposed to lie between a scanty thirty-one degrees thirty minutes and twenty-nine degrees; Rica de Plata, between thirty-four and thirty-three degrees north. Unamuno sailed various courses until July 28 when he sighted two small islands, each about three leagues in perimeter, and a league and a half apart, "lying north by west-south by east in latitude twenty-five degrees and a half." He sailed around them both, finding no harbor nor any sign of water, so he named them *Las sin provecho* or Useless Islands.

He fared on his way and reported that on August 12, twenty-seven days out, he arrived where Rica de Oro Island was supposed to be. One may note, parenthetically, that in these twenty-seven days' cruising, Unamuno had to average only about fifty miles a day to get to Rica de Oro's fancied location. He did not find it although "everything possible was done, and the said Island couldn't be encountered from which it became obvious that it didn't exist." Then, on August 22, Unamuno said he reached the chart location of Rica de Plata.

And having made every possible effort and unable to find it, for which reason it probably didn't exist, except that someone from hearsay perhaps ordered it to be drawn on his Chart. Sunday, in the night of 23 August, course was set to go in search of the Islands called the Armenian's which, according to their drawings upon some Charts, are twenty leagues from the Island named above, Rica de Plata, which lie along a track, one with the other, Northeast-Southwest, in latitudes of thirty-four degrees, and thirty-five and a third. We found ourselves in their latitude Wednesday the twenty-sixth of the said month of August, and their sighting was attempted with great care, making every effort possible, and it was learned that they do not exist.

It seems appropriate here to suggest an historical correction for, from the foregoing account, the Ar-

menian's Islands were separate and distinct from Rica
de Oro and Rica de Plata. Chapman appeared to have
been confused on this point; apparently, he hadn't
consulted Unamuno's log. He said:

> Moya wrote to the king, strongly urging the need of discovering
> and occupying a port on the Alta California coast, and intimated
> that he was about to send Gali again to the Philippines, with
> orders to explore and make maps of the coasts of Japan, the
> islands of the Armenian (as the islands later styled Rica de Oro
> and Rica de Plata were sometimes called), and the Californias.[15]

On October 18, 1587, they anchored in a mainland
bay which they named Puerto de Sant Lucas because
it was that saint's day. They shot the sun and found
themselves in "thirty-five and a half long degrees."
Unamuno disembarked leading twelve soldiers under
armor and arquebusses and some "Yndios Luzones" or
Filipinos, armed with their shields and swords. They
had sighted Indians before they disembarked; they
sighted more ashore who ran away. Nearby, there was
a large river of good drinking water which was blocked
from the bay by a big sandbar. As this seemed to be
worthwhile country, Unamuno disembarked the rest of
his crew and performed the act of possession.

Proceeding about four leagues up the river, they
came to a deserted ranchería having eighteen huts
made of tree branches, each capable of holding twelve
people and appearing to be about a month and a half
old. On October 20, they turned back to the frigate,
finding another abandoned ranchería of thirty huts, all
empty except for some fish nets. When they had arrived
about half a league from their ship, they were beset by
Indians who wounded four of the party by arrows and
lances and killed one of the Filipinos. As more Indians

---

15 Chapman, *A History of California*, p. 115.

closed in, the Spaniards killed some of them by gunfire and made all the Indians retire up a hillside. Unamuno's party then made a raft which they carried to a small boat they had left on the beach; embarked in both; and, went aboard the frigate. Here, they learned that, the day before, another party from their vessel had been engaged in a skirmish with Indians whom they drove off.

They sailed away coastwise against contrary winds on October 21 and pressed on until the twenty-third when fog shut off sight of the coast for five days despite their having been less than two leagues offshore. On October 28, they began to take soundings in thirty degrees north. It is presumed that this was a dead reckoning position because Unamuno said that he was still in cerrazón, heavy overcast. At any rate, their soundings got ten fathoms on rock bottom for a league and a half; then, a shoal; and next, they struck white water, very turbulent, which seemed to be a river.

Several factors prompted Unamuno now to stand down to New Spain. The fog was too thick to risk standing inshore again; he had to consider his wounded for whom he had no medicines; the coast below Cedros Island had been explored long ago; so, he set courses for Acapulco.

Unamuno cited some distances which seem remarkably accurate today. For example, he gave the distance from the port he named Sant Lucas to Cape San Lucas as two hundred ninety leagues. One may recall that, by his sun sight, the former was in thirty-five degrees thirty minutes – he stated that he found the latter in twenty-three scanty degrees. Thus, if his league is accepted at three nautical miles and his fixes as accurate, there is rather astonishing harmony between run and fixes.

Unamuno reached Acapulco November 22, 1587. He didn't state anything further about his wounded; perhaps they recovered without incident. One may hope so, anyway.

The next Alta California exploration after Unamuno's visit saw a recrudescence of the Manila Galleon idea which appeared to lapse into desuetude after Gali's 1584 run along the California coast. The royal planners fancied that the Galleon could easily assume a double role; that she could combine a survey of the Alta California coast southward from her usual landfall near Cape Blanco or Cape Mendocino with that leg of her *tornaviaje* to Acapulco. To them, this plan seemed feasible because that leg was the easiest sailing of all in the tremendous round trip, *viento en popa,* wind astern or sailing before the wind, continuously. True enough, but how about ships racked by wind and sea and overloading, patched canvas and uneasy cordage, crews retched by rotten and wormy meat and bread, devastated by scurvy and demoralized by whining passengers? Did they think of that? Who knows?

Yet, this scheme was the least expensive to the Crown of all which could be devised, and money was an item. Felipe II had been pouring treasure into armies, invincible armadas, and monasteries [16] faster than it could

---

[16] Felipe II spent on El Escorial alone in 1562-1598 more than $22,000,000.00 (5,800,000 ducados). See Julián Zarco Cuevas, *El Monasterio de San Lorenzo el Real de El Escorial y la Casita del Príncipe* (Madrid, 1955), p. 205.

"In 1623 [twenty-five years after Felipe II's death], the number of members in religious orders in Spain was 200,000 [*sic*] or thirty percent of the population. The Cortes [Congress] of 1623 said that there were then 9,088 convents in Spain. The income from the clergy's real estate exceeded half of the kingdom's total income. The annual income of the seven archbishoprics and thirty-nine bishoprics which existed in the Peninsula came to 21,740 ducados each. The archbishop and ecclesiastic community of Toledo collected

be extracted from the Indians and mines of Mexico and Peru and the pearl fisheries of Margarita Island, Cubagua, Río de la Hacha, and the Gulf of California. Despite the fact that Spain reached the zenith of her greatness under that monarch, he twice declared his kingdom bankrupt during his long reign and his borrowings brought the big Fugger banking firm to the verge of bankruptcy also.[17]

In fairness to the galleons, however, it seems proper to say that the "San Agustín," the 1595 ship which combined California exploration with her *tornaviaje* to Acapulco, should have gone into the yard for major overhaul before she departed. This became evident from the outset according to

> Cruise Log and Report of the exploration which sebastian Rodríguez cermeño made. By order of his majesty from the philipinas to ysla de cedros.[18]

The "San Agustín" sailed from Cavite on Tuesday morning, July 5, 1595, and anchored at the foot of El Fraile the same day. She got underway the next day in a strong southerly wind which, by four that afternoon, came on to blow with such force that she was forced to take shelter in the lee of Mariveles Island. One may wonder if that island wasn't Corregidor as named today. On the seventh, she got underway again in an

---

from 350 to 400,000 ducados annually," – Rafael Ballester, *Curso de historia de España* (Barcelona, 1929), p. 323. Note: The figure, 200,000, is believed to be a typographical error because this would indicate a total population of less than 700,000. Ballester said on p. 321, same work, that "During the seventeenth century only about ten millions of inhabitants were counted in Spain."

[17] Victor von Klarwill, editor, in preface to *The Fugger News-Letters* (London, 1925).

[18] Title page, Ms, Audiencia de Méjico 23, AGI. Except as otherwise indicated, Rodríguez Cermeño's cruise will be based hereinafter upon this manuscript.

offshore wind but she was forced to go into the shipyard on Mindoro Island on the eighth because she had
sprung so many leaks that she couldn't navigate until
they bailed and pumped her clear of water. At this
time also, they lightened her by unloading some clothing from her cargo and by putting ashore some pas-
engers, "Spaniards, as well as Indians and negroes."
They remained at Mindoro until July 14 because of
contrary winds, according to Cermeño, yet it seems
reasonable to suspect that a great deal of shoring up
timbers and caulking was done in the meantime.

By dead reckoning on August 6, Cermeño said that
they had reached seventeen scanty degrees north. Southerly setting currents had proved so strong on three or
four occasions as to carry him two degrees to the south
in a twenty-four-hour run.

A hurricane from the north struck them on August
13 with such force that, for safety's sake, they had to
throw overboard a deck load of chests, hencoops, and
big earthen jars of provisions. They appeared to sur-
vive this very well, however, and sailed on various
courses until October 29 when Cermeño shot the sun
and found that the "San Agustín" had reached forty-
two long degrees of north latitude. Later that day, the
weather became overcast and calm and Cermeño took
in sail by night because he was near land and didn't
want to risk running aground.

Cermeño did not mention longitude at any time in
his report, an omission common to all the Spanish sixteenth century cruise reports the writer has read. Apparently, he had decided that he was near the Alta
California coast by dead reckoning; that is, by calcu-
lating the amount of eastings made good on the basis of

the distance he ran on each course steered. Time, most probably, entered into his calculations also because ships of that day generally maintained a continuous watch on the sandglass "which, from the Middle Ages until after the nineteenth century had begun, was the only process for measuring time on board ship." [19] This watch was the special function of shipboard pages who scrupulously capsized the glass just as the last grain of sand was running out.[20] At any rate, Cermeño began sounding on October 29 and, in the morning of November 4 "the land and coast of New Spain appeared."

The land he sighted lay between two capes, twenty leagues apart; it was mountainous and heavily forested; and, they could make out very thick piney woods near the beach and farther inland. As Cermeño was looking for a safe port where also there was timber for building a launch, he ran on coastwise, close-hauled by night. He found this a very rough coast with reefs offshore. On November 5 they rounded Cape Mendocino and, that night, a strong northwester struck them which forced them to run before it under shortened sail. On November 6 they stood inshore and discovered a horseshoe-shaped bay with a clean, sandy bottom where they anchored in seven fathoms. A river flowed into this bay over a bar which carried three fathoms of water at high tide.

They found Indians settled near the river mouth who corresponded well with descriptions the Spaniards generally have given the natives on the California

[19] Julio F. Guillén, editor, *Catálogo guía del Museo Naval de Madrid* (Burgos, 1945), p. 166.

[20] Incidentally, sandglasses or *ampolletas* are on display in the Museo Naval, Madrid, which measure respectively, fifteen seconds, thirty seconds, one minute, thirty minutes, and two hours.

coast; the men with their genitals exposed – the women with theirs covered by woven grass or an animal's skin. The first of these men to come out to the ship arrived, moving very swiftly, by using a two-bladed paddle in a little craft woven of rushes similar to the *tule* or *reed mace* in the lake at Mexico City. As they gave this Indian some pieces of silk and blankets and other trifles, four others came aboard the next morning to see what they could cadge.

At this point, one encounters a very odd break in Cermeño's report; yet, there is no obvious indication of a change in its usual continuity. To the writer, at least, it seemed as if someone had censored the narrative, deleted two or more pages, perhaps; then, had rewritten the remainder so as to smooth the rejointing as well as possible. Without any break in his account of the four Indians' visit, he summed that up and spoke about his personal actions saying:

> They were on board and did the same as the first one and in order to see the lie of the land and to start what I was planning which was to build the launch in order to carry on the said exploration I embarked in the said ship's barge with twenty-two men seventeen of them arquebusiers three with bucklers and my lieutenant and sergeant and disembarked on the beach where close to it I found many Indian men women and boys who had their ranchería there in some caves dug in the sand and covered with grass according to the usage of the Chichimecas Indians they have bows and arrows and we couldn't find any sort of iron to form into a weapon or anything else they are a people who go painted in parts but the paint isn't thick like the Chichimecas' and the country according to what has been seen appears fertile through three leagues inland which I and the other Spaniards saw who were accompanying me *to hunt supplies we needed because the ship had been lost.* . . [Underscoring supplied.]

The foregoing translation corresponds with *Fojas,* sheets, 5va and 6 of the manuscript upon which this account is based. It is literal with respect to punctuation; almost so, in substance; and the principal departure from the original is in capitalizing words normally so written in English. This was done in order to emphasize the continuity mentioned above. This cavalier dismissal of the "San Agustín" was such a radical change from Cermeño's usual practice in his report that the writer could not escape the suspicion that higher authority had decided to keep the details of her loss secret as far as official records were concerned. As a matter of fact, the lost ship's name was not associated with her at all in this account.

After Cermeño had gone inland twice in search of foodstuffs, he sailed out of the bay which he named San Francisco, and which has no connection with the port one may enter today through the Golden Gate. His bay, Cermeño said, was also called Bahía Grande. He got underway in the launch he had built and named "Santa Buenaventura." As he did not mention the "San Agustín's" barge again, one might presume that it was hoisted in upon his return aboard and lost with the ship.

Cermeño said that his San Francisco Bay lay in thirty-eight degrees forty minutes; the keys in its entrance in thirty-eight degrees thirty minutes; and, that its two headlands were twenty-five leagues apart. While such distance between points renders identification difficult, other circumstances appear to point to Drake's Bay as the current name of Cermeño's port even if he did fail to mention anything about the brass plate Sir Francis Drake said he left there. Possibly that metal had been made into necklaces, nose rings, bracelets, and anklets by the Indians long before Cermeño arrived.[21]

Anyway, Cermeño, emboldened no doubt by a store of bitter acorns he had got from the Indians as rations, set forth to accomplish the mission His Majesty had assigned him. Also, he had some woven stuffs and trinkets for barter with the Indians along the way which had been salvaged from the "San Agustín," possibly the most valuable assets to him then which that wreck could have afforded. Manifestly, too, he had salvaged his astrolabe for he didn't shoot the sun the next day after he sailed because it didn't appear; that day being cloudy and very windy. He had lain to the night of December 8 after about a ten league run and, the day following, he ran twenty-two leagues coastwise until sunset when he anchored behind a point.

---

[21] Some clarification as to this locality seems to have been provided by Chief Pilot Francisco de Bolaños. He recommended in the council convened aboard Vizcaíno's flagship, the "San Diego," anchored in thirty-nine degrees, on January 7, 1603, that they go into a safe port two leagues to leeward. He stated that he had been in there aboard the "Ship 'San Agustín' when Sebastian Zermeño came to make the said exploration of this coast. . ." – Ms, Audiencia de Méjico, 372, fol. 16, AGI.

In the sailing directions composed during Vizcaíno's expedition, this port was called Puerto de Don Gaspar, perhaps in honor of the Viceroy of Mexico, Conde de Monterrey, whose patronymic was Gaspar de Zúñiga y Azevedo. The boatswain of the frigate "Tres Reyes," however, stated that this port, "called above Don Gaspar," was the Puerto de los Reyes where the ship "San Agustín" was wrecked. It was named Puerto de los Reyes also on the chart of the same port in these sailing directions. *Ibid.*, fols. 58 and 88v.

One may wonder why Francisco de Bolaños might not have insisted upon keeping one of Cermeño's two names for this port of tragic memory; perhaps he was imbued, however, with Vizcaíno's zeal for creating new toponomy. At any rate, they did not find it in a new latitude; they gave it the same thirty-eight degrees forty minutes where Cermeño had placed it. And, oddly enough, all these spotted it only ten minutes farther north than the "conuenient and fit harborough" Drake "fell with" in June 1579. Yet, Vizcaíno has said that he was unable to identify the places Cabrillo named!

He "began to navigate" on Sunday, the tenth, and discovered a very big cove which he named San Pedro Bay. Across its mouth, from point to point, was a stretch of fifteen leagues and, shooting the sun, he found that it lay in thirty-seven degrees. After he had gone seven or eight leagues farther south, he anchored behind a point in order to avoid travel at night.

He sailed on thus until December 13 when the need of something more to eat than bitter acorns began to tell upon both the seamen and the passengers, a total of seventy aboard the "Santa Buenaventura." All, depressed and ill, began begging Cermeño, for their lives' sake, to stop exploring and to run without halting again until they could reach a place where food might be found. He put them off with mollifying arguments as best he could, and fared along as before.

By December 17 he had come to an island, probably San Martín, which Cermeño said was named San Agustín. In the meantime, he had sighted Monterey Bay (his San Pedro), an Indian village on the Santa Bárbara Channel, Catalina Island, San Clemente Island, Point Loma, and San Diego Bay. Contrary winds held them in the vicinity of San Martín Island until December 22.

While they were here, they took on fresh water and made the best of a fish which had been stranded among some rocks, weakened by two mortal wounds. This fish was so big that it provided seven days' food for seventy people. Grateful as he was for this windfall, Cermeño decided, nevertheless, that he shouldn't draw any nearer the end of his tether. He felt, too, that the coast thence to Cedros Island was so well known that he probably could not contribute very much more by an additional survey.

Study of this report to December 22, 1595, when Cermeño had reached thirty-one degrees fifteen minutes, fails to indicate much basis for the unfavorable criticism which the viceroy of Mexico, Conde de Monterrey, expressed to the king in his letter of April 19, 1596.

> To me there seems to be convincing proof, resting on clear inference, that some of the principal bays, where with greater reason it might be expected harbors would be found, they crossed from point to point and by night, while others they entered but a little way. . .[22]

Cermeño's report shows that the night of December 14 was the first he spent underway. He had left a bay in thirty-four degrees and ran close offshore inside a cove which lay between two points thirteen to fifteen leagues apart because it was a clear night and no good anchorage was to be found. He cruised again at night on December 16, just before reaching San Martín Island. It is rather difficult up to this point to see just what constituted the viceroy's "clear inference."

Cermeño said that, from this island, he ran down to Cedros Island, thence to Cape San Lucas,

> and crossing the Gulf, I went to moor the launch and disembark the people in the Puerto de Hacalan which is the one they call Puerto de Compostela where we put an end to all this exploration.
>
> Dated in Mexico on 24 April 1596.
> (Signature and flourish) Sebastyan Rodrigues Cermeño.

The same *legajo* which has been used above contains also a copy of the letter which the royal officials of Acapulco wrote the viceroy of Mexico on February 1, 1596. They reported that, on the preceding day, a craft

---

[22] As quoted in Chapman, *A History of California*, p. 122.

which, in the Philippines is called a *viroco,* had arrived
in that port. Juan de Morgana was its pilot and with
him there were four Spanish sailors, five Indians, and
a negro. They reported the loss of the "San Agustín"
on a coast where she had struck and broken up. A des-
calced friar and some other persons were drowned;
seventy survivors embarked in the *viroco.* All of these,
except themselves, had remained with Sebastián Rodríguez Cermeño and disembarked from this craft in
La Navidad. Morgana swore to this account.

The officials stated that there were no goods of any
sort aboard the launch and that the men were practically naked. To them, it appeared a miracle that so
many could have made that long voyage in such a
small craft. It appears a miracle to the writer also.

Rarely in the history of any nation, if at all, has anyone offered a greater example of perseverance toward
accomplishing a mission than Cermeño provided from
the very day he sailed out of Cavite in that leaky old
tub. In the total absence of details about the manner of
her stranding, one may wonder whether Cermeño
might not have been trying to beach the "San Agustín"
in order to avoid total loss; if then, she might have
begun to leak so fast as to upset his calculations and
thus force him to drive her onto less favorable ground
for salvage.

Of course, it is possible that the determination he
manifested after her loss might have been born in
desperation for his was the unpardonable sea crime; he
lost his ship. Certainly a man of mark, as Cermeño had
been previously, might be impelled to extreme efforts
to redeem himself. Possibly, there was yet an Armenian's Island, a City of Cíbola, or a Los Angeles along
the Alta California coast which he might find; whose

vast riches would so overshadow the Manila Galleon's worth as to make her loss trifling; even to make her investors glad her wreck had led to the greater prize.

Well, whether such fancies motivated Cermeño or not, his actions did not mark him as a man obsessed by desperation; rather, he acted apparently in calm resolution. The writer, however, should have to be desperate indeed before he would sail out of Drake's Bay in December with seventy men aboard a little open launch and nothing but river water to drink and acorns to eat, even to go as far as San Francisco.

If Sebastián Rodríguez Cermeño had not lost the "San Agustín," and had striven to carry out his coast survey mission with the same zeal he displayed in the "Santa Buenaventura," it seems most probable that another survey would not have been considered necessary. In that case, there would not have been any reason to send Sebastián Vizcaíno up the Californias' coasts seven years later. The results of Cermeño's survey, also, would have been available to a viceroy highly favorable to establishing a supporting base in Alta California so it might not have been abandoned to the Indians as, in the following chapter, one may see that it was indeed.

X

Alta California Abandoned

After Juan Sebastián Vizcaíno sailed past San Diego Bay without stopping, about January 30, 1603, no other Spaniard, as far as the record shows, set foot on Alta California's coast until 1769. Thus, for 166 years, this great land lay abandoned to its aborigines.

Allusions and references to Vizcaíno have been made so frequently in the course of this study that it seems superfluous to dwell further upon his voyage to Alta California. Even if it has been the best documented of all the early Spanish nautical explorations along that coast; even if it formed the bases of written *pareceres* or opinions about the state's worth to the Spanish Empire for twenty-six years after it ended;[1] its place in historical high relief seems attributable largely to its high water mark status. High water mark? Yes, his voyage saw the end of efforts begun sixty-four years earlier; barring unconfirmed accounts, no other attempt to explore or settle Alta California was made by Spaniards during the next 166 years; no other seafaring expedition followed Vizcaíno.

And, those mythical islands, Rica de Oro and Rica de Plata, figured prominently as obstacles to navigation toward California, farfetched as that must seem physically. Instead of following up the plan to estab-

---

[1] Ms, Colección Navarrete, vol. xix, doc. 12, "Otro parecer de Fray Antonio de la Ascensión, 1629."

lish a supporting base for the Manila Galleon in California – actually ordered by Felipe III on August 19, 1606 [2] – the viceroy of Mexico seized upon the islands alleged to be rich in gold and silver as more expedient sites for support.

Chapman has very fitly stressed this change of policy as consonant with the change of viceroys in Mexico. The Marqués de Montesclaros relieved the Conde de Monterrey shortly after Vizcaíno's return from California in 1603 and, apparently, he was bent against finding any good in anything Monterrey had championed. He shunted aside and reduced the handsome rewards Monterrey had accorded Vizcaíno and his key personnel, even going so far as to hang Enrico Martínez, the expert cartographer. So, in 1611-1613, Vizcaíno fared over to Japan and into a fruitless search for the fabled islands.[3]

And, reverting to Friar Andrés de Urdaneta, one may wonder why he didn't verify the status of those islands on his *tornaviaje* in 1565. He, according to Friar Andrés de Aguirre, was responsible for spreading the legend about them so one might think that he would have been eager to locate them or to prove that they were just a myth. His 1565 homeward track passed about 150 miles north of Rica de Oro's presumed position; about forty miles north of Rica de Plata's fictitious locality. If Urdaneta was concerned about them at all, however, he apparently did not share his preoccupation with Pilots Esteban Rodríguez and Rodrigo de Espinosa for they didn't mention anything about them whatever in their log of that voyage.[4]

---

2 Venegas, *Noticia,* vol. I, pp. 145-150.
3 Chapman, *A History of California,* pp. 138-142.
4 *Colección de diarios,* vol. v, Lámina v, and pp. 113-135.

Pedro de Unamuno's 1587 report on them got very little attention, apparently, else none wanted to believe what he said regarding their non-existence. So, a will-o'-the-wisp lured Spain's nautical exploration away from California and left it abandoned to the Indians until 1769.

While the Spaniards and the Mexicans together actually occupied California from 1769 to 1848, they never gained, apparently, any comprehensive idea of its tremendous resources. The Spaniards, oddly enough, seemed to have as early as 1536 an appreciation of petroleum, certainly one of the greatest sources of wealth with which California has been endowed. From Valladolid, September 3, 1536, the Queen of Spain addressed a letter to the royal officials of Cubagua, an island which lies between Margarita Island and the Araya Peninsula, Venezuela. In that letter she said that some persons had brought to Spain *azeite petrolio* "of which there was a spring in that said island." While the queen's name for that product was indeed redundant, she obviously meant rock oil or coal oil as it was called in the United States many years ago.

The queen said that, to her, it appeared useful, so she ordered that as much of it as possible be sent to her in all the ships which should depart Cubagua bound for Spain.[5] As the amount of crude oil this source produced was scanty, however, the Supreme Council of the Indies lost interest in it.[6]

While one might be surprised by a remote appreciation of petroleum among Spaniards, one would be astounded if ever they had failed to appreciate gold.

[5] Ms, Audiencia de Santo Domingo 1121, libro 3, fol. 122, AGI.
[6] Ernesto Schäfer, *El Consejo Real y Supremo de las Indias* (Sevilla, 1947), vol. II, p. 338.

Yet, paradoxically, its discovery in Alta California, "the most famous and most important find being that by Francisco López in San Feliciano Cañon in 1841," [7] did not create any significant stir in either our state or Mexico. This might have been the same mine to which Greenhow had referred.

> The only mine as yet discovered in continental California is one of gold, situated at the foot of the great westernmost range of mountains, on the west, at the distance of twenty-five miles from Angeles, the largest town in the country. It is said to be of extraordinary richness. [8]

Gold failed, however, to motivate any Mexican rush to Alta California; there was no great movement to the scene at all; there was nothing whatever to compare with the surge of Americans into California in 1849 after gold had been discovered at Sutter's Mill in Coloma. So tremendous was this influx, that on September 9, 1850, California became a state in the American union, just one week more than thirty months after her cession to the United States. Apparently, not even gold discovery could rouse the Spanish-Mexicans from apathy toward Alta California.

Yet, some writers have insisted that Spain never lost interest in Alta California; never really abandoned that land to the Indians. As an indication of prolonged interest in this state, some have cited the numerous voyages which the Spaniards projected into the Gulf of California during the seventeenth century. The writer is willing to grant that the Spaniards looked constantly upon settling Baja California but that was in immediate self defense; they saw danger to all

---

7 John Walton Caughey, *California* (New York, 1950), p. 286.
8 Robert Greenhow, *The History of Oregon and California and the Other Territories on the North-West Coast of North America*, p. 14.

Mexico in the event that a foreign foothold were established there. They appreciated the same geographical features of Baja California which later prompted the United States to lease Magdalena Bay from Mexico in order better to provide naval defense of the Panamá Canal. Thus, in the writer's opinion, the Gulf voyages and the efforts to found colonies on the peninsula constituted negative approaches to Alta California.

It is conceivable, of course, that widespread settlement of Baja California might have been extended ultimately into the land to northward. Still, Spanish penetration into New Mexico in 1598 had no effect upon Alta California prior to San Diego's founding in 1769.

Settlement, evangelization among the Indians, discovery of mineral deposits and pearl oyster beds, and charting the coastline were extolled as motivations and assumed as obligations by the petitioners in all the proposed agreements with the Crown to undertake maritime expeditions into the Gulf of California. These, however, did not mention Alta California. As to this point, of course, it could be argued that Alta California and the peninsula which projected from it to the southeast were considered one big island until 1746. Such persistence in erroneous ideas, despite the evidence to the contrary which Ulloa, Alarcón, and Cabrillo had provided during the second quarter of the sixteenth century, probably emphasized Spain's decadence since 1588 as sharply as any other phase of her thinking could. And, consistent with this general deterioration, the matchless resources of Alta California were left to exploitation by a people who went almost naked, prowled the countryside constantly like other wild beasts, and fed partially on reptiles and larvae.

As indicated already, many cruises into the Gulf of California were made during the seventeenth century. In chronological sequence, the most important – if any could thus be characterized – were, in the writer's opinion, made by: Juan de Iturbi, 1616; Francisco de Ortega, 1632, 1633, and 1636; Pedro Porter y Casanate, 1644 and 1648; Bernardo Bernal de Piñadero, 1664 and 1667; Francisco de Lucenilla, 1668; Isidro de Atondo y Antillón, 1683; and, Fathers Eusebio F. Kino and Juan M. Salvatierra, 1697.[9]

Insofar as anything resembling a step toward Alta California was concerned, all these amounted to precisely nothing until January 1683 when Atondo established at La Paz, in Baja California, a colony which lasted until mid-July of the same year. He tried again in October 1683, establishing a colony at San Bruno, about fifty miles north of La Paz. This was the most nearly successful of all the efforts to colonize Baja California which had been made up to that time; yet, after two years of fitful life, this colony succumbed also.

Establishing a permanent settlement on this peninsula was to wait for the two Jesuit priests, Fathers Kino and Salvatierra, whose cruise as noted above resulted in accomplishing their mission at Loreto in 1697.[10] Perhaps their success was attributable more to personal character than anything else for only sterling manhood could gain admission into the Company of Jesus, an order which appeared immune to the decadence which had infected Spain since 1588. Besides the splendid leadership and inspired zeal which they bent to their

---

[9] Based upon Julio F. Guillén y Tato, *Repertorio de los M.SS., cartas, planos y dibujos relativos a las Californias, existentes en este Museo* (Madrid: Museo Naval, 1932), p. 23. Ortega's cruises were omitted in the chronological list but were picked up on pp. 32-34.

[10] Venegas, *Noticia de la California*, vol. I, pp. 159-169; vol. II, pp. 11-22.

task, however, their principal objective was to establish an operating base in order to project conversion to Christianity through the Indians in Baja California; not to build a mere adjunct to exploiting pearl oyster beds along its eastern coast.

Pearls had been the unofficial yet prime lure as far as all the seventeenth century maritime exploration was concerned in Baja California with the exceptions of Atondo's attempts and these two great Jesuits' efforts. While it is not the writer's purpose to dwell exhaustively upon that subject, some idea of the Gulf of California's vast pearl resources should be presented at this point.

For example, in 1636, Francisco de Ortega submitted to the King a list of thirty different pearl oyster beds which he said he had discovered in the Gulf of California in the period, 1631-1636. He gave the dimensions of twelve of these beds, the perimeters of four of them, and, more descriptions of the remaining fourteen; that is, these last lay between certain terrain features or occupied all or a certain portion of particular coves or bays. Obviously, one would require the chart to which he referred in order to gain an idea of those beds' aggregate area, so that part of his list cannot be used here.

The total of the perimeters he gave was 19.5 miles. If those miles had enclosed a perfect circle – which, of course, they did not – its diameter would have been a little more than six miles and its area more than twenty-eight square miles. The areas for which Ortega did give length and breadth aggregated 132.75 square miles.[11] He found quite a large area of pearl oyster beds, one might observe.

[11] Ms, Colección Navarrete, vol. XIX, doc. 35, fol. 19.

There is a more vivid but imprecise statement of these beds' extent in a report by Pedro Porter y Casanate. After stating that all who had gone to Baja California had traded for pearls and brought out a great many, he said:

> There are more than sixty leagues of beds and if all the people in New Spain should become divers, everyone would have a place in which he could gather pearls. Very good ones have been found inside the ports in shallow water – the natives use them in trade. And so, both men and women know how to dive for them.[12]

One may only guess just what "sixty leagues of beds" measured; what the total population of New Spain was when Porter made that undated statement; or, how much space each inhabitant would have required for efficient pearl diving if everyone had been so engaged at the same time.

On the same page, Porter went on to speak of the great numbers of pearls which Vizcaíno, Juan de Iturbi, and others had secured in the Gulf of California, either by trading with the Indians or by sending down their own divers. As to size, some of these pearls had weighed seven *adarmes* or 12.6 grams, about forty-four hundredths of an ounce avoirdupois. Wagner, treating pearls in the same area, has said: "The Marqués [Cortés] found one valued at more than five thousand ducats [$19,500], and there were many others of great value among the soldiers . . with him."[13]

---

[12] Pedro Porter y Casanate, "Memorial impreso," no location, addressed to "V. Magestad," in *Varios Papeles Tocantes a Indias*, MS 8,553, p. 118, Biblioteca Nacional, Madrid.

[13] Henry R. Wagner, "Pearl Fishing Enterprises in the Gulf of California: The Expedition of Sebastián Vizcaíno," *Hispanic American Historical Review*, May 1930, vol. x, no. 2, pp. 189-190, quoting from Baltasar Obregón, *Crónica comentario o relaciones de los Descubrimientos antiguos y modernos de Nueva España y del Nuevo Mexico*, 1584. "Original in Archivo General de Indias, 1-1-3/22."

While Spanish reports as to the extent of the fisheries and numbers, sizes, and values of the Gulf of California pearls could be cited at length, perhaps it is just as well to hear something from an American writer on these points.[14]

> The most important marine pearl fishery on the American continent is that of Lower California, the central point being at La Paz. Here the true pearl oysters, Meleagrina or Margaritophora, are found, on the eastern [sic] shores of the Gulf of California, from Cape San Lucas to the mouth of the Colorado River, taking in about 1,500 miles of coast, including the gulf islands. . . . After some intermittent work, the fisheries, about 150 years ago [1742], were again worked, with system and with great success, by one Juan Ossio, who took from them yearly from 300 to 500 pounds of pearls, actually packing them on mules and selling them by the bushel. . .

After describing the vicissitudes of pearl diving and the various methods employed in that industry, that author said that a perfect pearl weighing four hundred grains was secured at Loreto by a Mexican diver and another, almost equivalent to this one, had been taken in the Bay of Mulege. In 1883, they found

> a light-brown pearl, flecked with darker shades, weighing 260 grains and valued at $8,000.00. It was sent to Paris. Another one was pear-shaped, white, with dark specks, weighed 176 grains, and sold for $7,500.00. . . In 1881 a black pearl, weighing 162 grains, was sold in Paris for $10,000.00. During 1884 two other pearls, weighing respectively 140 and 124 grains, and of surprising lustre, brought $11,000.00.

From such accounts of great wealth in the Gulf of California pearl fisheries, it is easy to fancy their get-rich-quick appeal to the threadbare gentlemen of the seventeenth century. Of course, Porter y Casanate,

---

[14] George Frederick Kunz, *Gems and Precious Stones of North America* (New York, 1892), pp. 218, 219, 224.

whose views regarding these pearl fisheries have been expressed in part above, was anything but one of the threadbare gentlemen. Alvaro del Portillo definitely set him in a class apart, saying:

> After the epoch which we have just considered; that of obscure explorers, very heroic, and, very much soldiers of fortune; the history of the voyages to California is indeed adorned by the togated figure of Don Pedro Porter Cassanate.[15]

Porter, without doubt, was an ornamental figure compared with his predecessors in the latter half of the sixteenth and the first half of the seventeenth century for he was a member of the Order of Santiago, the first Spanish seafarer into the Pacific who belonged to one of their four great military orders since Knight Commander Pedro de Alvarado departed from the scene. And, as far as the writer has been convinced, he was just that – ornamental.

Porter wrote, yes; as a relatively young naval officer he published *Reparos a los errores de la Navigación* (Corrections of Errors in Navigation) which was printed in 1634. A copy of it is on exhibit today in the Museo Naval, Madrid,[16] but, from conversations with that museum's staff, the writer gathered that no popular demand for its reproduction had been noticeable up to May 1956. Several of the archives in Spain carry his *memoriales* or briefs which cite his services to king and country. As far as the writer has been able to determine, these have been principally restatements of the same claims and, certainly as far as the Californias have been concerned, those services amounted to little

---

[15] Portillo, *Descubrimientos y exploraciones en las costas de California*, p. 245.

[16] José F. Guillén, editor, *Catálogo guía del Museo Naval de Madrid*, p. 164.

more than much ado about alleged perseverance against "the slings and arrows of outrageous fortune."

Withal, Porter has enjoyed a splendid press. For example, Pérez Embid, in his review of Portillo's work, said:

> Don Pedro Porter Cassanate, an Aragonese admiral, an educated man, energetic and generous servant of the King, a significant personality from various points of view, carries away all of Chapter VII. . . Whenever some investigator may decide to dedicate to him that special monograph which, with much less justification has been dedicated already to many figures in Spanish actions in America, he will encounter in the pages of this chapter a résumé of his own book, in which he will be able to rectify few important things.[17]

With the addition to that field of *Genial Adventurer* or *Adventurero genial,* title of a work dedicated to Porter by a very laudatory fellow-Aragonese,[18] that investigator might indeed find a dismaying scarcity of unused data for his monograph.

Before the writer had read Chapman's work, he had reached approximately the same conclusion the historian expressed:

> In 1650 Porter disappears from the record. A royal order of that year required the viceroy to assist him unless there were serious objections, but the authorities wanted an explanation of Porter's delays, making the observation that his license was not unlimited in time. It seems likely that the viceroy recommended against any further dealings with Porter. One wonders whether the latter had sincerely endeavored to fulfil his contract. For fifteen years he had devoted himself to this project, and, so far

[17] Florentino Pérez Embid, "Notas bibliográficas, Portillo y Diez de Sollano, Alvaro, Descubrimientos y exploraciones en las costas de California" in *Revista de Indias* (Madrid: Enero-Marzo, 1947), Año 8, no. 27, p. 201.

[18] A Gascón de Gotor, *Aventurero genial: Aragón en América* (Zaragoza, 1950).

as the evidence goes, had made but two rather unsatisfactory voyages. . .[19]

The writer agrees completely with Chapman on doubt as to whether Porter had endeavored sincerely to fulfill his counteract – the writer does not think he did. That conclusion, of course, is based upon the assumption that Porter was capable of fulfilling it.

Although Porter on this exploration advanced farther into the interior of the Gulf than his predecessors, he did not sight the end of it. With the hope of reaching it, or believing he could find a strait which would demonstrate California's insularity, or perhaps to encounter the famous Northwest Passage which would enable him to return to New Spain through the Atlantic; our man undertook his voyages of 1649 and 1650. He was inclined to this last idea after his final California expedition when, on August 18, 1651, he wrote the Viceroy, Conde de Alva, that "what until now was distrusted has finally been assured; that there is a navigable strait to the North Sea."[20]

It seems idle to note the refreshing naïveté which both Portillo and Porter displayed in this quotation. As for Portillo, he seemed blandly unaware that previously he had recorded in this same work that Ulloa in 1539 and Alarcón in 1540 had reached the northernmost part of the Gulf of California.[21] Just how Porter could state that the existence of a navigable strait to the Atlantic Ocean had been assured when he never reached even the mouth of the Colorado River is something which must be left to an imagination far more fecund than the writer can claim.

According to Portillo, Porter's 1649 voyage carried him up the gulf to a point very close to thirty-one

---

19 Chapman, *A History of California*, pp. 166-167.
20 Portillo, *Descubrimientos y exploraciones*, pp. 281-282, and quoting from Porter's letter in Ms, Audiencia de Guadalajara 134, fol. 1, AGI.
21 Portillo, *op. cit.*, pp. 151-152.

degrees. At his northernmost position, he encountered some currents with which he was not familiar. These were so strong as to menace his vessels with shipwreck and to prevent his sailing north of Angel de la Guarda Island. So he fell off to leeward and christened the islands which flanked the channel in which he turned back, *Salsipuedes,* "Get out if You Can." To Porter's Pepys, this name was indeed indicative of the difficulties his idol encountered on this cruise despite the fact that it was made during summer months.

Conditions must have been trying indeed when they could baffle a man of Porter's parts, for Portillo has said that he was a seaman of great theoretical and practical learning. "He understood to perfection arithmetic, geometry, navigation, military architecture, and other sciences useful to mariners." Furthermore, he had amplified his knowledge notably during many voyages in the Royal Spanish Navy on the *Carrera de Indias* or Indies Run.[22] Yet, even with all these accomplishments, Porter failed to get within one hundred and fifty miles of the Colorado River's mouth, a goal which Ulloa and Alarcón had reached respectively, 110 and 109 years previously. Perhaps they weren't educated enough to know any better.

This dreary history of seventeenth century Spanish voyages into the Gulf of California does not afford a happy ending to any discussion concerning them. Possibly too many Spaniards, cast from the same mold which had formed such figures as Cortés, Ulloa, Alarcón, Alvarado, Cabrillo, and Cermeño, had been washed up on the English Channel and North Sea beaches and laid beneath the Low Countries' sod to leave any of their sort available for maritime explora-

---

[22] *Ibid.,* pp. 282, 288.

tion along the coast of the Californias. Mediocrity and poorer than mediocre were the prevalent characteristics among the Spanish seafarers in the seventeenth century.

Yet, paradoxically, the records of some of these men, threadbare in character as well as in clothing, are the most complete of all. The writer has chosen one such record as base for the final portion of this work; partly because, chronologically, it falls within the last four voyages of that century; partly, because it carries an extremely rare feature, individual character summaries of all the personnel embarked, barring the clergy. Withal, it is typical in failure. Thus, one may learn what one may from

A Summary Account of the Voyage Which Captain Francisco de Lucenilla Made to the Californias by Commission from the Most Excellent Marqués de Mancera, Viceroy of New Spain. Written by Father Friar Juan Cavallero Carranco, Lecturer in Theology, and Commissioner of This Voyage by the Holy Tribunal of the Inquisition, and by the Most Reverend Father Commissioner General, Friar Fernando de la Rua.[23]

Captain Francisco de Lucenilla, a native of Paradas in Andalucía, arrived in New Spain in September 1665 with a stock of assorted merchandise; some of it belonged to him, some of it had been entrusted to him on consignment. As the sum total of his stock did not move very fast, he was forced to stay so long in Mexico City trying to sell his wares that he missed the return voyage of the ship which had brought him to New Spain. While he was thus occupied, he heard reports of the imaginary wealth in the Californias.

23 Frontispiece, Ms 18,758, no. 14, Biblioteca Nacional, Madrid. Except as otherwise noted hereinafter, all the following will be based upon this manuscript.

At the instances of some flatterers, Lucenilla developed a fervent desire to make a voyage to the Californias as others had done. He was told that he could make it for less than four thousand pesos, in less time than a year, and, that he could gain thereby great riches and even greater honors. In Friar Juan Cavallero Carranco's opinion, he was "gullible to all such tales both on account of what had been written about that realm and also because, at the same time, a gentleman called Don Bernardo Bernal de Piñaredo [*sic*] was in Mexico City who, with the title of Admiral, had gone to the Californias twice." Friar Juan said that, although Piñadero had not accomplished anything in service to God or King, he was still insisting very much on being allowed a third voyage to those lands.

Lucenilla consulted a number of people; read various accounts; and, all of this fanned his desire to go. He found himself with some money; he was presumptuous and yearned for riches and honors; so, he presented a petition to the viceroy. In company with Captain Alonso Matheos, he offered to populate the Californias within a year; to build two big ships for that purpose; and, to take on this expedition fifty men and twenty horses together with everything necessary for their maintenance. Above everything else, he would take also two priests to initiate the conversion of those lands to Christianity.

Then, a lawsuit developed between Francisco de Lucenilla and Bernardo Bernal de Piñadero which resulted in the viceroy's decision that the former would make the voyage and that the latter would cease and desist. Litigation ensued also between the Jesuits and the Franciscans over the question as to which of those two orders should be represented on this voyage. The

decision was favorable to the Franciscans on the basis
of their primacy in New Spain, their participation in
such undertakings since Cortés had begun them, and,
because conversion of the Indians had been entrusted
to them by a special *cédula* from His Majesty. So,
Father Friar Juan Cavallero Carranco, a native of
Guadalcanal, Estremadura [*sic*], and Father Friar
Juan Bautista Ramírez, born in Ayamonte, Andalucía,
were appointed to Lucenilla's expedition.

After getting the viceroy's authorization, Captain
Alonso Matheos left Mexico City with thirty comrades
in February 1667 to build the ships at an appropriate
site on the Pacific. For reasons of timber and subsistence available there, Matheos decided upon Chacala
in the jurisdiction of Compostela, Tepic.

So great was everyone's desire to make this voyage,
that all of them worked manually in the shipyard to
the wonderment of everybody living in the surrounding
countryside; all marvelled upon seeing Spaniards in
person working so devotedly and painstakingly. As
hard as they tried, however, the work did not progress
as they wished. Instead of finishing the ships in four
months, as they had thought they could, they couldn't
complete the job under fourteen.

One reason for the delay was that they had only one
yard master; the other, Miguel de Cadis, had returned
to Mexico City as a result of disputes with Alonso
Matheos. Another reason was that all of them were not
workers for some of them had been pampered types.
Also, it disgusted those who worked to see that others,
who just ate and slept all the time, were the favorites
with the captain.

While these people worked in the shipyard, Captain
Lucenilla was in Mexico City attending to other mat-

ters necessary for the voyage. Captain Juan de Cavueñas, seeing that Captain Lucenilla had run out of funds, spent money in the latter's behalf with great zeal and gathered up the remaining men necessary to meet the number required by the contract.

When everything had been arranged, they left Mexico City during the afternoon of Corpus Christi Day, accompanied by carriages loaded with friends as far as Chapultepec, a league from the city. In unusual applause and gayety goodbyes were said here and they fared on their way, taking more than two months to reach the shipyard.

Friar Juan spoke of the "Señores Saucedos" who, in their *hacienda* in Guarache, entertained them most sumptuously for two days. He said they entertained everyone who passed that way according to his quality and, for that practice, they enjoyed more praise and a better reputation than any gentleman in New Spain.

In Guadalajara City, they were entertained by the president and members of the *Audiencia* and by the bishop. The bishop gave Friar Juan the title of "Judge and Vicar General of the Kingdom of the Californias" for, as Cavallero explained it, the bishop assumed action as prelate of that territory and, consequently, he wanted all who went there to go as his ministers.

When some business had been dispatched in Guadalajara, the party went on to Compostela where a man was selling merchandise on the Captain's account in order to provide necessities for the men working in the shipyard. After they had rested a few days, it was decided that Friar Juan Bautista and the men should go on to the shipyard where this Friar would say mass and console those in need. Friar Juan Cavallero was to remain in Compostela to attend to such business as might need attention and to conserve his health for the shipyard was a sickly place during the rainy season and an emergency would arise if both clergymen should fall sick and be unable to make the voyage. "And so," said Friar Juan, "I remained in the city and my companion went with the men to Chacala where he stayed to the great pleasure and consolation of everybody."

Friar Juan related that all were in a state of peace and tranquillity; his companion was attending to the company and he to such business as arose, hearing many confessions and preaching many sermons which were heard with great approbation, until the beginning of December. Then, "the Licentiate Christopher War came to introduce war between the Captain and ourselves" – *vino el Licenciado Christoval Guerra a introducir la guerra entre el Capitan y nosotros.* According to Friar Juan, Guerra came to embark upon the California voyage without the viceroy's authority and without having advised the Father Commissary General of his intentions. All the authority Guerra had, consisted in dispatches from the Bishop of Guadalajara.

When Friar Juan had seen these, he wrote the captain that Father Guerra's coming would be an affliction and, in order to obviate that, the captain should give Cavallero permission to write to his prelate to find out if the latter were pleased to have Guerra accompany them or not.[24] For this reason, great quarrels ensued between the Franciscans and the captain. These reached such a stage that Lucenilla wrote secretly to Mexico City in terms unfavorable to the Franciscans; indeed,

---

[24] Friar Juan Cavallero used *nosotros,* meaning "we" or "us" in his accounts of arguments with Lucenilla. The context indicates that, in these expressions, he referred to himself and his fellow-Franciscan.

he requested that no priest other than Father Guerra accompany him on his voyage.

Friar Juan said that Lucenilla was thus actuated by some malicious secular clergy, envious of the monastic priests, who, as always, had been authorized to take part in the expedition. "But," he observed,

> God, who always favors the causes of little people and, especially those in my sacred Order, willed that, in Mexico City, they order the Captain to take us and to leave the secular priest ashore for this was appropriate and obligatory, a result which the Captain regretted very much and was painful to the malevolent but pleasing to the good-intentioned.

When everything had been provided and the ships were water borne, the captain reconciled himself with the Friars and set May 1 as the sailing date. Before that day arrived, a solemn procession was formed with four priests carrying the "Sovereign Queen of the Angels" on their shoulders from her church to the beach. There, in sight of the ships, Friar Juan Bautista said mass and Friar Juan Cavallero preached with the greatest spirit he could muster and everyone thus became consoled and fervent toward the voyage. They said goodbye to the neighboring people who came to see them off and, according to Friar Juan Cavallero, those were the most joyful days which had ever been seen in those parts.

As soon as mass was over, all embraced each other and shed copious tears. In order that all might recognize the state of affection and peace in which they were sailing, the captain pulled off his shoes and embarked the two friars on his back. Friar Juan Cavallero did not give the details of this maneuver but one may reasonably surmise that small boats from the ships were lying off the beach as near as they could get without grounding and that the Captain simply waded out to them twice with a friar pickaback each time. In the meantime, the relater said that the captain begged the friars' pardon time and again for the tribulations he had brought them. They not only begged his pardon, too, but also that of everybody in the ships' companies, and asked everyone present to take special care to commend them all to God.

When everything had been supplied and embarked, with arms and supplies for fifty-four people, they set sail at dawn on May 1, 1668. They began the voyage with extraordinary pleasure; seeing how well the two ships had been turned out, big enough to make the run to Spain, fleet and well-finished. The second day, the ships sailed coastwise in a fresh breeze and, when within sight of Puerto de Matanchel, the *capitana's* foremast broke. They put in to this port which, according to Friar Juan Cavallero, was a very good one, twelve leagues from Chacala. Another foremast was shipped and they went on their way rejoicing.

Mazatlán was their next port of call for they had chosen it as point of departure for crossing the gulf to Baja California. At the cost of some very hard work, they took aboard water and firewood, as the water was six leagues away and there was very little wood nearby. During their stay at Mazatlán, a "prodigious event" materialized. While everybody was regretting that they had no bell at all on board, Domingo de la Rocha found one in the sea. It was a medium-sized bell with a good tone although, in the course of time, it had become somewhat damaged.

The Friar said there were some pearl oyster beds at Mazatlán like those in the Californias. Some pearls they found in the oysters they ate were lackluster although, indeed, as they learned from the local inhabitants, good pearls also were to be found there.

After everything had been made ready for sailing, they began to navigate across the Vermilion Sea, thus named on modern maps, as Friar Juan Cavallero observed; however, he said he couldn't see why because it was the same in color as all the rest of the oceans. It was possible, of course, that he hadn't been up the gulf far enough to see the red water which had suggested that name.

As the wind was contrary, they required six days for the crossing although the Friar said that Cape San Lucas was only eighty leagues from Mazatlán and that both were in the same latitude, twenty-three degrees thirty minutes north. He spoke then about the islands along their track from Chacala and the different types of fish which abounded in those waters. Ideas were prevalent, according to him, that amber or ambergris should be found along the Gulf of California coasts because of the whales teeming in the gulf.

Friar Juan observed that the prevailing winter winds were northwesterlies, very good for the run from the Californias to New Spain; during the summer, southwest and south winds prevailed and favored runs to the Californias and along their coasts northward.

> And anyone who may wish to make this trip, or sail to discover the strait so desired by the Kings, should take note of this: it can be made by sailing in April or May and travelling through the Gulf from southeast to northwest. But returning to our voyage, I say that we crossed the Gulf from east to west without any alteration at all in the sea because it is very pacific and quiet.

From this fine beginning, one might have expected a happy and successful cruise but such was not to be the case; least of all, from Friar Juan's point of view;

hardly at all, from any other measure of success one might apply to it. For example, they sighted land in Baja California on Sunday morning, May 20, "the first day of the Paschal of the Holy Ghost."

> As I was aboard the *capitana,* I asked the Captain many times for permission to say mass for augury of a good voyage and on account of the solemnity of that day. They impeded me on this, as on other occasions, because the least of their concerns was following the divine will by complying with its holy laws. As soon as they saw the California hills, the question rose as to shares in order to see what was to fall to each one's lot, as if the hills were gold, pearl, or amber. It was a matter of great unpleasantness and thus, nothing was adjusted; not a word was heard regarding the conversion of souls for everything said was in discussion over riches.

One may wonder just what circumstances on a Sunday morning would justify a captain's disapproving his chaplain's request for permission to conduct divine services aboard an American man of war.

Anyway, they anchored near the shore that night in a large and very deep bay which they named Bahía del Espíritu Santo.[25] There was a *ranchería* of about a hundred Indian men and women nearby who made big bonfires and kept up a great deal of tumult and outcry all night. Agitation was hardly less in the ships for rarely did anyone go to sleep and the hours still to pass before they could see the pearls seemed like centuries to them, according to Friar Juan Cavallero.

At dawn, Monday, the crews were put into good order and the Indians were invited to come aboard. They came out in their rafts very happily although, at first, they declined to come over the side. Later, they did so, both men and women; something never seen

---

25 Didn't they know that it had been named San Bernabé many years before their arrival or were they merely presumptuous?

before, according to those who had been there on other occasions, for the Indians usually kept their women very much out of sight. The Friar said that all went naked except the women who were very chaste and wore a little petticoat of net, made from closely-woven thread, caught in many folds at the waist and reaching down to the ankles.

As soon as the Indians arrived, they told the Spaniards that water was to be found in two places nearby, one of them a brook. Friar Juan said that the Indians were given corn and hardtack whereupon they made presents of some little cords, feathers, and shells, none of it worth very much. They were very gentle Indians, strong, well-proportioned, and grateful for what was given to them. They were offered some gourds in which they might bring the Spaniards water and they fetched it on the run; water of the richest sort, it was entirely full of gilded marguerites.

The Friar said that all that day the crew was urging that they be allowed to go ashore to reconnoiter the water sites and the lay of the land but, much to their disappointment, the Captain did not want them to do so. As soon as dawn had broken and the Indians arrived on board, these were asked to trade pearls, called *voho,* for knives, and this went on all day; but, what was obtained in trade had very little value.

As the ship was anchored in complete calm, Friar Juan said he wanted to say mass because it was still the Paschal of the Holy Ghost and mass had not been said the first day of it. The captain opposed his request, saying that it didn't appear convenient to hold that service because everyone was busy trading. The friar insisted at length and finally said it while many Indians were on board with their chief. Seeing the mass aroused great wonderment among all the heathen, both men and women, who stayed aboard the ship all day in great happiness.

At ten o'clock that night, they sailed out of Espíritu Santo Bay northward, looking for Puerto de la Paz and some islands near that port because they had received reports that these were rich in pearls and that many could be garnered by trading along the coasts. The captain was determined to sail coastwise in order to get all he could by trading before going ashore and, after that, if he had gained little, to anchor offshore and look for more. Although he was advised several times that his first endeavor should be to land, fortify himself, and build a church and dwellings; he didn't want to do so, saying that he wanted to see first what wealth there was. The rations were being damaged rapidly at sea; they advised him to consider this and come to a halt soon; but, he considered only the possible existence of pearls, having no room in his mind for anything else.

Tuesday morning found them six leagues from Espíritu Santo Bay, in sight of another Indian *rancheria* and an island. Upon drawing near the *rancheria* and anchoring, they traded for some pearls, scanty in number and poor in quality. Because pearls were scarce, the Indians priced them very highly.

According to Friar Juan, they spent Wednesday where, four years earlier, Don Bernardo Bernal had left Pedro Escandan and Don Luis behind. When they asked the Indians about these men, they were told by signs that an enemy tribe, the *Guaiaros* – possibly, the Guaicuri? – had come and killed them. At this point, Friar Juan expressed the hope that God might pardon them and reward an act as great as that was where only two men had remained among barbarous Indians who were at war among themselves. If the two men had done so with good motives, they would receive a great reward in glory; but, if they had done so from cupidity, it was great foolhardiness.

At this place, they did not get any pearls at all; nor, in a beautiful bay which lay farther ahead, although great efforts to do so were exerted among the Indians. By their fear and wariness, these let it be understood that they were the ones who had killed those two miserable Spanish lads in order to rob them of what they had – about such barbarous people, anything could be believed.

The Spaniards were looking for a port which would afford trade and security for their ships – only security was available there – so, they went looking for Puerto de la Paz, greatly depressed because of the few pearls they had collected. The land they saw was distasteful to the eye, cinder-colored hills devoid of trees and grass, with no signs of metals.

Friar Juan observed that the first site they reached, the bay they named Holy Ghost, was the place which had proved most agreeable to the friars who wanted to stay there. He said there was mystery in their arrival on the Holy Ghost's Day, the day "when that sovereign dove came down in tongues of flame to sear hearts with his preaching." There, too, the Indians built more fires and showed more signs of rejoicing than others had; they gave the Spaniards their trinkets and pearls more liberally than the rest. At that bay, they had found a brook abundant in water and beautiful sand filled with golden marguerites, a great amount of firewood, and large stretches of plains. The Indian women came on board the ships, something they did not do elsewhere.

Finally, according to Friar Juan, be it mystery or be

it the affection engendered by the first encountered, those Indians stole the friars' hearts away; and, they would have remained there gladly to preach to them.

> For, when Christ Our Life sent the apostles into the world to preach, they did so, beginning at the place in the Kingdom or Province where they arrived, and thence they proceeded into the rest of it. But, on this voyage, the objective was to gain pearls and not souls and thus, the latter were scorned in order to seek the former, and our pleasure was not fulfilled. Moreover, I told them all that if they didn't start the conversion in that place, they could rest assured that the voyage would fail. I am tenacious in my opinions and I usually hit the mark; may God grant that I do not err in this.

That Wednesday, they anchored opposite Cerralbo Island near a big sierra whose three-league perimeter enclosed high land, useless and uninhabitable. Again they sailed on, reaching some red mountains which appeared like mining areas; but, although some men familiar with mines prospected them carefully, they said that there was not even a color of ore in them, a nondescript land with no hope whatever of offering anything good, just heaps of burned earth, uninhabitable in the last analysis.

For these reasons and because the sea was getting rough, they got underway and reached the bay beside Puerto de la Paz. Friar Juan said that it was most beautiful to look upon for twelve to fourteen leagues roundabout it; but, with so little depth anywhere that on Saturday, Most Holy Trinity Eve, they saw themselves almost lost there with the *capitana* aground.

> I recalled to everyone on this occasion what I had preached when we were embarking; that the sea was to go dry on us and the earth was to become sea, unless we carried as our objective service to God and to Peace and, as all that was lacking, we found ourselves already with the sea dry.

On Most Holy Trinity Day, we again accounted ourselves lost by groundings; punishment, no doubt, because they had not let me say mass on a day of such great solemnity, but God willed that we should enter the port through the channel.

As all that bay was so shallow, it was necessary to keep very close to land going through the channel. The mountains roundabout were barren, with little firewood; but, alongside the port, there were trees and patches of plain which they did not examine to see whether they were arable land. There was a patch of reed grass nearby with fresh water in it, water so bad that it could have given them the plague if they had drunk it.

Friar Juan found the Indians at this port hideous. Their noses were pierced through the cartilages, and their ears were split and also pierced in order to carry tubes they had thrust into them. They were very coarse and belligerent, keeping their bodies striped with colors; and, they would not come aboard the ships however much they were offered welcome. They weren't maritime Indians like the others the Spaniards had encountered and, against their opposite types, they waged continual war. As far as could be learned, these Indians owned nothing of any value.

So, that place appeared a bad site for settlement and, by common consent, they sailed the next day and looked over the big island which lay opposite the bay, thinking they would find many Indians and pearls there for, according to its reputation, it had some of everything. There wasn't a single Indian to be seen anywhere on it, not a drop of water nor any other convenience to mankind; all was most barren, lacking wood, water, or anything good. For these reasons, they left that place and turned back toward Espíritu Santo Bay in order to take on water, wash clothing, and to rest withal, if a port should be found nearby, for the supplies were being damaged and expended without any return at all.

On Corpus Christi Day, the ships entered a roadstead where there was a pretty patch of reed grass in which they found a lot of fresh water. High mountainous ground stood about the roadstead and appeared as if it contained mineral deposits. The land was suitable for settling but there was no port; the ships anchored near the fresh water for that was mainly what they had been searching.

Tame Indians, although just a few, approached the Spaniards who gave them some presents then got underway, passing by sundry Indian *rancherías,* all poor and miserable like the rest they had seen, without finding any site with the accommodations desired for founding a settlement.

In this way, they sailed on to Cape San Lucas and into San Bernabé Bay. There, they found over four hundred people, all naked like the other Indians they had seen; without houses, and with no means of livelihood other than eating what they could get by hunting and fishing. In this bay, there was a great deal of fish of all sorts, including tunny like that in Spain. There was a reed grass patch containing fresh water and there was also some salt along the beaches, but they did not see anything else for human consumption. The Indians were very gentle and friendly; yet, according to the friar, as only riches were desired, it was decided to cruise northward from *ranchería* to *ranchería,* trading for what pearls there might be and looking for a suitable port; although already, they had been losing heart.

Everything had been done in reverse order from

what had been planned because practice was opposite to promise, according to Friar Juan. He said that, since the day they reached the Californias, it was desired first to look for pearls and gold mines in order to be able later to further God's cause through using these means.

"Seek first," says Christ, "the Kingdom of God for yourselves and for your neighbors and with this you will have everything at your command"; but all was done to the contrary and came out contrary to what was desired.

The good friar's account became repetitious, a rather dreary record of Lucenilla's efforts which bore fruit only in futility. He said that, as they cruised coastwise, they saw no signs of minerals because, by then, they were looking at the land with desires to get away from it; or, because what they saw were ranges along the seacoast and, obviously, there were never mines to be seen in such sites, least of all when searching from the decks of ships. Without doubt, according to him, those men believed that they were to find mountains of refined silver visible from the vessels.

They went ashore several times, both on the mainland and on all the islands nearby. On the islands, they found no water, firewood, or Indians. On the mainland, they got mostly so few and such inferior pearls that everyone became dispirited to such a degree that they began shouting, "Let's get away from this country or we'll stay here forever!"

On the mainland, opposite the island named Espíritu Santo, they found shelter for the ships, water, and firewood, and there were very wide trails which led into the interior. On account of this, the captain decided to go inland, taking Friar Juan Bautista and twenty soldiers along, to look at the country. Three leagues

inland, they found a handsome plain where they encountered a spring and some Indians, naked and
shelterless. The party travelled about eight leagues in
all, then returned, because the rest of the land appeared
to be bad hill country with scanty produce.

Here, it was decided very sorrowfully to run farther
along the coast toward the north to seek good fortune
and not to return soon to New Spain without prestige
as those with few obligations wanted to do. On Saints
Peter and Paul's Day, they arrived at "the best port
God has placed in His seas." As Friar Juan described
it, it was more than eighteen leagues in circuit; it had a
good bottom and was sheltered from all winds; and,
around it, there were many Indians who were "more
blonde" than those they had seen elsewhere on the cruise
and lighter in color than the Indians in New Spain.
There was fresh water in several places here; there
were good hill lands and plains in its environs; in short,
it would have been a good port in which to settle at the
beginning.

However, as they did not see any riches there, all
became despondent and began clamoring despicably
to go home. In view of this, a council was convened on
July 2 which decided that they return and give an unfavorable report about the land in California. So then,
they "turned back to New Spain, misguided and without honor."

Although it was intended to return to Chacala from
which they had sailed, winds and currents were so
contrary that, however hard they tried for many days,
they couldn't make any headway at all. The currents
carried them northward; some storms struck them so
severely that the *almiranta* lost all the mooring cables
and anchors or grapnels that she carried. As she was on

the point of shipwreck, they decided to beach her on the Sonora coast where some pagan Indians and some Christians called *Los Guaimas* came to her assistance. So, it was necessary for the *capitana* to go there also and thus ended the voyage, some twenty leagues north of Río de Loque.

Friar Juan said that this place in Sonora wasn't twelve leagues distant from California. From the beach, the California highlands were clearly visible and, because the two coasts were so close together, the hills and the valleys on either side appeared to be part of the same stretch of terrain. He noted also that the more one travelled northward, the closer the land in New Spain drew to California. When they crossed the Gulf, sailing from Mazatlán, they found eighty leagues of water in between; whereas, when they went from California to Sonora, there were no more than twelve leagues to cross. It could be, that more to the north, the two lands came together and thus would make conquest easier. "I believe it is that way," Friar Juan said.

All tried to get to the Christians' settlements; the laity went from there in order to find the means of livelihood; the clergy, in order to find means for returning to their ecclesiastical province in Mexico. The ones and the others felt like men beguiled – that voyage must have been a dream – for they had begun and ended the cruise in less than three months while two years had been spent in preparation for it.

Their misfortune soon became known everywhere.

And I bring to an end the true account of this tragic voyage and go on to write some of the causes of its failure. May they serve as a warning hereafter to those who may want to go to the Californias and may these try to remedy them.

THE PRINCIPAL CAUSES OF
THIS VOYAGE'S PERDITION

Friar Juan Cavallero Carranco thought that the first
and most important cause of their failure should be
ascribed to divine will; that the time it had set for the
California Indians' conversion had not arrived; or,
because of the Spaniards' sins, God was not motivated
to exercise His loving-kindness toward the Indians on
that occasion. At any rate, He didn't want this voyage
to succeed. The human causes as a whole, however,
were numerous and any one of them would have sufficed to spell failure.

Friar Juan said the business was very serious for it
was nothing less than to conquer, pacify, and convert a
vast realm like the Californias and other realms to
follow in turn. This was to be undertaken with such
puny force as were fifty men of the quality Friar Juan
would indicate later and with such little capital as the
six or eight thousand pesos which the captain had,
believing these assets sufficient for the task. Obviously,
this was either imprudence or insanity. The friar supported his point with the Biblical parable regarding
the man about to build a tower who should first consider the cost in order to be sure he had funds enough
to complete the job. He said that the captain built
castles in the air; fancied himself Lord of the Californias; and, everything turned out just as windy.

Captain Francisco de Lucenilla, according to Friar
Juan, was not a man capable of executing such an enterprise. He had no experience in seafaring matters nor
in serious business ashore and thus he did not succeed
in managing anything. He had no background in wars
or conquests, so he did not hit the mark in anything he
ordered. If, as the politicians say, ruling or governing

is the art of arts, how could Francisco de Lucenilla govern, being only a poor gentleman, a native of the town of Paradas, reared in abject poverty, with no management of serious affairs?

Lucenilla, according to Friar Juan, was so timorous that he feared both the great and the small. He bore himself in everything with no appearance of authority or self-esteem, so everyone depreciated him. He was irregular in command; disgruntled those whom he should have kept contented, the key men, and cherished those who didn't matter. For a long time, he would show fondness and consideration to some, then lose these friends in an instant by some very little thing, done without prudence or civility, and thus he did not have a firm friend. Worse yet, Friar Juan said that Lucenilla

> put himself in opposition to the church, or to its ministers, try-ing to discredit us, giving ear to gossip and talebearers. How could he have a good ending if, at the outset, he tried to affront God's ministers? How many a kingdom has been lost on account of this sin! He did not dare to punish anything, no matter how serious; and so, each day the soldiers lost respect for him and lost respect for us priests. Indeed a voyage must fail where there was no respect or obedience for our Lord and King's minister nor for the ministers of God.

As Lucenilla's capital was scanty, he embarked very few conveniences; little was available for the soldiers to wear and little to eat for all the food was reduced to maize and wormy dried meat. And, as the soldiers found themselves eating badly and dressed worse with no financial reward in sight, they became disgusted. The captain was partial to those who worked least and to these he showed favors, something which bred dis-satisfaction among the rest who noted that some did the work and others loafed.

Friar Juan said that Lucenilla was very grasping indeed, as everyone knew, so the men expected that if a lot of wealth were acquired, all would have to take their share in it by force. A rumor was afloat that he had spent over twenty-four thousand pesos on the voyage although, in reality, he had expended but little more than twelve thousand. It was believed that he intended to conceal the gains from the cruise, usurping the fifth due His Majesty and what was due the poor crew members for their labor.

The friar listed other accusations against the captain which included misuse of funds derived from goods consigned to him in Spain, neglect of his young wife and children there, failure to have his people eat fish on Fridays and other fast days, and his having placed obstacles against saying mass. He said also that the timber which went into Lucenilla's ships had belonged to some poor people in Compostela whose only recompense was harsh words and having the fruit in their orchards eaten by his men to whom, as the king's soldiers, all property appeared as if it were owned in common.

With respect to causes of failure due to the men embarked, Friar Juan said that the majority were useless people, failures in New Spain, who had joined the expedition just to be able to eat. Without exception, all who wanted to sign articles were accepted as soldiers, without verifying what each could do or without telling him what he was expected to do. Thus, most of them were useless; many were irresponsible people, indifferent to despicable failure of the expedition. There were many from Jerez who, because they were a numerous group, tried to gain control over the others and even the captain himself. The friar then noted,

parenthetically, that he was speaking thus about everyone except some in particular whom he would mention
later.

Friar Juan said that the useless people would start a
riot over a *tortilla;* they held meetings continually in
the forecastle, all to promote discord and grievances.
Among very few of them, could fear of God or respect
for His ministers be discernible. Either because they
were flaccid or unserviceable, most of them did not
want to work and thus disheartened those who were
willing to work. They came along only to look for
pearls and, as they saw very few, they became dismayed
and clamored, "Let's go! Let's go!" without a thought
to making a settlement.

In order to found a colony, according to the friar,
they looked for safe shelter for the ships, a good port
which also would have, within an arquebus shot, fresh
water, firewood, arable land, rich mines, pearl oyster
beds, and many Indians; and, if some of all this were
lacking, they would say it was a bad site. He admitted
that the California land was displeasing to the eye;
they arrived "in the rigors of summer"; and then, as
they didn't find riches or comforts and were tired from
so much work, they didn't want to stay.

Besides all this, Friar Juan said, the captain and the
pilots lacked experience in such cruises and did not
carry good cables, anchors, shrouds, or sails, and the
vessels consequently lacked proper equipment, a matter
which depressed the ships' companies very much. As
there was no one to advise the captain correctly, he
erred in what he did, doing nothing which didn't turn
out to be a blunder afterward. A fault much greater
than the captain's lack of understanding, however, was
that he listened to the worst opinions, disregarding

especially the advice of the friars who accompanied him.

These were causes why, in the friar's judgment, not only an expedition but also a kingdom should be lost; but, there were yet other faults, extremely serious, for the captain did not fulfill his contract with the viceroy nor heed what everyone in Mexico advised him to do. He was to carry supplies and munitions necessary at sea and on land; carrying also twenty horses in order to reconnoiter inland terrain; and, he was to leave a man in Chacala, provided with two thousand pesos in order to supply the ships quickly with additional subsistence and clothing. Above all, before he should go hunting pearls or mines, he was to land with all his personnel; fortify himself; proceed gradually to learn the local language; penetrate inland when the heat was least; and, only after this, to look for wealth.

According to Friar Juan, none of this was done — everything to the contrary. Sufficient munitions were not provided; not even one horse was brought; not a single peso was left in New Spain. The first effort was to find pearls without any attempt to found a settlement, and, as the crews did not see the means they desired, they got hot under the collar. There were no horses to ride inland; the local dialect was not learned; they saw that the captain did not have money enough to feed and clothe them; and, there was no material for repairing the ships.

Friar Juan said that, if one of their ships found itself with the sea abeam, its crew became disconsolate and began shouting, "Let's go home!", preferring ignominious failure of the expedition to exposing themselves to discomfort and danger. Accounts of conquests made by honest efforts did not suffice to reanimate them; it did no good to scold them or plead with them; and, finally, nothing sufficed to keep most of them from forming mobs and yelling, "Let's go back!"

SOMETHING ABOUT THE QUALITY OF THE PERSONS WHO CAME ON THIS CONQUEST OF THE CALIFORNIAS

Under this heading, Friar Juan Cavallero Cerranco began his analysis of the individuals who composed this expeditionary force. He prefaced his characterizations by observing that:

Undertakings aren't gained by a multitude of subjects unless they are as they should be. Usually, a few good men accomplish more than numbers of wretches; from this, few and wretched participated since those in the *capitana* were the following:

1. First, Captain Francisco de Lucenilla, native of the town, Paradas, Andalucía. As leader of a conquest, he'd make a good farmer — *bueno para labrador, y malo para esto.*

2. Esteban de Silva came as pilot. He was the son of a Portuguese, native of the town, Las Canarias. He was little pilot and much visionary, a man who always talked about gaining new worlds and never had a shirt to his back. He did very badly here for he was a major cause of discontent among the crew, running down the Californias and assuring all that their lives would be imperilled unless we turned back soon. He wanted some of his comrades to buy our ships for him so that he could sail them on discovery of new worlds and talked other nonsense.

3. Francisco Ramires, boatswain, native of Tiamonte. He came only to look for wealth; and, at the instant he saw there wasn't any, he clamored for turning back and stirred up the rabble so that all would clamor, "Let's go!" A man with a sour stomach, he could not be kept contented.

4. Joseph Fernandes, shipyard master, a Portuguese, as unruly as the most. He worked well in building the ships but he was so puffed up, he galled his companions. He wanted to dominate and order everyone around, wanting them to

take orders only from him, and committed many other excesses. When everything didn't go to suit him, he stirred up the rabble and caused a thousand headaches.

5. Domingo de la Rocha was a Portuguese, one of the best in every respect on land or sea. Very few like this man came along.

6. Pablo Fernandes de Córdoba, native of Murcia, was a silkweaver but had neither hands nor feet because of sickness. He had a long tongue; was widely read; and, always talked against the captain and the expedition and in favor of more contented common people.

7. Juan Bautista Escorza came as ensign of the voyage, a Biscayan gentleman of very good sense and intentions. The captain's conduct displeased him and his timidity in punishing evildoers fretted him. As he was very young, he committed some boyish pranks of little importance. He had a high reputation and great spirit. As he had been reared in ease, he couldn't work as was necessary on sea duty.

8. Juan Montero, a native of Paradas, was a man of little capacity, a moderate worker, and sick from the start.

9. Domingo Moreno, a native of Viruega, was a competent man, prominent in his country, who functioned well because he had health and repute.

10. Joseph de Arrones Navarro, reared in ease, he worked as much as he was able but always followed the malcontented.

11. Juan Sarmiento was a laborer boy, raised in the country, a native of Ronda, rustic in capacity, and thus was like a weathervane, now on the captain's side – now with the rabble, but he worked very well.

12. Juan de Acosta was a creole from Mexico City, of few years and less brains, very much a little rascal and shameless, who could work very well but, most of the time, didn't want to.

13. Don Antonio de Vedoia from Arazena, a well intentioned gentleman, impassioned on subjects of honor; but, as he was very old and could not work, he became a hindrance and an expense like all those who couldn't perform manual labor.

14. Luis de Flores, a native of Sevilla, very young, reared in ease, and wasn't made for work, although he did well as far as he was able because he had a good reputation to uphold.

15. Diego de Salazar, a creole from Aguacatan, Nueva Galicia, a young lad, good for little work and hard to stomach because he was too presumptuous, but he was not one of the worst.

16. Marcos de Valvas, a creole from Chimaltitan Real de Minas, well born, a good worker, good in everything and for all things.

17. Agustín Quijada, a creole from Mexico City, barbarian with a good disposition but worked little and let himself be led by the rabble.

18. Diego Hurtado, a native of Triana, an elderly man who wanted only to eat, not intended for these labors, yet did more than others much younger.

19. Francisco Vastos, from San Lúcar de Barrameda, little sense. He was a shoemaker and, as such, he didn't work as was necessary on this enterprise.

20. Sebastián López, a native of Baeza, couldn't work because he was sick and hadn't been raised to work, although he understood the science and other matters pertaining to the sea.

21. Don Fernando Ponce de León, from the city of Jerez de la Frontera, bad judgment, not raised to work and thus useless.

22. Don Baltasar de Medina, also from Jerez de la Frontera, good disposition but raised in ease and, for that reason, useless on this mission.

23. Martín Calderón, Jerez also, a barber evilly disposed for all he wanted was to stir up mutiny among the crew and be insolent to the captain and the priests. He spoke ill about everybody and, on another occasion, he persuaded the crew into mutiny against Don Bernardo Bernal [de Piñadero] and caused the voyage's perdition and he tried the same thing with these people. God deliver us from such an accursed man.

24. Andrés Peres, from the same city, a good worker, but became corrupted by his fellow-countrymen and thus he went wrong.

25. Don Juan de Ibarra, a creole from Guadalajara, little sense, but not the worst for these occasions.

26. Alonsillo, a boy, the captain's servant.

27. Juan de Gragalva, a *mestizo,* good worker, but already aged.

28. Juanillo, *mestizo,* an agile boy.

29. Damianillo, a mulatto from Guadalajara, good-for-nothing.

30. Alonso de Glaguotoca, not a bad boy.

31. Periquillo, a little Indian boy.

32, 33, 34.[26] Two lassies of the world, one an Indian and the other half-Spanish, little sense, although they didn't work badly at what was offered them.

These were the people who embarked in the *capitana.* Only God knows what I suffered from their unreasonable conduct and the continual strife among themselves and between them and the captain.

35. In the *almiranta,* embarked with my companion, was Captain Alonso Matheos who commanded that ship. He was from the city of Jerez de la Frontera, an elderly man of some experience and, with his bad temper, he offended the ship's company. He was concerned only with eating and drinking and speaking ill about priests; a bad man.

36. Juan Matheos, the other's nephew, most harum-scarum, and good for nothing except being rude to the others, taking advantage of the protection his relationship with the master afforded him.

37. Juan de Jerez, a lad of few years and little sense, but a good worker.

---

[26] The manuscript doesn't indicate definitely why there are three numbers here when only two individuals are mentioned. It may be conjectured that the third number referred to the general statement about all the *capitana's* personnel.

38. Rodrigo Camacho, from Jerez, a good man, well-meaning, and apt for everything.

39. Andrés Pérez, a native of Sevilla, very sickly, harum-scarum, of no use for anything.

40. Martín Delgado, an Andalusian, old and sick, little sense and very stubborn; worthless.

41. Juan Felipe, a creole from Guadalajara, a spirited lad and a worker.

42. Juan Núñez, from Sevilla, a lad, good worker ashore and afloat but with little sense; he followed the rabble.

43. Juan de León, from Sevilla, a first class carpenter with a bad disposition as he was too presumptuous; no good for this affair.

44. Juan de Anaia, from Mexico City, a druggist; meant for drugs – not for conquests.

45. Juan de Valenzuela, Sevillian, a humble lad but not meant for so much work.

46. Don Alonso Rogel, from Puerto de Santa María, a sick gentleman, unable to work at all.

47. Francisco García, a sorrowful pilot, a sick man with little sense but good at sea.

48. Francisco Martín, Sevillian, little capability but a good worker.

49. Agustín Maldonado, from Mexico City, a carpenter, not a bad worker.

50. Pedro de Salamanca, an Andalusian, a noble and presumptuous lad but not meant for so much work.

51. Agustín Guerra, an honest sailor and a great worker; in everything good and good for everything.

52, 53. Diego Porras, an Indian from Xala, a good worker who behaved like an honest man. He was married to Juana, an Indian woman, who helped very well afloat and ashore.

54. Gaspar de Pastrana, from Old Castille, was also embarked in the *capitana*. Worthless afloat and ashore, he always followed the mob.

So, as Friar Juan went on to say, these were the people who came to conquer the Californias; he would let the reader judge whether they were fit for the job where there were no friendly Indians or hired help to do so much work. Thus, it was not astonishing that the product of so many months' labor, at such great cost, could be lost so quickly. It was a case which called for many good, industrious men, so how was success to be won with so few and such inferior people? Along with many good men, much capital was demanded; not such scanty means as the captain had.

The friar said he confessed that some of them worked hard, and that some behaved like honest men; however, these were few; few were the workers; and, few were those of good repute. The sorry sort were numerous so, of necessity, failure was to prevail and the cause was to be lost. A few inferior people could never do anything important.

It was Friar Juan's conviction that only the king could conquer or convert the Californias. The main objective should be conversion of all the people there; although indeed, there might be wealth in pearls and metals as the sea and the land had indicated. His Majesty could overcome all such difficulties as encountered by the individuals who had gone there by taking many people and much livestock to be landed in various parts of that country, defraying expenses and supporting the colonists until the land should bear fruit, as had been done in the Philippines, New Mexico, Sonora, and other places. This was something private persons did not do because they spent a little then wanted to get a hundred in profit to one they had expended.

The friar believed also that the Californias should

be explored in the rainy season; if arrival there preceded the rains, exploration should wait until wet weather came on. The writer presumes that this measure would obviate concern over the general scarcity of water inland there, although he might also have had in mind the lesser prevalence of vermin during the rainy season. He said that horses should be available for exploring inland and the writer can certainly agree with him on that point. As for the Indians, no resistance at all was to be expected from them, he thought; yet, one might ask, what about such tribes as the Guaicuri?

As for inhabiting the country, Friar Juan recommended that only working people be chosen and that these should be in salaried status in order that, if they shouldn't see any quick return for their efforts, they wouldn't lose heart as they had done thitherto, because the pay would be a reward for their labor. Besides this, soldiers assigned to the conquest should be assured that His Majesty would reward their travail and heroic action, even if the land should not bear fruit, because none of them exerted himself unless there was a prize dangling before his eyes.

> God, in His loving-kindness, grant His Majesty rest and freedom from wars in order that he may use his patrimony in this affair of continuing conversions; for, the heathen in those parts not only do not resist us but receive us with pleasure, and regret that we do not stay in their lands as the case has been just now.

The friar said that, on this cruise, they probably sailed more than two hundred leagues coastwise from Cape San Lucas to the big port they named San Pedro y San Pablo, opposite Sonora. Along this part of the California coast, there were many inlets and some fair ports. There were some places with water and small trees; places with long stretches of plain which might be suitable for livestock and cultivation. The safe step upon beginning colonization, he thought, would be to take in everything necessary for life and to leave some-one in New Spain to replenish supplies until, by experiment, it was determined what produce and livestock could be raised in the Californias. All should go there persuaded that the first two years were to be spent only in converting souls, learning the language, and travelling over the country, crossing it from coast to coast. According to statements by those who knew something about cosmography, the distance across the country could not be very great because the coast on either side ran from southeast to northwest and thus, that land was long and narrow.

Friar Juan reverted to his Argonauts' specifications for a site suitable for a settlement. He said that the captain and the others had been looking for a very secure port which, along its shores, should have fresh water, groves, arable land, mines, pearl oyster beds, and many tame Indians; a combination, he said, which could not be found in the entire world. He might have said, possibly, that they were like the man who specified a Pegasus when he went to buy a horse. Ports, he thought, were usually incommodious and useful only as havens for ships; the other elements were to be sought inland. For example, the Sonora coast was worse than the California and more unsightly; yet, twenty leagues inland, there were riches and every other re-source – the same could be the case, perhaps, in the Californias. He again expressed the pious hope that the king would make this enterprise his personal con-cern because private individuals were sure to fail.

The friar thought the Californias had been praised too much for their riches; indeed so, by those who had never gone into the interior there. He pointed out many obvious flaws the land presented but did insist that there were a few sites fit for small initial occupation. One such was six leagues from Cape San Lucas – presumably eastward – and another was at the cape itself. The best of all, he insisted, was the last port they saw before they turned heels to the Californias. He repeated the praises he had bestowed earlier upon that place and stressed one feature which the Spaniards might have given very serious consideration; namely, it was only twelve leagues from the Sonora coast, a very short line of communication from a good supporting area. Possibly, the relative proximity to Sonora had some influence upon Kino's and Salvatierra's choice of Loreto.

According to Venegas, the port where Lucenilla's expedition ended was near the mouth of the Yaqui River;[27] if so, it could have been Guaymas. Be that as it may, the writer hasn't been able to find any part of the Gulf of California south of thirty-one degrees as narrow as twelve leagues, mainland to mainland. The stretch between Tiburón Island and Cape San Miguel measures less than that distance, but it would seem overly generous to consider that island part of the Sonora coast.

As for the paucity of pearls in the Gulf of California, Friar Juan's opinion was surprising, to say the least, in light of the abundance and quality of these gems which others found there as noted in this paper. He said that they obtained very few and very inferior pearls from the Indians. There were indeed many oysters but all the oysters did not contain pearls; he

[27] Venegas, *Noticia de la California,* vol. I, p. 158.

"certified" that he had seen many oysters opened and had never seen a pearl taken from any oyster at all. He must have forgotten that he had said earlier that they found some lackluster pearls in oysters they were eating in Mazatlán prior to starting across the gulf. At any rate, Friar Juan reached the conclusion that it was a great blunder to spend money on building and equipping ships just in order to seek pearls.

To the writer, it seems highly probable that no one among Lucenilla's crews knew anything about selecting pearl-bearing oysters; certainly, the friar did not mention any such qualification among his characterizations of those men while he did mention such as barber, carpenter, shoemaker, druggist and "two lassies of the world." One might suspect that Martín Calderón had learned something about pearl oysters while cruising with Piñadero; yet, according to Friar Juan, he was bent only toward slander and inciting to mutiny; "God deliver us from such an accursed man." The friar spoke only about trading for pearls; he never said anything about diving for them. With divers along, the latter part of his story might have been different, insofar as seeing a pearl extracted from an oyster was concerned.

There are three indications on which pearl fishers rely for detecting from the outward aspect of the shell the presence of pearls. These are, first, the thread, that is, the recess or elevation extending from the vertex to the edge; second, the kidney-shape of the shell, that is, an indentation on the ventral side; and third, the contortion of both shells toward the middle plane of the animal.[28]

Quite likely, the oysters the friar saw opened had been tonged haphazardly.

[28] George Frederick Kunz, *Gems and Precious Stones of North America*, p. 217.

Friar Juan insisted that, if "God's cause" were made the prime endeavor among those *gentiles* or pagan Indians, "His Majesty" would give as recompense many pearls and riches in this life and glory in the next [*sic*]. Those who went to the Californias primarily to seek wealth, however, were sure to fail because they would not find riches there. The Indians were extremely poverty-stricken – literally, they did not have a shirt to their backs – and there was no use in seeking gain among them for none could get rich even if every Indian there gave one everything he had.

> I conclude, saying again that no private person should attempt this conquest nor, least of all, poor men; because, all would end up ruined and lost as has been the case in more than twenty voyages which have been made. But, if our Lord and King, whom God preserve, should make it, I advise all to go and they will perform the greatest service to God imaginable, extracting from the Demon's power so many souls as there are in it.
>
> So then, I bring to an end this true account of the Unhappy Voyage to the Californias, and I solemnly declare that it is not my intention in this nor in other writings to say anything against the opinion of our Roman Catholic Mother Church. Finished in the Real de San Miguel, Sonora Province, on September 20, 1668.
>
> (Signed) Fr. Juan Cavallero Carranco

Ill feeling between Lucenilla and Friar Juan Cavallero must have developed prior to the beginning of December 1667 when Father Cristóbal Guerra came to join the expedition. One may recall that Friar Juan Bautista had been sent to the shipyard in Chacala while Friar Juan Cavallero was kept in Compostela. It appears reasonable to presume that Lucenilla did not consider it expedient to allow Friar Juan much contact with the bulk of the expeditionary personnel. Furthermore, it is likely that Lucenilla grasped at the first opportunity to get rid of Friar Juan; glad to accept one secular priest in exchange for two Franciscan friars just in order to keep Friar Juan on the beach.

It may be recalled also that on the one occasion when Lucenilla went exploring well into the interior, he selected Friar Juan Bautista from the *almiranta* to go with his patrol instead of Friar Juan who was conveniently at hand aboard the *capitana*.

Oh well – the cases in history are legion where expeditionary and other leaders have been at loggerheads with missionaries. However one's sympathies might be inclined, though, one must be grateful to Friar Juan for his having provided this rare document wherein reasons for an expedition's failure have been pinpointed so minutely. In fact, despite Friar Juan's aspersions against his captain, one might even be disposed to hoist the "well done" signal to Lucenilla for having gone as far as he went with such sorry personnel at his disposal.

And this episode among a sorry series spanning the sixteenth century is just part of Alta California's abandonment to the Indians until April 11, 1769 when, again a Spanish ship, the "San Antonio," dropped an anchor in San Diego Bay.[29] Although that bay's fine bottom had lain unfurrowed by anchor flukes for more than one hundred sixty-six years, it was again a maritime expedition which first provided the means whereby Spaniards, during two hundred twenty-seven years, had been enabled to gaze upon that beautiful harbor "where the mountains meet the sea."

Thus, the equivalents of millions of dollars which Cortés, Alvarado, Mendoza, and the Spanish govern-

---

29 James M. Keyes, *Las misiones españolas de California* (Madrid, 1950), p. 32.

ment had expended in early nautical exploration along the coasts of the Californias had not produced any direct dividends upon the investment. To be sure, Ulloa, Cabrillo, Cermeño, and Vizcaíno furnished increments to geographical knowledge, but Spain did not exploit these; she left Alta California to her aborigines. And, the ultimate effect of this abandonment may be seen in the last stage of this study in general conclusions to be drawn from the background herein provided.

XI

Conclusion

Looking back on history, over the reach of time, it seems strange that so little attention was paid by Spain to the rich lands lying northwest of Mexico. Perhaps Spain became so weakened internally that the spirit of adventure died away, and as for the explorers themselves they sought only treasures which they could load on their ships and haul away, to enrich themselves.

Yet California, bordering upon the same South Sea, was susceptible of incomparably greater exploitation than Mexico and Perú combined. Possibly Cortés' sea captain, Ulloa, touched and left its beaches, ignorant of its resources. Cortés' great rival, Antonio de Mendoza, sent out one of the great conquistadores, Juan Rodríguez Cabrillo, to cruise its coastline and he saw and reported, first of all, on that part of great Alta California.

Others, Gali, Cermeño, Unamuno, and Urdaneta, sighted or touched that California's headlands or beaches, sailing southerly, but none of these planted a permanent foothold upon its soil. Juan Sebastián Vizcaíno went plowing Cabrillo's old furrows sixty years after the conquistador had broken the way; Vizcaíno left a voluminous report behind but nothing solid in Alta California.

The Manila Galleon probably lumbered southerly along Alta California's coast after making its landfall

somewhere between Cape Blanco and Punta Concepción. It never sailed through the Golden Gate, however; it was always too anxious to pass its cargo through
the rustic gate into the annual Acapulco Fair.

Withal, nautical expeditions toward Alta California
were almost entirely Spanish American undertakings
by private enterprise. The only exception was Vizcaíno's 1602-1603 voyage which was financed by the
royal treasury. All had royal sanction, to be sure; none
would have dared openly to fare far abroad without
that license. Yet, while the crown invested nothing in
those voyages, it exacted much from prospective gains,
usually beginning with the *quinto real* or royal fifth.
From His Majesty's point of view, the arrangements
were literally a case of "heads, I win; tails, you lose."
If ever fraud in connection with a contract could be
condoned, one's sympathies would go to the impresario
who reduced the value of the royal fifth or evaded
paying it entirely.

Royal avarice also denied industrial development to
the colonies, and this, too, played its part in the failure
to appreciate the future of California. Only necessity –
or greed – brought about any exploitation of natural
resources of the New World, such as the use of indigenous timber for shipbuilding. It soon became evident
that Spain could not gain in the New World through a
home monopoly in ship construction while she produced no wood which could resist the ravenous little
marine borer, *broma,* which quickly made honeycombs
of European hulls.

Cabrillo went into the pine groves near Guaxalcingo
to make tar a substitute for pitch in caulking Cortés'
bergantines preparatory to his assault on Mexico City.
Rope, lines, shrouds, and hawsers were made from

nequén or *henequén* (sisal hemp, in English) and proved stronger than like cordage produced in Spain. Canvas, woven from cotton, gave excellent service in its manifold uses aboard ship from sails to sandals.[1] *Estopa de coco* or coir, proved better than hemp as a source of oakum for caulking the ships built along the Pacific Coast of Mexico and Central America. It was claimed to be "incorruptible as long as the sea bathed it."[2] Possibly, also its lightness commended it because even the heaviest coir hawsers will float.

Thus, it is seen that much of Spain's monopoly in seafaring materials was ineffective in the New World. One might wonder, withal, why iron was not produced locally also. That, always, was an important item, scarce and extremely expensive because of transportation costs and squeeze. The abundance of high grade iron ore in Venezuela must have kindled in some immigrant from Bilbao, Spain, speculation over the possibility of exploiting it. Still, the iron ore deposits in California have been exploited only during the last eleven years after nearly a century under the American flag.

In the last analysis, early Spanish nautical exploration along the coast of California had no measurable effect upon that land's ultimate destiny. Spanish failure to make a permanent settlement at Monterey Bay in 1606 did not invite incursions by foreigners any more than their settlements at San Diego in 1769 and at San Francisco in 1776 prevented the Russians from establishing Fort Ross in 1812.

Still, after 1769, inferior types of Stone Age people were no longer to rove untrammeled through one of

[1] Cappa, *Estudios críticos*, vol. x, p. 95.
[2] *Ibid.*, pp. 116-117.

earth's most remarkable and most variegated garden spots. Almost within a generation thenceforth, California's rich endowments were to begin appealing to yet another set of men; these unparalleled resources, then, kept calling to somewhat Nordic outsiders to come and give them what they so definitely deserved, their opportunity to support and maintain one of the most enterprising settlements the world had ever known.

Appendix

Appendix

JUAN RODRIGUEZ CABRILLO'S LEGACY

Although, as mentioned earlier, J. J. Markey has challenged Juan Rodríguez Cabrillo's right to remain established as the first European to sight Alta California's coast, he has not published evidence sufficient to supplant Cabrillo with Francisco de Ulloa. So, the writer will proceed to cast such additional light as he may upon this great man who, perhaps, has yet to receive the full meed his deeds deserve.

Alvaro del Portillo has said that, as a result of "the exacerbating of the patriotism of the Lusitanian historians," Cabrillo has received excessive fame as a discoverer, based upon his California expedition. In his footnote on the same page, that author listed "the most important" works in Cabrillo bibliography. There are six books in his list; three by American, three by Portuguese authors. It does not include any of Henry Raup Wagner's works. As for Cabrillo's other claims to fame, Portillo either was not aware of them or he deliberately ignored them. He said nothing about Cabrillo's services in the conquests of Mexico and Guatemala, his contribution in no mean measure to the seaworthiness of Cortés' bergantines, nor about his supervising the construction of Pedro de Alvarado's second armada.[1]

As Cabrillo's record unfolds, one cannot but regret that his background prior to 1520 is opaque. The writer has yet to find any data or even any reasonable conjectures as to the date or the place of his

---

[1] Portillo, *Descubrimientos y exploraciones en las costas de California,* pp. 154 *et seq.* In December 1955, the writer spent the better part of two days in the Portuguese National Archives, Torre do Tombo, and in the National Library, Lisbon. In the Torre do Tombo, an assistant librarian and two file clerks assisted the writer in searching for material relating to Cabrillo and Bartolomé Ferrelo (Ferrer or Ferrel) who, according to Celestino Soares, *California and the Portuguese,* p. 43, was Portuguese also. Not even the name of Cabrillo or Ferrelo could be found in the Torre do Tombo. In the National Library, only the works of Soares and E. Goulard da Costa, *Portugal descobridor: Apuntamientos respeitantes a descoberta de California,* could be found.

birth or his upbringing. To be sure, some statements, highly general-
ized, have been made about his place and date of birth. One writer,
Lummis, has said: "He was born in Portugal late in the 15th century; came to America a young man; had proved himself; and was
past fifty when he added to the world's knowledge."[2]

While lengthy *probanzas* of Cabrillo's merits and services have
been submitted and now form parts of trial proceedings in suits begun
before his death and continued for years thereafter, none of these
shows anything pertaining to his life before he entered Spain's service.
That he was experienced and expert in navigation is well emphasized,
but there is no hint at all as to how he became so.

Even his surnames have elicited conjecture. Soares said:

> The surname Cabrilho is not known in Portugal . . . it
> seems probable that Cabrilho was the surname of his Spanish
> mother, or a corruption of the surname Cabrilha, which still
> exists in Portugal.[3]

Alves de Azevedo implied that, in the conquest of Mexico, Cabrillo
changed his name to Juan Rodríguez de Villafuerte in order thus to
pass as a Spaniard; evade prejudices toward Portuguese; and, to gain
dispensations as a native Spaniard.[4]

Ample evidence shows conclusively that these Rodríguez were two
entirely different men. "Juan Rodríguez de Villafuerte, a native of
Cortés' home town of Medellín, came to New Spain with the
captain-general."[5] Juan Rodríguez Cabrillo, as noted earlier, went
to New Spain more than a year later with Pánfilo de Narváez. More
evidence than this could be cited but let it suffice that Villafuerte was

---

[2] Chas. F. Lummis, *In Memory of Juan Rodríguez Cabrillo Who Gave the
World California* (Chula Vista, Calif., 1913), pages not numbered but
correspond with pp. 3-4. Lummis did not state the source which provided him
this information. Possibly it was the same, or a similar source which, as
noted earlier, had informed him about the effect that the death of Doña
Beatriz de la Cueva had upon her husband, Pedro de Alvarado, who had
been dead more than two months when she was killed.

[3] Soares, *California and the Portuguese*, p. 39.

[4] Alves de Azevedo [which particular one of many such surnames was not
indicated], "Cabrilho e a sua viagem," *Boletim da Sociedade de Geografia
de Lisboa,* Julho e Agosto 1944, p. 519.

[5] Gardiner, *Naval Power in the Conquest of Mexico,* p. 139, citing Villafuerte's *probanza* of services.

a resident of Zacatula, Guerrero, as of March 11, 1528;[6] on March 18, 1528, the Cabildo, Santiago de Guatemala, acknowledged Cabrillo as a resident of that city.[7] He had been serving continuously in Central America since his original entry with Pedro de Alvarado in 1523.

With the question of Cabrillo's identity settled categorically, one may proceed to examine other features of his legacy. Let it be recalled from prior disclosures in this study that, on September 1, 1541, Cabrillo submitted a petition, *ad perpetuam rei memoriam,* in which he established certain claims for compensation for goods and services rendered to Pedro de Alvarado; also, that prior to departure on his epochal voyage, he entered suit for possession of the *encomiendas* Tacuba and Jumaitepeque which Alvarado had granted him.

The record shows that it set in slow motion a trial which was to last for years. The caption on the record, Ms, Justicia 280, no. 1, Audiencia de Guatemala, Año de 1543, AGI, states: "This suit began on June 6, 1542 and continued until December 22, 1550." While one's sympathy may go involuntarily to unfortunates, caught for so many years in legal trammels, one also may be grateful to law's ponderous proceedings for biographical and historical data which could not be found elsewhere.

The same record shows that, in Santiago de Guatemala, on December 6, 1543, more than eleven months after Cabrillo's death, his widow, Beatriz Sánchez de Ortega, gave full power of attorney to Juan García de Madrid to safeguard her interests and those of her two minor sons by Juan Rodríguez Cabrillo, Juan and Diego.

. . . and because she said she couldn't sign her name, one of the witnesses to this letter, who are Juan Maldonado and Luys López, being in the said city, signed it in the register.

(Signed) Juan Maldonado

Together with this power of attorney, she delivered to Juan Pérez de Ardón, *alcalde ordinario* or, possibly, justice of the peace, Santiago de Guatemala, the proof, *ad perpetuam rei memoriam,* which has been cited herein.

---

[6] A. Millares Carlo and J. I. Mantecón, *Indice y extractos de los Protocolos del Archivo de Notarías de México, D.F.* (México, 1945), vol. I, p. 256, no. 1155.

[7] *Libro viejo,* vol. XII, p. 32.

Most of Cabrillo's services as established by this trial have been mentioned already. The purpose to be achieved by proving them in court was to show that his heirs were entitled to all the favors and privileges which the emperor had decided to be the lot of those whose services had brought New Spain into his realms. It is regretted, withal, that more of Cabrillo's background should not have been considered germane to the issue; perhaps, however, ink, quills, paper, and scribes were, relatively, just as expensive then as now.

The encomiendas for which Cabrillo had initiated this suit stemmed, of course, from the *repartimiento* or parcelling out lands and inhabitants thereon to the conquerors. This practice, the writer believes, was mainly to transfer Spain's feudal system, the only social organization the invaders knew, to the New World. He believes, furthermore, that as far as New Spain was concerned, the situation there was made to order for the Spaniards because that land also was definitely feudal. All resolved itself simply into the Spaniards' occupying by military force the upper strata of a society already divided into horizontal layers. That this, at least, entailed serfdom cannot be doubted.

While the Spanish crown was opposed to enslaving Indians; while it insisted that these were its subjects on the same footing with Spanish-born citizens; while the crown, at one time, even went so far as to order encomiendas abolished in New Spain; yet, despite all this, the emperor had to take a realistic view of the situation and temporize with the encomenderos as he became convinced that, without encomiendas, the new realm could not be populated by Spaniards. And why should this have been the case? Perhaps it was due to what was, possibly, one of the most fundamental Spanish characteristics. Speaking of Spain, it has been said that

no other European country so stigmatized manual labor, which was not accorded legal dignity until the reign of Charles III in the eighteenth century, in the course of the invasion of rationalist ideas from foreign lands, an invasion which affected only the epidermis of Spanish life. . .

"No sooner has a merchant or a worker or a peasant enough to buy a government pension worth 500 ducats a year than he buys with this income a pension for his eldest son, whereupon not only this son but all his brothers become ashamed to occupy themselves at the humble tasks with which that money was originally earned," for "those who are not nobles aspire to make themselves nobles, and those who are aspire to rise to higher places still." [8]

This author proceeded thence – where, apparently, he had been quoting in part from Pedro Fernández de Navarrete, *Conservación de monarquías* – to illustrate an effect of this characteristic under certain conditions abroad.

> . . . When the Spaniards got to the Indies, they implanted and perpetuated their way of life there. In 1590 the inhabitants of Buenos Aires wrote to Philip II in desperation, complaining of the poverty of the Argentine land (which for the English Puritans would have been a paradise), because it is not the land which makes the man but the reverse, even though the importance of natural conditions and the historical moment are not to be denied. In Argentina there was no gold or silver, nor were there native cities, as there were in Mexico and Peru, and the Spaniard, incapable of creating things, did not know what to do: "We are so poor and needy that we could not be more in want, in proof of which, *we do our plowing and digging with our hands.* . . The people wait on themselves as if it were the tiniest village in Spain."

While the writer does not agree at all with Castro relative to the Spaniard's incapability of creating things, he must admit that the Spanish aristocrat, or would-be aristocrat, seemed to believe that a fulsome life, without having to work, was his inherent due. This becomes all too manifest as the court records unfold; *hidalgos,* or aristocrats, definitely deserved fat encomiendas.

Now, as the lawsuits develop the fact that a number of encomiendas had been granted Cabrillo, Senior, it seems manifest that Pedro de Alvarado was by no means entirely inconsiderate of his followers. He has been portrayed, however, as having made his grants with such utter recklessness as practically to grant nothing at all. Helps appeared convinced that Alvarado was prodigally careless in designating the encomiendas he granted in Nicaragua where, one may recall, Cabrillo, Senior, was given Teota é Cotela. Helps seemed to base his

---

[8] Américo Castro, *The Structure of Spanish History,* trans. by Edmund L. King (Princeton, 1954), pp. 630-631.

belief mainly upon a letter which Francisco de Montejo wrote the emperor on June 1, 1539, Ms, Colección Muñoz, tomo 81, which he quoted in a footnote:

> He gave a province to one person, and he distributed all of the towns and farms in it to others; and to another he gave a town by three or four names to three and to four persons, and to others he gave hills and mountain ranges and rivers in allotments of territory.[9]

While Montejo most probably viewed everything Alvarado did with a jaundiced eye on account of rivalry with him and animosity toward him, some fire did smolder beneath this smoke. For example, on May 6, 1530, Gonzalo Ortiz, a procurator, requested the town council of Guatemala City to ask Don Pedro de Alvarado to make a new and general distribution of territory. He pointed out that, during the previous six years, many captains had been there who conquered "piecemeal" with pieces rebelling sometimes and having to be conquered anew. Alvarado and his captains had made many temporary grants, not knowing what they were giving, because it was notorious that there were three and four deeds to one town and likewise for many others. For this reason, many lawsuits and contentions sprang up every day which put the residents to great expense and mutual vexations. The worst of it was that those who had issued the grants knew only from the Indians' accounts what provinces and towns existed. As the Indians were "evil and untruthful," it appeared that they were never accurate, according to Ortiz. Alvarado agreed to all this and promised to travel over his bailiwick and to make an entirely new and equitable distribution of lands as soon as possible.[10]

While some question regarding multiple ownership did rise in the suit now under consideration, the principal factor as one may recall was that Francisco de la Cueva, acting governor of Guatemala, "jumped" Cabrillo, Senior's, claim to the last two encomiendas Alvarado had given his admiral. If either Cabrillo or Alvarado had lived a few years longer, it is very doubtful that Cueva could or would have persisted in his stand. At least in one competent opinion of him, he was not quite the sort to stand long against a strong character like that of either of the two conquistadores.

---

[9] Arthur Helps, *The Spanish Conquest in America* (London, 1855-1861), vol. III, pp. 339-340.

[10] *Libro viejo*, pp. 115. *et seq.*

According to Bishop Marroquín, Francisco de la Cueva had not been the most desirable candidate to succeed Pedro de Alvarado in the governorship of Guatemala even if Pedro had made him governor *pro tempore*. The bishop said that Cueva was a youth in both age and works; he was not careful in administering justice; did not set a notable example; and, in nothing, was he a friend of good men.

Bishop Marroquín expressed misgivings as to the state of affairs in Guatemala, fearing uprisings, and recommended that the governorship be given to Juan de Alvarado, Pedro's nephew. Juan was the son of one of Pedro's brothers who had died in the conquest of Tierra Firme and Pedro had brought the youth to New Spain when he returned from the homeland in 1530. Juan, thenceforth, had followed the uncle in all of his expeditions, acquitting himself so well that, when Pedro put to sea with his armada, Juan went as "colonel (as a person in whom the governor confided most)." [11]

The cabildo apparently shared the bishop's opinion of Cueva for, as soon as they learned of Alvarado's death, they elected Doña Beatriz, his widow, as governor of Guatemala. She accepted the appointment, then appointed Cueva, her brother, lieutenant governor. It seemed difficult to get rid of Cueva but, after the death of Doña Beatriz, the cabildo ameliorated the situation by electing Bishop Marroquín co-governor with him. Finally, the viceroy of New Spain took a hand in the situation and appointed a member of the Audiencia of Mexico, Alonso de Maldonado, governor of Guatemala, pending instructions from the crown.[12]

At the outset of this trial, apparently, the complainants had to prove that Juan Rodríguez Cabrillo was in fact, dead, for the witnesses were asked if an accurate report had not arrived in Santiago a few days previously, stating that he had died while on his discovery voyage. This was substantiated and, if it is assumed that a month elapsed between arrival of Cabrillo's ships at La Navidad and the time the report of his death reached Santiago, this testimony was probably given about mid-May 1543.

Proof seemed to be required, too, that Doña Beatriz Sánchez de Ortega had been Cabrillo's lawful wife. While, as noted earlier, they were married in Spain, and this was duly proved, it is most regrettable

---

[11] Letter, Bishop Marroquín to emperor, Ciudad-Real de Chiapa, August 10, 1541. Letter, Bishop Marroquín and officials to emperor, Santiago de Guatemala, November 25, 1541. In *Cartas de Indias*, pp. 429-431, 432-433.

[12] Bancroft, *History of Central America*, vol. II, pp. 312-313; 323.

that the exact date, the place, and the name of the church were omitted. These items would have been a boon to California historians of the nineteenth and twentieth centuries. If Doña Beatriz had taken the stand in her own behalf and related the events leading into their marriage, she might have provided clues to much which yet remains obscure in the explorer's background.

As to the legitimacy of Juan Rodríguez Cabrillo, Junior, there was ample affirmative evidence, although some could not say whether he was the oldest son. Bernal Díaz del Castillo helped on this point as did also Bishop Marroquín, Francisco López, and Pedro de Ovide.[13]

In folios 17v. and 18 of this manuscript, the fifth question dwelt upon Cabrillo's services in Mexico and Guatemala where he did everything expected of a conqueror and, in so doing, had been required to spend a great sum of money. Diego Holguín, as one of Cabrillo's comrades, confirmed this and, with respect to the expenses incurred, he said that all of them spent whatever they owned because a horse cost six hundred pesos and more and supplies and other things they required sold at very high prices. His Majesty gave them no pay whatever; so, for this reason, it appeared to this witness that Cabrillo could not have failed to spend very copiously like the rest. Juan de Espinar testified likewise, adding that neither the emperor nor their captains gave them anything. The remaining witnesses spoke to like effect, although Bernal Díaz del Castillo and Pedro de Ovide could not confirm the matter of great expense with direct reference to Cabrillo.

Two features of this practice seem highly noteworthy at this time: one is the obvious transfer of ancient feudal exactions to the New World whereby vassals, according to their quality, were to furnish arms and military services to their overlords; the other is the inescapable need to extract compensation or reward from the conquered. From this, the so-called rapacity of the conquistadores stemmed as an inevitable sequel; the encomienda or allotment of native settlements, services, and tribute, was the only means at hand to support hidalgos, or persons of quality, in a manner befitting their status; that is, without having to work. Such will be further illustrated in later pages.

As to Cabrillo's highly important part in the development and operation of Alvarado's armada, ample affirmative evidence was adduced in subsequent folios. Then, in addition to showing that he

---

13 Ms, Justicia 286, fols. 17-17v., AGI.

was legally entitled to the towns, Tacuba and Jumaitepeque, and that he had rendered value received for them, they attempted to prove that Francisco de la Cueva lacked authority to preempt them.

So far, so good, apparently; yet, to current thinking, the Cabrillo party appeared to weaken its case by what might be termed emotional appeal. They attempted to show that Cueva drew a salary of six thousand pesos per annum from the royal treasury. As to the rental the two towns in litigation paid, the evidence was rather indeterminate; the motive seemed to be to show that Cueva had ample means already; that to preempt Cabrillo's grant was sheer greed.

Next, Cabrillo's party established Cueva's length of residence in Guatemala, manifestly to show him as an upstart in comparison with the conquistadores. They proved that he arrived in company with Pedro de Alvarado when the latter returned to the governorship from his last trip to Spain which, as noted already, was in April 1539.

The plaintiffs returned to Cueva's financial status, trying to prove that, since his arrival in Guatemala, he had held the town of Zacatepeque in encomienda in His Majesty's name. This, they alleged, was one of the best allotments in the province; that it paid a rental of four thousand pesos a year. The witnesses in general agreed that it was one of the best encomiendas in the country but they either didn't know at all or knew only by hearsay how much tribute it paid. Juan de Espinar had seen its assessment from which he estimated its capacity to pay annually about two thousand castellanos. Garçi López and Bishop Marroquín testified, in effect, that it came to Francisco de la Cueva through his marriage to Alvarardo's daughter, Leonor.

That Cueva had a side to present was, of course, to be taken for granted. Bishop Marroquín's opinion that Cueva was careless in legal matters appeared justified by the *probanza* he submitted for, apparently, he did not learn beforehand just what all of his witnesses could or would testify. First, was the usual question as to the witnesses' acquaintance with the parties to the trial, but Cueva asked also whether they had any knowledge about the towns, Jumaitepeque, Xicalapa, Aguacatlan, Comitlango, and Xocotenango. If so, the next question to be asked was if they knew that Xocotenango and Aguacatlan formed one encomienda, which one Diego Sánchez de Ortega had owned for a long time prior to and up to his death, and, that Xicalapa and Comitlango were another encomienda which Juan Rodríguez Cabrillo had owned and that both now belonged to Juan Rodríguez, his son. This, incidentally, indicated much more generosity to Cabrillo on Alvarado's part than Cabrillo's statement of his services to the governor have manifested. Perhaps one may assume safely that Alvarado considered Cabrillo so important in connection with his seafaring plans that no favors should be spared in retaining his services.

Substantiation of these points by Cueva was not apparent, however, for the testimony by one of his witnesses, Pedro de Ovide, was inconclusive. Another of his witnesses, Pedro de Losa, stated that he knew only that Cabrillo had owned Xicalapa.

In the third question, Francisco de la Cueva tried to establish the point that Alvarado's grant of Tacuba and Jumaitepeque was made in Colima, more than two hundred leagues away, and, therefore, was beyond the jurisdiction of Guatemala. He tried to show, also, that Alvarado made the grant because of the request and importunings of Bishop Marroquín and others who told him that Don Francisco had given these towns to one Juan de Ortega; and, if the governor had known Cueva was holding them, he would not have given them to Cabrillo.

Pedro de Ovide said that he deferred to the encomienda deed. Pedro de Losa, however, testified that he was in Colima while Viceroy Mendoza and Alvarado were there. The bishop and others told the governor that one Marmol, the former encomendero, was dead and that Cueva had given the towns to Juan de Ortega, his armorer. Alvarado became angry at this and said that His Majesty did not want an official to have Indians and, for this reason, he gave the towns to Cabrillo.

Juan de Ortega said he was the Ortega in question; that Cueva did not give him either of the towns but kept them for himself until the audiencia took Tacuba from Cueva and granted Jumaitepeque to Cueva. Martín Díaz had heard that the cédulas were issued in Colima; also, he had seen them and noted that they were written in La Navidad. It seemed to him that Alvarado would not have issued them to Cabrillo if he had known Cueva was keeping the towns, in view of the latter's necessities. Bishop Marroquín knew only that Alvarado had issued the cédulas in La Navidad because he was there with the governor. He did not refer to the accusation in reference to Juan de Ortega.

In folios 27 and 27v., Cueva's fourth question indicated some elements of complication which may be very well one of the reasons why sixteenth century lawsuits seemed interminable. He asked if the encomienda which he gave himself had become vacant or available at the death of Sebastián Mármol who had previously possessed the towns; if Cueva thenceforth had received their rental until "the president and members of the Royal Audiencia of the Boundaries which resides in this city" took them, declaring them vacant; then, gave him Jumaitepeque while giving Tacuba to Pero González Nájara and Juan Resino; and, that the two Juan Rodríguez never had held nor possessed these two towns.

Pedro de Ovide merely deferred to the cédulas and the pertinent judicial acts, saying that all the "question says" may be seen therein. Pedro de Losa confirmed all the allegations and Martín Díaz did likewise, adding that he was the agent who took possession in Cueva's behalf.

The highly important element of high family quality or *hidalguía* was introduced next. While to current thinking this might have been obvious since it had been proved that Cueva was governor *pro tempore* of Guatemala, the defendant possibly wanted to draw an invidious comparison between himself and young Cabrillo. At any rate, Cueva's aristocracy was established, Martín Díaz testifying that he had known the defendant's parents and relatives. With folio 28, the invidious comparison came into the open. De la Cueva established his status as married to Doña Leonor, daughter of Pedro de Alvarado, who had served His Majesty many years, and gloriously, and had died in his royal service. By Doña Leonor, the defendant had five legitimate children – Juan Rodríguez was a minor in age and unmarried. Bishop Marroquín knew that Francisco de la Cueva and Leonor de Alvarado were married because he performed the ceremony.

The next point, no doubt, had moral effect; Cueva's administration of Jumaitepeque benefited Guatemala City. He showed that he had a farm within Jumaitepeque's limits where he raised livestock and grew a great deal of wheat. The city provided itself with this wheat and received great benefit therefrom. In order that the city dwellers shouldn't lose this boon, the audiencia gave Don Francisco Jumaitepeque in encomienda.

Pedro de Ovide knew Cueva raised livestock and planted wheat and corn there but nothing about the rest of the question. Pedro de Losa confirmed everything except the reason for the Audiencia's action. Juan de Ortega testified likewise but Martín Díaz confirmed all the allegations as Bishop Marroquín did also. Oddly enough, nothing was said with regard to the conditions under which the produce was provided the city; whether gratis or at what prices, high or low.

Cueva's *probanza* developed an odd contradiction on his part with respect to authority to award encomiendas. He did not question Alvarado's authority to grant Tacuba and Jumaitepeque to Cabrillo; rather, he tried to prove that his father-in-law had done so because others had misrepresented the facts in the situation, much as heirs to an estate might bring suit to show that improper or unethical influence had been exercised upon the testator to favor a certain heir unduly. Yet, when he showed that the Audiencia of the Boundaries had taken Tacuba from him but granted him Jumaitepeque, he acquiesced in a step directly opposed to his assumed right as acting governor to grant himself this encomienda. Certainly, Bishop Marroquín was correct; Francisco de la Cueva was careless in legal matters.

At any rate, Don Francisco lost the first round for Licentiate Maldonado found in favor of Beatriz Sánchez de Ortega, widow of Juan Rodríguez Cabrillo, and Juan Rodríguez Cabrillo, Junior. The defendant appealed to the Real y Supremo Consejo de Indias who, on May 27, 1560, reversed Judge Maldonado's finding. The Cabrillo plaintiffs appealed to the same body but these, on December 12, 1568, sustained their finding of about eight years previously.[14]

So much for this suit – another was already in the making. In Ms, Justicia 290, AGI, the frontispiece reads:

Guathemala. Año de 1563.

Juan Rodríguez Cabrillo, vecino de la Ciudad de Santiago de Guathemala, *con* el Fiscal de S.M. *sobre* los yndios de los Pueblos de Coban, y Acotenango.

Relator Vaños   Secretario Luyando

Thus, the younger Cabrillo, a resident of Santiago de Guatemala, was suing the crown, represented by His Majesty's attorney, over the Indians in the towns Coban and Acotenango, with Relator Vaños and Secretary Luyando keeping the record of proceedings, twenty years or more after Juan Rodríguez Cabrillo's death. He had ready proof that Pedro de Alvarado had granted his father this encomienda because he held the deed thereto dated March 31, 1540. A copy of

---

[14] Ms, Justicia 286, no. 4, ramo 2, Audiencia de Guatemala, AGI.

this cédula, authenticated by Juan de Camano, appears on folio 7 of the manuscript cited above.

In folios 49 *et seq.*, young Cabrillo established the contention that Dominican friars had moved into Coban before he could succeed in possession of it and, as a result, the Cabrillo heirs, since then, had not received any income whatever from that encomienda. This, together with the loss of income from Tacuba and Jumaitepeque, had reduced the family to straits of poverty. He was married "with Doña Ysabel Aldana, a person of much quality," by whom he had three children, and all suffered from great need and penury because "the Indians I now possess do not provide me enough to sustain my house and family six months in the year." An impossible situation for an hidalgo, but more of that later.

On April 4, 1566, the Audiencia de Guatemala found in young Cabrillo's favor. The crown attorney, Licentiate Gerónimo de Ulloa, appealed, however, to the Council of the Indies and the venue was changed to Spain. Here, the crown attorney seized upon a point which, possibly, had not weighed heavily with the audiencia. There, the crown had proved that an agreement was made in 1537 between Alonso Maldonado, acting governor of Guatemala, and the Bishop of Chiapa, Friar Bartolomé de las Casas, whereby the Bishop and the friars of his order would "reduce" the allegedly rebelling Indians in Coban to the service of Our Lord God and His Majesty. When this should have been accomplished, Maldonado promised on the crown's part that these Indians would never be given to any Spaniard in encomienda.

Perhaps the audiencia considered Maldonado's agreement superseded by Alvarado's cédula of March 31, 1540, or, as the plaintiff claimed, that this deed merely replaced a joint cédula issued many years previously to Juan Rodríguez Cabrillo, deceased, and to Diego Sánchez de Ortega, his brother-in-law. That is to say, Alvarado merely issued a new deed in 1540, after Ortega's death, in order to confirm Cabrillo as sole owner.

Perhaps the audiencia, too, gave full credence to the testimony of Francisco de Castellanos, "thesorero en la probinçia de guatimala" – treasurer of the province of Guatemala. He had seen the agreement between Maldonado and the bishop and knew at the time that Coban had been at peace since 1529 when he had conquered it. He couldn't recall the date when Alvarado gave it jointly to Cabrillo and Diego

Sánchez de Ortega but he knew that both received its tributes a long time and that this encomienda remained in Cabrillo's possession after Ortega's death.

He knew that Cabrillo and Ortega had enjoyed the Coban Indians' tributes because he had personally seen those Indians serving them and delivering produce to them. Also, he had seen them bringing supplies to the slaves who were working Cabrillo's and Ortega's mines along the Uzpantlan and Tequiçiztlan Rivers. How many parts of a man was this Cabrillo?

Furthermore, he said, the land called Vera Paz was formerly Teculutlan; Coban was nearby but a land apart, not subject to Vera Paz, and it served its masters peacefully from "twenty and nine" onward. The Coban Indians even spoke a different tongue from those in Vera Paz. Other witnesses testified to like effect in general. What seems most damning to Bartolomé de las Casas and his cohorts, however, was the testimony which Gonzalo Ortiz gave. He testified that when Juan Rodríguez, deceased, left to serve His Majesty in Alvarado's armada, leading up to his death, and, because of his absence, the "frailes de la horden de santo domingo" – the friars of the Order of St. Dominic – intruded into Coban and other towns, without exercising any moderation or self-restraint [*sin ylles a la mano*], and today have them, possess, and enjoy them. From their assumption onward, Cabrillo's heirs had not received any benefit from the Indians in Coban.

In the appeal trial, however, the crown tried to controvert this testimony despite the apparent weight of evidence in the plaintiff's behalf. The crown asked also, if, in Guatemala and other parts of the Indies, a matter "public and notorious" was, that no one could have two encomiendas and that, if Cabrillo were given Coban, he would have two repartimientos; "let the witnesses say what they know believe and understand." Of course, the crown had a technical point there, yet, the law it invoked had been honored in the breach to such an extent throughout the Indies, that custom had long since taken precedence over the letter of the law.

Perhaps with the Council of the Indies, however, Friar Bartolomé de las Casas, Bishop of Chiapa and Apostle of the Indians, really turned the scales against young Cabrillo. He testified under oath that he and the Bishop of Vera Paz, Friar Pedro de Angulo, "reduced and attracted" to the service of God and His Majesty the town of Coban in question, which, at the time, was in a state of open rebellion.

It was in the "kidney of the Bishopric of Vera Paz," he said, one of the most "principal towns of that province" and had been chosen as seat of the cathedral church of said bishopric. He testified further that Coban had always been and was still a crown possession and had never belonged to a subject nor paid any tribute whatever unless it were to royal officials in His Majesty's name. All this, he said, was common knowledge, very "public and notorious," among all who had any information concerning that country.[15]

After one has read the testimony recorded for both parties to this suit, one cannot escape a grave suspicion that this Most Reverend Bishop perjured himself.

At any rate, the crown won; Cabrillo was sentenced to "perpetual silence"; but, he didn't keep silent long. On May 23, 1567, he petitioned the king, asking that the council's sentence be set aside and that the audiencia's finding be confirmed. He insisted that the weight of evidence rested upon his pan in the scales; that injustice had been committed against him; and, that all the rental from Coban be paid to him from the date his father had been despoiled of that encomienda. He insisted that the evidence submitted by both parties proved that Coban had never been in rebellion but, on the contrary, had facilitated penetration into Vera Paz in order to subdue that area.[16]

Apparently, Bartolomé de las Casas' credibility did not rank very high; perhaps, too, the council suffered a twinge of conscience for they remitted the costs. This really meant something in those days because all plaintiffs had to post fifteen hundred *doblas* prior to trial, a sum probably equivalent to about fifty-four hundred dollars today, to be forfeited to the crown if they lost their case.[17] The council went on to say that they had consulted His Majesty and, considering the services of Juan Rodríguez Cabrillo, the elder, the monarch graciously awarded the son three hundred *pesos de minas* annually for the rest of his life. This sum was to be paid him from the first Guatemalan encomienda which should become vacant.[18] Thus, some measure of justice was rendered the great explorer's heirs.

This, of course, did not cost the King anything for those pesos were to come from tribute already imposed upon Indians for the benefit of another citizen of Guatemala. All the younger Cabrillo

[15] Ms, Justicia 290, fol. 125, AGI.
[16] *Ibid.*, fols. 142 *et seq.*
[17] Schoenrich, *The Legacy of Columbus*, vol. I, p. 345.
[18] Ms, Justicia 290, fols. 142 *et seq.*, AGI.

had to do was to wait until some other encomendero should die without legitimate issue or until some other should pass away who had been granted a like encomienda for his lifetime only. Possibly, in the meantime, the Cabrillo heir could support his wife and children, "and his brothers and his sisters and his cousins and his aunts" on the fifty-four hundred dollars forfeit His Majesty had forgiven him.

Bibliography

Bibliography

Aiton, Arthur Scott. Antonio de Mendoza First Viceroy of New Spain. Durham, N.C: Duke University Press, 1927

Alcedo, Antonio de. Diccionario geográfico de las Indias Occidentales o América. Madrid: Benito Cano, 1786

Alves de Azevedo. "Cabrilho e a sua viagem." In Boletim da Sociedade de Geografia de Lisboa. Julho e Agosto, 1944

Anónimo, El Conquistador. Relación de algunas cosas de la Nueva España, y de la gran ciudad de Temestitlán, México. Mexico City: Editorial América, 1941

Artíñano y de Galdácano, Gervasio de. La Arquitectura Naval Española (en madera): Bosquejo de sus condiciones y rasgos de su evolución. Barcelona: Oliva de Vilanova, 1920

Ballester, Rafael. Curso de historia de España. Fourth edition. Barcelona: Talleres Gráficos de la S.G. de P., S.A., 1929

Ballesteros y Beretta, Antonio (editor). Historia de América y de los pueblos americanos. Madrid and elsewhere: Salvat Editores, S.A., 1954. Vol. VII

Bancroft, Hubert Howe. The Works of. San Francisco: A. L. Bancroft and Company, 1882-1887:
VI-VII: History of Central America. Vols. I, II
IX: History of Mexico. Vols. I, II
XV: History of the North Mexican States. Vol. I
XVIII: History of California. Vol. I

Benzoni, Girolamo. La Historia del Mondo Nuouo. Venice: Heirs of Giovan Maria Bonelli, 1572

Beristain de Souza, José Mariano. Biblioteca hispano-americano septentrional. Mexico City: No publisher named, 1816

Biblioteca "Goathemala" de la Sociedad de Geografía e Historia. Libro viejo de la fundación de Guatemala y papeles relativos a D. Pedro de Alvarado. Guatemala: Tipografía Nacional, 1934. Vol. XII

Bolton, Herbert E. Coronado, Knight of Pueblos and Plains. Albuquerque: University of New Mexico Press, 1949
——. Spanish Explorations in the Southwest, 1542-1706. New York: Charles Scribner's Sons, 1925.
Brebner, John Bartlet. The Explorers of North America, 1492-1806. Garden City, N.Y: Doubleday & Company, 1955
Brown, Lloyd A. The Story of Maps. Boston: Little, Brown and Company, 1949
Cappa, Ricardo. Estudios críticos acerca de la dominación española en América. Madrid: Librería católica de Gregorio del Amo, editor, 1894. Vols. x-xii
Carrasco y Guisasola, Franco. Documentos referentes al reconocimiento de las costas de las Californias desde el cabo de San Lucas al de Mendocino recopilados en el Archivo de Indias en los años 1584 a 1602. Madrid: Dirección de Hidrografía, 1882
Casas, Bartolomé de las. Historia de las Indias. Edición de Agustín Millares Carlo y estudio preliminar de Lewis Hanke. México: Gráfica Panamericana, 1951. Vol. I
Castro, Américo. The Structure of Spanish History. Translation by Edmund L. King. Princeton: Princeton University Press, 1954
Castro, Rodolfo Baron. Pedro de Alvarado. Madrid: Ediciones Atlas, 1943
Caughey, John Walton. California. New York: Prentice-Hall, Inc., 1950
Cervantes de Salazar, Francisco. Crónica de la Nueva España. Madrid: Hispanic Society of America, 1914.
Chamberlain, Robert S. The Conquest and Colonization of Honduras, 1502-1550. Washington: Carnegie Institution, 1953
Chapman, Charles E. A History of California: The Spanish Period. New York: The Macmillan Company, 1951
Clavijero, Francisco Javier. Historia de la Antigua o Baja California. Translated from Italian by Nicolás García de San Vicente. Méjico: Juan R. Navarro, 1852
Collis, Maurice. Cortés and Montezuma. New York: Harcourt, Brace and Company, 1955
Cortés, Hernán. Cartas de relación de la conquista de Méjico. Madrid: Espasa-Calpe, s.a., 1942
Costa, E. Goulard da. Portugal descobridor: Apuntamientos respeitantes a descoberta de California. Lisboa: Depositaria Livraria Moraes, 1928

Cuevas, Mariano. Cartas y otros documentos de Hernán Cortés novísimamente descubiertos en el Archivo General de Indias de la ciudad de Sevilla e ilustrados por el P. Mariano Cuevas, s.j. Sevilla: F. Díaz y Compa., 1915

——. Monje y marino: La vida y los tiempos de Fray Andrés de Urdaneta. México: Galatea, 1943

Dantin Cereceda, Juan. Exploradores y conquistadores de Indias: Relatos geográficos. Madrid: Instituto-Escuela, 1934

Davidson, George. "Voyages of Discovery and Exploration on the Northwest Coast of America, 1539-1603." In United States Coast and Geodetic Survey, Report for 1886, Appendix vii

Descola, Jean. The Conquistadors. Translated from French by Malcolm Barnes. New York: The Viking Press, 1957

Díaz del Castillo, Bernal. Historia verdadera de la conquista de la Nueva España. Madrid: Espasa-Calpe, 1928

——. Verdadera y notable relación del descubrimiento y conquista de la Nueva España y Guatemala. In Biblioteca "Goathemala." Guatemala: Tipografía Nacional, 1933-1934. Vols. x-xi

Dorantes de Carranza, Baltasar. Sumaria relación de las cosas de la Nueva España. México: Museo Nacional, 1902

Drake, Francis. The World Encompassed by Sir Francis Drake. London: T. Richards, 1628

Ediciones de la Vicesecretaría de Educación Popular. Grandes de España: Primera serie: Capitanes: Alvarado. Madrid: 1945

Engineer Department, U.S. Army. Report upon United States Geographical Surveys West of the One Hundredth Meridian. Washington: Government Printing Office, 1879. Vol. vii – Archeology

Espasa-Calpe, S.A. Enciclopedia Universal Ilustrada Europeo-Americana. Madrid and elsewhere: No date. Vols. xxxii, xl, lxv

Estrada y Arnaiz, Rafael. La influencia del mar en la historia de España. Zaragoza: El Noticiero, 1950

Fernández Duro, Cesáreo. A la mar madera: Libro quinto de las disquisiciones náuticas. Madrid: Rivadeneyra, 1880

Fernández de Navarrete, Martín. Colección de los viajes y descubrimientos que hicieron por mar los españoles desde fines del siglo xv. Madrid: Imprenta Real, 1829

—— (posthumous). Biblioteca marítima española. Madrid: Viuda de Calero, 1851

Fuentes y Guzmán, Francisco Antonio de. Historia de Guatemala o Recordación florida. Ms, 1690. Madrid: Justo Zaragoza, 1882

Gallardo, Bartolomé José. Ensayo de una biblioteca española de libros raros y curiosos. Madrid: M. Rivadeneyra, 1863-1866

García Icazbalceta, Joaquín. Colección de documentos para la historia de México. México: J. M. Andrade, 1858

Gardiner, C. Harvey. Naval Power in the Conquest of Mexico. Austin: University of Texas Press, 1956

Gascón de Gotor, A. Aventurero genial: Aragón en América. Zaragoza: Imprenta Estilo, 1950

Gerhard, Peter. Pirates on the West Coast of New Spain, 1575-1742. Glendale, Calif: The Arthur H. Clark Co., 1960

Greenhow, Robert. The History of Oregon and California and the Other Territories on the North-West Coast of North America; from Their Discovery to the Present Day. Boston: Freeman and Bolles, 1847

Guillén, Julio F. Catálogo guía del Museo Naval de Madrid. Burgos: Imprenta Aldecoa, 1945. Ninth edition

——. Repertorio de los M. SS., cartas, planos y dibujos relativos a las Californias, existentes en este Museo. In Publicaciones del Museo Naval, 1. Madrid: Museo Naval, 1932

Hakluyt, Richard. The Third and Last Volume of the Principal Navigations, Voyages, Traffiques, and Discoveries of the English Nation . . . any time within the compasse of these 1600 yeres . . . London: George Bishop et al., 1600

Hammond, George P., and Agapito Rey. Narratives of the Coronado Expedition, 1540-1542. Albuquerque: University of New Mexico Press, 1940

Haring, Clarence Henry. Trade and Navigation Between Spain and the Indies in the Time of the Hapsburgs. Cambridge, Mass: Harvard University Press, 1918

——. The Spanish Empire in America. New York: Oxford University Press, 1947

Helps, Arthur. The Spanish Conquest in America. London: John W. Parker and Son, 1855-1861. 4 vols.

Herrera, Antonio de. Historia general de los hechos de los castellanos en las islas y tierra firme del mar oceano. Madrid: Imprenta Real, 1601

Iglesia, Ramón (editor). Estudios de historiografía de la Nueva España. México: El Colegio de México, 1945

Illescas, Gonzalo de. La historia pontifical y cathólica. Madrid: Melchor Sánchez, 1652

Instituto Histórico de Marina. Colección de diarios y relaciones para la historia de los viajes y descubrimientos. Luis Cabreiro Blanco, editor. Madrid: Escelicer, S.L., 1943

Keyes, James M. Las misiones españolas de California. Madrid: Consejo Superior de Investigaciones Científicas, 1950

Klarwill, Victor von (editor). The Fugger News-Letters. London: John Lane The Bodley Head, Ltd., reprinted 1925

Kunz, George Frederick. Gems and Precious Stones of North America. New York: The Scientific Publishing Company, 1892

Lamb, Harold. New Found World: How North America Was Found & Explored. Garden City, N.Y: Doubleday & Company, Inc., 1955

Libro viejo . . . See Biblioteca "Goathemala"

López de Gómara, Francisco. Conquista de Méjico. Barcelona: Daniel Cortezo y Cia., 1888

Lorenzana, Francisco Antonio. Historia de Nueva-España escrita por su esclarecido conquistador Hernán Cortés. México:Imprenta del Superior Gobierno, 1770

Los Angeles Herald Express. August 30, 1955

Los Angeles Times. February 11, 1957, Part III

Lowery, Woodbury. The Spanish Settlements Within the Present Limits of the United States. New York: G. P. Putnam's Sons, 1911

Luengo Muñoz, Manuel. "Poder adquisitivo de la moneda en Indias," Anuario de Estudios Americanos. Sevilla, 1951. Vol. VIII

———. "Regulación jurídica de la explotación y comercio de las perlas del Mar Caribe en el siglo XVI." Doctoral dissertation, Universidad Central de España, Madrid, 1952. Unpublished

Lummis, Charles F. The Spanish Pioneers. Chicago: A. C. McClurg and Company, 1899

———. In Memory of Juan Rodríguez Cabrillo Who Gave the World California. Chula Vista, Cal: Denrich Press, 1913

MacNutt, Francis Augustus (editor and translator). Letters of Cortés: The Five Letters of Relation from Fernando Cortés to the Emperor Charles V. New York: Knickerbocker Press, 1908

Madariaga, Salvador de. Hernán Cortés. Buenos Aires: Editorial Sudamericana, 1945

Malaret, Augusto. Diccionario de americanismos. San Juan, Puerto Rico: Imprenta "Venezuela," 1931. Second edition

Mange, Juan Matheo. Luz de Tierra Incógnita en la América Septentrional y Diario de las Exploraciones en Sonora in Publicaciones del Archivo General de la Nación. México: Diario Oficial, 1926
Manuscripts
  Archivo General de Indias, Sevilla, Spain:
    Audiencia de Guatemala: 9; 128
    —— México: 23, ramo 1, 1595; 372
    —— Santo Domingo: 1121, libro 3, folio 122
    Indiferente General: 111
    Justicia: 280; 286, no. 4, ramo 2, 1556; 290, "Autos Fiscales, año de 1563 . . ."; 1041, no. 2, Audiencia de Guatemala
    Patronato: 20, no. 1, ramo 1; 20, no. 5; 21, ramo 4; 68, no. 2, ramo 3; 87, no. 2, ramo 4, Audiencia de Guatemala; 180, ramo 52; 182, ramo 28
  Biblioteca Nacional, Madrid, Spain:
    3165, folio 182; 8,553; 18,758, no. 14; 19,243
  Museo Naval, Madrid, Spain:
    "California, historia y viajes," tomo 1, no. 1
    Colección Navarrete; tomo XVIII, doc. 41; tomo XIX, nos., 12; 15; 20; 523, "Capitan Jhoan de Escalante de Mendoça, Ytenerario de Navegacion de los Mares, y tierras Oçidentales"
Martínez Guitian, Luis. Aportación a la historia de Santander: Construcción naval y navegación en corso durante el reinado de Felipe II. Santander: Vda. de F. Fons, 1935
Mártir de Anglería, Pedro. Décadas del Nuevo Mundo. Translation, Latin into Spanish, by Joaquín Torres Asensio. Buenos Aires: El Ateneo, 1944
Mason, A.E.W. The Life of Francis Drake. Garden City, N.Y: Doubleday, Doran & Company, Inc., 1942
McElroy, John W. "The Ocean Navigation of Columbus on His First Voyage." In The American Neptune, vol. 1, no. 3, 1941
Millares Carlo, A., and J. I. Mantecón. Indice y extractos de los Protocolos del Archivo de Notarías de México. México, D.F: El Colegio de México, 1945
Ministerio de Fomento. Cartas de Indias. Madrid: Manuel G. Hernandez, 1877
Monleon, Rafael. Construcciones navales: Bajo su aspecto artístico: Catálogo descriptivo. Madrid: Original paintings and manuscript, Museo Naval, 1889

Mosk, Sanford A. "The Cardona Company and the Pearl Fisheries of Lower California." In Pacific Historical Review, vol. III, 1934

Muñoz, Juan Bautista. Historia del Nuevo Mundo. Madrid: Viuda de Ibarra, 1793. Vol. I, perhaps the only one published.

Obregón, Baltasar de. Historia de los descubrimientos antiguos y modernos de la Nueva España. México: Departamiento de Educación, 1924

Orozco y Berra, Manuel. Historia de la dominación española en México. México: Librería Robredo, 1938.

Oviedo y Valdés, Gonzalo Fernández de. Historia general y natural de las Indias, islas y tierra-firme del mar océano. Madrid: Imprenta de la Real Academia de la Historia, 1855

Pardo, Joaquín. Documentos para la historia de Guatemala. Guatemala: Anales de la Sociedad de Geografía e Historia de Guatemala, 1935

Paso y Troncoso, Francisco del. Epistolario de Nueva España. México: Librería Robredo, 1939

Pérez Bustamante, Ciriaco. Don Antonio de Mendoza, Primer Virrey de la Nueva España, 1535-1550. Santiago de Galicia, Spain: El Eco Franciscano, 1928

Pérez Embid, Florentino. "Notas Bibliográficas, Portillo y Diez de Sollano, Alvaro. . ." In Revista de Indias. Año 8, no. 27, Enero-Marzo, 1947

Portillo y Diez de Sollano, Alvaro del. Descubrimientos y exploraciones en las costas de California. Madrid: Escuela de Estudios Hispano-Americanos de Sevilla, 1947

Prescott, Wm. H. History of the Conquest of Mexico. Paris: Baudry's European Library, 1844.

Ramusio, Giovanni Battista. Primo volume & Seconda editione Delle Navigationi et Viagge. Venice: Stamperia de Giunti, 1553

——. Delle navigationi et viaggi. Venice: I. Giunti, 1606

Real Academia Española. Diccionario de la lengua española. Madrid: Espasa-Calpe, S.A., décimoséptima edición, 1947

——. Diccionario manual e ilustrada de la lengua española. Madrid: Espasa-Calpe, S.A., segunda edición, 1950

Real Academia de la Historia. Colección de documentos inéditos relativos al descubrimiento, conquista y organización de las antiguas posesiones españolas de América y Oceanía, etc. Madrid: José María Pérez, 1870.

Recinos, Adrián. Pedro de Alvarado: Conquistador de México: Fondo de Cultura Económica, 1952.

Remesal, Antonio de.   Historia general de las Indias Occidentales, y particular de la gobernación de Chiapa y Guatemala.   Guatemala: Biblioteca "Goathemala," 1932

Riva Palacio, Vicente.   El virreinato: Historia de la dominación española en México desde 1521 a 1808. In Tomo ii of Resumen integral de México a través de los siglos.   México: La Carpeta, s.a., 1951

Robertson, William.   The History of the Discovery and Settlement of America.   Edinburgh: University Press, 1829

Rodgers, William Ledyard.   Naval Welfare Under Oars, 4th to 16th Centuries: A Study of Strategy, Tactics and Ship Design. Annapolis, Md: United States Naval Institute, 1939

Rogers, Woodes.   A Cruising Voyage Around the World.   London: A. Bell, 1712

Rumeu de Armas, Antonio.   Los viajes de John Hawkins a América. Sevilla: Escuela de Estudios Hispano Americanos, 1947

Sahagún, Bernadino de.   Historia general de las cosas de Nueva España.   México: Alejandro Valdes, 1829-1830

San Luis Rey Historical Society, Bulletin, 9.57 – LPS.   Oceanside 1-18-57

Schoenrich, Otto.   The Legacy of Christopher Columbus. 2 vols. Glendale, California: The Arthur H. Clark Company, 1949

Schäfer, Ernesto.   El Consejo Real y Supremo de las Indias. Sevilla: Escuela de Estudios Hispano-Americanos de Sevilla, 1947

Simpson, Leslie Byrd.   The Encomienda in New Spain.   Berkeley: University of California Press, 1950

Smith, Donald E.   The Viceroy of New Spain.   Berkeley: University of California Press, 1913

Soares, Celestino.   California and the Portuguese.   Lisbon: Secretariado de Propaganda Nacional, 1939

Solís y Rivadeneyra, Antonio de.   Historia de la conquista de Méjico. Buenos Aires: Emecé Editores, s.a., 1944

Solórzano y Pereyra, Juan de.   Política indiana.   Madrid: Imprenta Real de la Gazeta, 1776

Southern California Rancher (Oceanside, Calif.), February 1952

Suárez de Peralta, Juan.   Noticias históricas de Nueva España. Madrid: Justo Zaragoza, 1878

Torquemada, Juan de.   Ia. parte de los veynte y un libros Rituales y Monarchia Yndiana, etc.   Seuilla: Matias Clauijo, 1615

Torres Campos, Rafael. España en California y en el noroeste de América. Madrid: Rivadeneyra, 1892

Vaillant, George C. Aztecs of Mexico: Origin, Rise and Fall of the Aztec Nation. Garden City, N.Y: Doubleday & Company, Inc., 1953

Vedia, Enrique de. Historiadores primitivos de Indias in Biblioteca de autores españoles. Madrid: M. Rivadeneyra, 1858

Venegas, Miguel. Noticia de la California y de su Conquista Temporal y Espiritual hasta el tiempo presente. Mexico City: Luis Alvarez y Alvarez de la Cadena, 1943. From ms. of 1739

Villagutierre Soto-Mayor, Juan de. Historia de la Provincia de el Itza. Guatemala: Tipografía Nacional, 1933

Villasana Haggard, J. Handbook for Translators of Spanish Historical Documents. Oklahoma City: Semco Color Press, 1941

Wagner, Henry Raup. California Voyages, 1539-1541. San Francisco: John Howell, 1925

——. "Francisco de Ulloa Returned." In California Historical Society Quarterly, vol. xix (September 1940), pp. 242-243

——. Spanish Voyages to the Northwest Coast of America in the Sixteenth Century. San Francisco: California Historical Society, 1929

——. Juan Rodríguez Cabrillo, Discoverer of the Coast of California. San Francisco: California Historical Society, 1941

Waterman, Ivan R. John Rodrigues Cabrillo, Discoverer of California. California State Board of Education: 1935

Wright, Irene A. The Early History of Cuba, 1492-1586. New York: The Macmillan Company, 1916

Yáñez, Agustín. Crónicas de la conquista de México. México, D.F: Universidad Nacional Autónoma, 1939

Zarco Cuevas, Julián. El Monasterio de San Lorenzo el Real de El Escorial y la Casita del Principe. Madrid: Sucesores de Rivadeneyra, 1955. Eighth edition

Zweig, Stefan. Magallanes: La Aventura más audaz de la Humanidad. Buenos Aires: Editorial Claridad, tenth edition, 1943

Index

Index